TRANS EXPLOITS

ANIMA Critical Race Studies Otherwise
A series edited by Mel Y. Chen and Jasbir K. Puar

TRANS EXPLOITS

Trans of Color Cultures and Technologies in Movement

JIAN NEO CHEN

Duke University Press   *Durham and London*   2019

Designed by Courtney Leigh Baker
Typeset in Whitman and Avenir by Copperline Book Services

Library of Congress Cataloging-in-Publication Data
Names: Chen, Jian Neo, [date] author.
Title: Trans exploits : trans of color cultures and technologies
in movement / Jian Neo Chen.
Description: Durham : Duke University Press, 2019. |
Series: Anima / a series edited by Mel Y. Chen and Jasbir K. Puar |
Includes bibliographical references and index.
Identifiers: LCCN 2018008215 (print) | LCCN 2018009564 (ebook)
ISBN 9781478002338 (ebook)
ISBN 9781478000662 (hardcover : alk. paper)
ISBN 9781478000877 (pbk. : alk. paper)
Subjects: LCSH: Transgender people. | Minorities. | Transgender
artists. | Minority artists. | Transgender people—Political activity. |
Minorities—Political activity.
Classification: LCC HQ77.9 (ebook) | LCC HQ77.9 .C44 2018 (print) |
DDC 306.76/8—dc23
LC record available at https://lccn.loc.gov/2018008215

Cover art: Yozmit, *Sound of New Pussy* music video, 2012.
Image design by Yvette Choy. Courtesy of Yozmit.

For kindreds

Contents

Acknowledgments

Although this book was conceived, written, and produced during a five-year time span concentrated within the academic world, it has been shaped by a longer and wider scope of learning and engagement. Most of all, I want to thank the artists, organizers, and scholars whose work I have only been able to highlight in the book and whose imaginations and labor have enabled me to create and build points of description, connection, and context. The many people and groups whose work I was not able to discuss in this limited collection of writings, although they have contributed to my thinking and growth in relationship to trans, queer, feminist, disability, and racial justice movement building and cultures, include, among others, Christopher Lee, Tamara Ching, Bamby Salcedo, Chandi Moore, Emi Koyama, Ignacio Rivera, Ryka Aoki, Lexi Nepantla Adsit, Pauline Park, Kortney Ryan Ziegler, Amita Swadin, Andy Marra, Ola Osaze, Cecilia Gentilli, Ashlee Marie Preston, Kay Ulanday Barrett, Trish Salah, D'Lo, Kai M. Green, Leeroy Kun Young Kang, Imani Henry, Leah Lakshmi Piepzna-Samarasinha, Pablo Espinoza, Willy Wilkinson, Kit Yan, Kris Hayashi, Alex Lee, Chino Scott-Chung, Ryan Li Dahlstrom, Elliott Fukui, Aren Aizura, Janani Balasubramanian, Alok Vaid-Menon, Mashuq Mushtaq Deen, Ren-yo Hwang, the Trans Women of Color Collective, the Audre Lorde Project, Sylvia Rivera Project, Translatina Network, Peacock Rebellion, Queer Rebels, Fresh Meat Productions, the Transgender Law Center, and El/La Para TransLatinas.

I am deeply grateful to Duke University Press series editors Jasbir Puar and Mel Y. Chen and executive editor Courtney Berger for trusting, supporting, and guiding my unfolding work from inception to completion. I thank editorial associate Sandra Korn, project editor Susan Albury, designer Courtney Baker, and copywriter Chris Robinson for their artistry, work, and patience in materializing this book.

At the Ohio State University (OSU), Joe Ponce has been an unwavering mentor, friend, and co-conspirator. Debra Moddelmog, Judy Wu, Lynn Itagaki, Robyn Warhol, and Shannon Winnbust have created spaces of vitality and support for my research, teaching, and cultural organizing. I am grateful to have the opportunity to work with brilliant, devoted colleagues Pranav Jani, Jill Galvin, Valerie Lee, Jim Phelan, Christopher Jones, Andreá Williams, Wendy Hesford, Koritha Mitchell, Sean O'Sullivan, Nancy Yan, Thomas Davis, Beverly Moss, Frederick Luis Aldama, Adéléké Adéèkó, Tracee Mohler, Wayne Lovely, Merrill Kaplan, Deb Lowry, Pablo Tanguay, David Adams, Michelle Ann Abate, Brian McHale, Nan Johnson, Sandra Macpherson, Ethan Knapp, Roxann Wheeler, Amanpal Garcha, Molly Farrell, Jared Gardner, Elizabeth Hewitt, David Brewer, Mike Bierschenk, Cynthia Selfe, Ryan Friedman, Kathleen Griffin, Lauren Squires, Breanne LeJeune, MaryKatherine Ramsey, Ruth Friedman, Jesse Schotter, Sarah Neville, Jacob Risinger, Nicole Cochran, Tiffany Quattlebaum, Christa Teston, Zoe Brigley Thompson, and Mira Kafantaris in the Department of English. I have appreciated intellectual and programmatic collaboration with Amy Shuman, Margaret Price, Namiko Kunimoto, Theresa Delgadillo, Daniel Rivers, Nick Spitulski, Toni Calbert, Jonathan Branfman, and other participants of the Diversity and Identity Studies Collective (DISCO) that brings together American Indian, Asian American, Latina/o, Disability, and Sexuality Studies programs. Special thanks to Tayo Clyburn and the Office of Diversity and Inclusion for bringing Janet Mock, in conversation with bell hooks, to OSU in 2013 and for bringing such impactful LGBT programming to OSU. Special thanks also to Maurice Stevens for guiding the early stages of my book-writing process. I have appreciated the collegial presence and support of Jill Bystydzienski, Jennifer Suchland, Vera Brunner-Sung, Amna Akbar, Sa'dia Rehman, Tanya Saunders, Binaya Subedi, Marc Johnston, Annabelle Estera, Mollie Blackburn, Treva Lindsey, Juno Salazar Parreñas, Noah Tamarkin, Guisela Latorre, Mary Thomas, Julia Watson, and Leslie Alexander. My work has been especially energized by conversations with present and previous graduate students Mercedes Chavez, Ariana Steele, James Harris, Zachary Harvat, Indya Jackson, Krista Benson, Joy Ellison, Nicholas "Nic" Flores, Debanuj DasGupta, Adrienne Winans, Juwon Lee, Leila Ben-Nasr, Pritha Prasad, Ryan Schey, Meredith Lee, Natalia Colón Alvarez, Alison Cummins, Jonathan Gillett, Kaiya Gordon, Misha Grifka, Arielle Irizarry, Xiyue Zhang, Deja Beamon, Allison Hargett, Elizabeth Blackford, Bonnie Opliger, Victor

Smith, Swati Vijaya, Nicole Pizarro, Nathan Richards, Erik Scaltriti, Chen Wang, Babette Cieskowski, Lindsay Hodgens, Danielle Orozco, Josh Ziri, Ali Alhajji, Joshua Anderson, Sidney Jones, Marie Franco, Molly Olguin, Luke Bauer, Sara Cieto, Brooke Felts, Michael Harwick, Joey Kim, Sharon Stein, Rebecca Sullivan, Maria Celleri, Han Chen, Melissa Stidams, Divya Sundar, and Drew Young. Lastly, I thank David Filipi, Chris Stults, and Jennifer Lange at the Wexner Center for the Arts for hosting film screenings with Tanwarin Sukkhapisit and Wu Tsang.

Much appreciation to Wendy Hui Kyong Chun for engaging critically and generously with an early version of my manuscript through a workshop organized by osu Asian American Studies in 2014. Heartfelt thanks to Jack Tchen, Laura Chen-Shultz, Alexandra Chang, Amita Manghnani, Ruby Gómez, and the Asian/Pacific/American (a/p/a) Institute at New York University (nyu) for hosting me as a visiting scholar in 2012. Yozmit, Tanwarin Sukkhapisit, Elle Mehrmand, Felix Endara, and Jasbir Puar's exciting participation in the "Transmitting Trans-Asian" exhibition and conversation at the a/p/a Institute provided the original impetus for this book. I also thank Susan Stryker, Paisley Currah, Aren Aizura, Yolanda Martínez-San Miguel, Sarah Tobias, Celine Parreñas Shimizu, Kara Keeling, Heather Love, Anita Mannur, Lisa Nakamura, and Kale Fajardo for opportunities, critical feedback, and conversations that have strengthened my book and work.

At nyu, I am indebted to E. Frances White for creating the university-wide Academic Diversity Postdoctoral Fellowship program and for her mentorship through the fellowship program and at the Gallatin School of Individualized Study. I thank Susanne Wofford, Ritty Lukose, Valerie Forman, Vasuki Nesiah, Millery Polyné, Myisha Priest, Alejandro Velasco, Hannah Gurman, A. B. Huber, Stacy Pies, Hallie Franks, Michael Dinwiddie, Nina Cornyetz, Sinan Antoon, Rachel Plutzer, Patrick McCreery, and Jessica Lee at Gallatin for supporting my work. In particular, the encouragement and contributions of Lisa Duggan, Karen Shimakawa, Ann Pellegrini, Jung-Bong Choi, Radha Hegde, Ella Shohat, Mara Mills, Yukiko Hanawa, José Esteban Muñoz, Gayatri Gopinath, Tavia Nyong'o, Wendy Cheng, Lissette-Tatiana Olivares, Imani Kai Johnson, Marie Cruz Soto, Jennifer Williams, Lisette Garcia, Alexander Galloway, Zhen Zhang, Crystal Parikh, and Marcial Godoy-Anativia have enlivened my relationship to academic scholarship and community. I enjoyed and learned from my conversations and work with previous graduate and undergraduate students Aaron Evans, Wesley Wollet, Thomas Casteneda,

Elizabeth Perry, Melissa Salm, Anna Mullen, Dana Droppo, Olivia Kendall, Ashley Oh, Janet Lee, Paolo Lopez, and Dorianne Loshitzer.

At the University of California, Irvine (UCI), I am grateful to Laura Hyun Yi Kang, Rei Terada, Jennifer Terry, and Ackbar Abbas for their guidance and support on my PhD dissertation and for laying the foundations for my academic work. Lindon Barrett, Akira Lippit, Glen Mimura, Inderpal Grewal, Eyal Amiran, Linda Trinh Vo, R. Radhakrishnan, Bliss Cua Lim, Mark Poster, Annette Schlichter, Gabriele Schwab, Ngugi wa Thiong'o, Jane Newman, Dina Al-Kassim, Étienne Balibar, Jonathan Hall, J. Hillis Miller, Fred Moten, Arielle Read, and June Kurata each contributed to my academic growth. Special thanks to Gayatri Chakravorty Spivak, Judith Butler, Mel Y. Chen, Glen Mimura, and Deborah Vargas for their generous participation in the "Global States" conference, hosted by Comparative Literature graduate students, and to David Theo Goldberg, Kim Benita Furumoto, and the UC Humanities Research Institute for the opportunity to join the "Present Tense Empires, Race, and Bio-Politics" Seminar in Experimental Critical Theory. I appreciated the academic companionship of previous graduate students Cindy Cheng, Shalini Fernandez, Donna Tong, Priya Shah, Neha Vora, Linh Hua, Natalie Newton, Jane Hseu, Michelle Cho, Wendy Piquemal, Erin Trapp, Tim Wong, Anna Cavness, Rosemary Kwa, Rose Jones, Janet Neary, Lindsay Puente, Lan Duong, Mariam Lam, Anna Kornbluh, Travis Tanner, Randy Ontiveros, I-Lien Tsay, Stewart Chang, Jane Griffin, Katherine Mack, Juan Buriel, Margaux Cowden, and Emma Heaney.

I could not have navigated the challenges of the academic industry and culture and life's many transitions without the care and inspiration of friends and comrades including Maritza Penagos, Stacy Kono, Gabriel Martinez, Nancy Cato, Dolores Garay, Laura B. Johnson, Noel Yin, Michelle Rivera Gravage, Jason Luz, Rima Añosa, Jason Alley, Maya and Chino Scott-Chung, Lisa Fujie Parks, Oscar Trujillo, Leeroy Kun Young Kang, Dani Heffernan, Lissette-Tatiana Olivares, Cheto Castellano, Un Jung Lim, Imani Henry, Felix Endara, Kadji Amin, Grace Nam, Milyoung Cho, Jennifer DeClue, Cecilia Gentilli, Pauline Park, Laimah Osman, Ninotchka Rosca, Sockie Laya Smith, Carrie Hawks, Wendy Cheng, Imani Kai Johnson, Yvette Choy, Ola Osaze, Kit Yan, Sel Hwang, Julian Liu, Tara Hart, Jeannine Tang, Vanessa Huang, Erica Cho, Sheena Malhotra, Gina Masequesmay, Gil Mangaoang, Maylei Blackwell, Karen Tongson, Richard Haberstroh, Tan Nguyen, Elizabeth Lee, Suparna Bhaskaran, Kris Long, Nancy Yan, Pejmaan Fallah, Wendy Ake, Sandhya Kochar, Noah Demland, Alcira Dueñas, Vera Brunner-Sung, Sam

Meister, Tayo Clyburn, Tara Polansky, Rashida Davison, Timothy Singhara-jah, Danielle Marilyn West, Dkéama Alexis, and Wriply Bennet. I give my deepest thanks to healers Trinity Ordona, Kit Yoon, and Donna Sigl-Davies and to dear friends and mentors E. Frances White, Ellen Eisenman, and Mel Y. Chen. My chosen siblings, Jabu Pereira, Iyatunde Folayan, Prajna Paramita Choudury, and Joyti Chand; my birth parents, Frances and Yuan Chen; and my birth sibling, Billy Chen, have journeyed every step with me.

INTRODUCTION

Racial Trans Technologies

They used to do that to us all the time, just come at the bar and the lights would go on and everybody would just stream out, . . . you knew that's what the routine was and it was just a night that it simply wasn't gonna happen. You know, . . . it's a feeling that you get like when you all go to a movie and see something together and everybody ah's and gasps at the same time? *That's the feeling.* You just knew. Everyone just looked at one another and sat down. *Not* leaving. *Not* going anywhere. —MISS MAJOR GRIFFIN-GRACY on the 1969 Stonewall Rebellion from *MAJOR!* (2015, dir. Annalise Ophelian and StormMiguel Florez)

Here on the gender borders at the close of the twentieth century, with the faltering of phallocentric hegemony and the bumptious appearance of heteroglossic origin accounts, we find the epistemologies of white male medical practice, the rage of radical feminist theories and the chaos of lived gendered experience meeting on the battlefield of the transsexual body: a hotly contested site of cultural inscription, a meaning machine for the production of ideal type. —SANDY STONE, "The *Empire* Strikes Back: A Posttranssexual Manifesto" (1987)

Time magazine's June 9, 2014, issue features actress Laverne Cox on the cover, looking boldly at the reader/viewer in a tall, elegant stance. While portraits often appear on *Time*'s covers, Cox's image is distinctive in its stature. The crown of her head appears above *Time*'s logo and her head and neck overtake and stand in for *m* in *t-i-m-e*. Instead of a close-up shot of Cox's face, the photo captures her full figure from head to toe, filling the entire space of the cover from top to bottom. The portrait not only claims to represent Cox

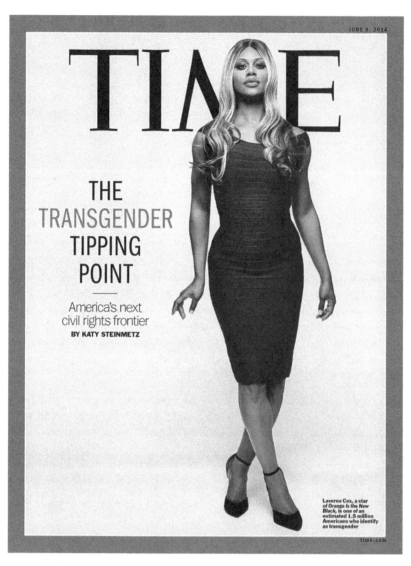

FIGURE I.1. *Time* magazine's "The Transgender Tipping Point" cover issue (June 9, 2014).

as a figure but stages her visually as a body to be encountered. It also interrupts *t-i-m-e* to become an integral part of time. Cox's image announces the "transgender tipping point" as the moment when trans people obtain just enough critical mass to tip over the dominant majority.[1] Drawing from sociological, biological, and technological popular theories, the concept of the "tipping point" attempts to absorb the gains won by trans justice movements into a "free" market populist vision of social change in which the particular interests of a minority group circulate just enough and under the right conditions to overtake or even "infect" the majority. While this concept may seem to validate the power of the few to change the whole, it actually cancels out the struggles, courage, labor, and creativity of social justice movement building to instead credit what is believed to be automated natural laws internal to American populism.

Additionally, the issue's cover story, "America's Transition" by Katy Steinmetz, highlights life stories of trans people but diminishes the complexity of their lives to translate them into signs for progress in medical science, cultural self-expression through the Internet and social media, and state-sponsored laws and policies. The article ultimately attempts to fold the intersecting trans struggles that have made these advancements possible into the time and space of a nation-state that supposedly has transcended the "frontiers" of racism, sexism, and more recently homophobia (with the then-imminent federal legalization of same-sex marriage) and is now ready to conquer the new frontier of transphobia. *Time*'s transgender issue reveals not only the technical administering of civil rights to deactivate social movements but also the managed harnessing of civil rights to advance the internal and external frontiers of American empire. We can view the magazine cover's insistence on capturing the full image of Laverne Cox from head to toe, in contrast to *Time*'s usual close-up cover portraits, as exploiting the overwritten hyper-visibility of Black trans embodiment to mark American civil progress—and to renew a claim on the racially gendered Black body for the continued expansionism of the settler colonial nation-state. Cox's studied crossed stance, however, seems to offer a visual impasse in response to *Time*'s demands.

Trans Exploits: Trans of Color Cultures and Technologies in Movement describes and theorizes the displaced emergences of trans of color cultural expression and social movement building through performance, film/video, literature, and digital media by the second decade of the twenty-first century. Approximately fifty years after state-managed civil rights reforms and two decades after white-dominated trans movements became organized in the 1990s, trans of color cultures and movements surface at the crossings between subcultural modes of self-determined representation and dominant regimes of visibility. Through close engagement with the work of artists, scholars, and activists, the book produces visual and perceptual strategies for analyzing and amplifying the liminal internal/external, private/public, sense/thought aesthetics of trans of color embodiments. I argue that these aesthetic practices address and attempt to rework subjective and social orders of (cis)gender dominance and the technologies and histories of racial and colonial gendering that have established binary gender/sex as one of the primary faultlines for securing and differentiating the national body of the white settler U.S. state and civil society. *Trans Exploits* explores—and assembles potential relationships between—the cultural practices and imaginings created by trans and gender nonconforming Asian, Black, Indigenous, and Latinx peoples in transnational locations incorporated by the U.S. empire inside and outside the U.S. national body and territories.

Trans of Color Displacements

In this book, I use *trans* in addition to *transgender* to potentially reorient transgender studies, cultures, and social identities toward a detachment from—and disruption of—the Western, racially constituted white gender/sex system that continues to root gender social formation. As Paul B. Preciado has argued, far from intervening in naturalized biological and visual regimes of sex, *gender* as a category was created by U.S. psych-medical industries by the 1950s to re-entrench binary sex, especially through forced gender assignment surgery and biochemical treatments on intersex people. However, the foundational U.S. histories of racialized gendering and sexualization that trans of color cultures remember and embody speak to the limitations of only critiquing and resisting gender as it has been prescribed and regulated through Western science, without attention to the deep entanglements between Western rationality, liberal governance through the nation-state form, and the different modes of colonization and racism on which liberal governance relies. Engaging with trans of color cultural workers and organizers, queer feminist of color and queer of color critiques, and women of color and transnational feminisms, I use trans of color as a set of counterimaginaries and analytics that mobilize potential points of solidarity and kinship between those who experience embodiment as a form of racial gender displacement and subjugation within radically different *yet interrelated* transnational U.S. histories and systems of genocide, captivity, colonization, and imperialism. Trans of color expressions and practices use the *surplus* that constitutes racial gender embodiment as the material for social struggle, reconstruction, and transformation. In addition to the hope of enlivening trans of color and other solidarities, my work aims to contribute to creating revised lexicons for perceiving and understanding trans of color and trans bodies and experiences—lexicons that acknowledge and describe the trans of color and trans politics and social labor of intervening in and reconstructing gender. The cocreation of these lexicons is challenging not only because of conflicting understandings of transgender communities and identities that are still emerging, but also and primarily, I would argue, because the gender/sex system continues to fundamentally structure the social and territorial body of U.S. neoliberal civil society at the scale of nature.

I use *trans* in connection with Miss Major Griffin-Gracy's frequent use of the term along with *transgender* in her public talks; her use, it seems to me serves, less to mark a stable identity than to describe and bring together those who share experiences and (otherwise undocumented) histories of devaluation by—and resistance against—gender policing, racism, and enforced poverty. Miss Major mobilizes *trans* and *transgender* to shatter the common-sense supremacy claimed by cisgender reality, to humanize gender variant and nonconforming people, and to keep *trans* and *transgender* adaptive and ungovernable as tools for gender liberation.[2] Additionally, Susan Stryker, Paisley Currah, and Lisa Jean Moore emphasize the relational possibilities of *trans* in *transgender* when the hyphenated status of *trans-* as a prefix is used to open up *trans* to other connections and meanings besides the suffix *gender* (2008). My use of *trans* is also aligned with the open-ended inclusiveness of *trans** in bringing together multiple gender nonconforming and variant identities and expressions, including *nonbinary*, *agender*, *gender queer*, *gender fluid*, and *gender free*, and those yet to self-name.

My discussion of trans of color cultures seeks to contribute to emerging U.S. transgender studies and cultural life, while potentially intervening in and expanding their subjects, approaches, and politics of knowledge and cultural production as they become more visible within dominant society. As described by Susan Stryker, transgender studies is "concerned with anything that disrupts, denaturalizes, rearticulates, and makes visible the normative linkages we generally assume to exist between the biological specificity of the sexually differentiated human body, the social roles and statuses that a particular form of body is expected to occupy, the subjectively experienced relationship between a gendered sense of self and social expectations of gender-role performance, and the cultural mechanisms that work to sustain or thwart specific configurations of gendered personhood" (2006, 3). The academic field emerged in the 1990s in connection with transgender movement building and a politicized social identity that included all people marginalized or oppressed based on deviance from social norms of gendered embodiment. This broad definition of transgender identity and political community drew from Leslie Feinberg's popularized activist work, Allucquère Rosanne (Sandy) Stone's critical manifesto (1996) against the renaturalizing of binary gender/sex by versions of second-wave feminism, activism around Nancy Jean Burkholder's expulsion from the Michigan Womyn's Music Festival, and other shifts and emergences in popular culture, academia, and activism (Stryker 2006, 4–5). Additionally, Stryker suggests that transgender studies appeared within the larger historical context of the "disintegration of the Soviet Union, the end of the cold war, the rise of the United States as a unipolar superpower, the development of the European Union as the first multinational state, and the elaboration of new global forms of capital" (8).

Stryker's expansive and politicized situating of the emergence of transgender studies and self-identified transgender communities works against what was already the semi-institutionalizing of transgender social identity and movement building through white Euro-American binary frameworks of gender, sex, and sexuality by the beginning of the twenty-first century. The majority of the first transgender-identified organizations formed in U.S. urban centers by the 1990s, especially those with 501(c)(3) status, were founded and accessed by white transgender people. These organizations and the broader movements they helped to activate tended to focus on transgender struggles with single-issue focuses on gender identity oppression and gender transition. Thus, many of these first organizations were male-to-female (MtF) or female-to-male (FtM) support groups geared toward helping members to navigate the pathologized complexities of transgender identification and embodiment, while privileging narratives of identity and bodily *transition from biologically assigned gender to self-determined gender in alignment with the white gender binary under the management of psycho-medical professionals.* Many of the first organizations were also oriented toward obtaining legal recognition, protection, and rights for transgender people. While legal advocacy is an important aspect of transgender activism, the legal frameworks adopted by these organizations often could not address the experiences of trans people of color who struggled with racist and classist forms of anti-trans cis-hetero-patriarchy. These legal frameworks also often presumed the possibility and desirability of a productive relationship with the U.S. state without addressing the impact of state divestment, policing, imprisonment, militarization, and direct and administrative violence on the lives of low- and survival-income trans people of color and immigrant communities. The single-issue agendas set by the predominantly visible white leadership of the "first wave" of transgender community organizations and transgender movements in the 1990s muted the work of earlier trans of color activists such as Christopher Lee, Bamby Salcedo, Janetta Johnson, Emi Koyama, Chandi Moore, Pauline Park, Imani Henry, Ignacio Rivera, Alex Lee, Pablo Espinoza, and Chino Mei Beck Scott-Chung, while further displacing the founding trans of color community building of Marsha P. Johnson, Sylvia Rivera, Miss Major Griffin-Gracy, Stormé DeLarverie, and Tamara Ching.

Trans of color cultures, social embodiments, and movement building contributed to the emergence of politicized and culturally mobilized U.S. transgender identity in the 1990s. Yet their experiences of interlocking oppression and cultural and political lives were sidelined by the more linear and one-dimensional gender identity–focused narratives of white-dominant transgender movements and communities. Trans people of color not only survived and opposed white cis-hetero-patriarchal settler society and state regimes. They created ways to thrive and build kinship at the edges of transgender, queer, women's, immigrant, ethnic, indigenous, and racial communities shaped by ongoing histories of subjugation—communities that often perceived them as *internal* threats to social fabrics already under attack. Trans people of color did not—and still do not—appear as a materialized coalitional identity bringing together trans Native, Black, Latinx, Asian, Arab, mixed-race, and other racialized American peoples. In contrast to *people of color*, which emerged in the mid-1950s as a term that mobilized political solidarity between racialized and colonized peoples based on nationalisms repurposed from Western European models of the nation-state, *trans of color*, *trans women/femmes of color*, *trans feminist of color*, *trans people of color*, and *racial trans* imagine affinities based on cultural memories and experiences radically dislocated from the times and spaces of nation-states and nationalisms (Wright 1956).

The transiting of gender by trans people of color has been shaped by white settler colonial histories and technologies of racial gender and sexual formation (HoSang, LaBennett, and Pulido 2012; Omi and Winant 1994). This gender shifting also draws from reassembled cosmologies and lineages of embodiment, relation, desire, and belonging that exceed what can be extinguished by these histories and technologies. Returning to historical accounts of Hernando De Soto's 1540 expedition through Indigenous Southeast territories, Qwo-Li Driskill has argued that European colonization occurred through successive attempts that relied not only on shared information on geography, Indigenous nations, and resources but also on "mapping European gender and sexuality onto Indigenous nations and bodies" (2017, 49). Driskill remembers and reimagines a third *asegi* Cherokee queer and Two-Spirit history that inflicts chaos on colonial binary gender systems through a "re-storying" of the Lady of Cofitachequi, who was kidnapped and forced to guide De Soto through Cherokee Southeast territory (2017, 3–20, 39–100). C. Riley Snorton has tracked historical moments when the queer excess of black masculine sexuality has been perceived and managed as public crises within the visual regimes of U.S. anti-Black racial capitalism (2014, 1–36). Through the figure of the plantation overseer, who is charged with watching over, punishing, and extracting labor from slaves, Snorton provides a rendering of Michel Foucault's panopticon that can account for the rationalized forms of surveillance and control exercised over black bodies within contemporary society and culture (2014, 37–66). Marcia Ochoa has delimited and revised U.S.-based concepts and theories of gender, race, and nation through an analysis of Venezuela's national construction of femininity through its mass-mediated transnational beauty pageant industry. Through queer diasporic ethnographic practices that shift identities and methods within different geopolitical contexts between the U.S. and Latin America, she describes the uses of the symbolic resources of the beauty pageant by *transformistas*, who were assigned male at birth, to materialize embodied femininity and to become women in Venezuela (2014, 1–58, 155–200). Ochoa's migration between different systems and locations of gender knowledge production puts pressure on U.S. understandings of transgender and gender that do not address the racial, indigenous, and cisgender hierarchies mobilized through gender within European colonial legacies and their modernization in Latin Americas within and adjacent to the U.S. Developing ethnographic approaches that emphasize migration over settlement in the moving oceanic spaces and times between nation-states, Kale Fajardo has offered a critical account of Filipino seamen who provide much of the ship labor needed to transport 90 percent of the world's commodities in the twenty-first century. His research details the queer complexity of their working class masculinities, which remain available to nonheteronormative intimacies that include tomboys, counter to the Philippine neoliberal state's efforts to produce exportable hypermasculine heteronormative national subjects and U.S. colonial histories of engendering Filipino and other Asian migration for labor extraction (2011, 1–76, 148–76).

Each of these groundbreaking approaches to gender variant and sexual histories, geopolitics, and social embodiments traces the centrality of gender and sexuality to the diverging modes and histories of settler colonialism, white supremacist racism, territorialism, and imperialism that constitute the U.S. national and territorial body and state inside/outside of Indigenous territories, and Latin Americas, the Black transatlantic, and the Indigenous and Asian transpacific. They also address the mediating role that gender and sexuality continue to play in the neoliberal restructuring and continuation of these modes and histories of subjugation within colonies, plantations, and territories turned democracies and free markets.

Contemporary Technologies of Racial Gendering

Trans of color cultures and social movements emerge at points of convergence and displacement between dominant culture and society and dispossessed countercultures and communities by the second decade of the twenty-first century, following fifty years of state-managed civil rights reforms in response to mass movements for racial, gender, sexual, economic, migrant, and decolonial justice. While these reforms enabled the limited entry of women, communities of color, and immigrants and refugees into domains of American civil society, they failed to directly address systemic social structures and cultures of cis-hetero-patriarchy, white settler colonialism, and capitalism. Federal civil rights reforms, including the Equal Pay Act of 1963, the Civil Rights Act of 1964, the Voting Rights Act of 1965, and the Immigration and Nationality Act of 1965, in addition to the extension of the constitutional rights of citizenship to include women, people of color, and immigrants, have provided the legal scaffolding that social justice movements have used toward broader demands for systemic transformation. Yet these reforms in and of themselves have only provided incremental protections against what these laws treat as private acts of discrimination, with the burden of redress resting on those impacted. Nonetheless, national civil rights reforms marked a formal restructuring of the U.S. nation-state from apartheid to neoliberal attempts to incorporate deviantly gendered, sexual, indigenous, and racialized communities as multicultural minorities. During this moment of restructuring, the racially engendering ideologies of the Black matriarch, Latinx culture of poverty, and Asian model minority were mobilized through national discourse and social policy to *privatize* the logics of systemic subjugation and the responsibility for their impacts within families of color.

The U.S. Department of Labor's notorious 1965 Moynihan Report identifies the "matriarchal structure" of the Black family as the root cause for ongoing socioeconomic inequality between Black and white Americans despite state-legislated civil rights protections. The report authored by Assistant Secretary of Labor Daniel Patrick Moynihan under President Lyndon B. Johnson's administration attributes the "deterioration of the Negro [sic] family" to its matriarchal structure, which "because it is out of line with the rest of American society, seriously retards the progress of the group as a whole, and imposes a crushing burden on the Negro male, and, in consequence, on a great many Negro women as well" (1965, 29). In a series of imposed substitutions, correlations, and internalizations, it recodes systemic racial dispossession into deracinated socioeconomic disparities between Black and white populations that originate in the failure of low-income Black families in particular to reproduce the patriarchal model of the white gender and sexually normative middle-class household. This failure is diagnosed as a "tangle of pathology" internal to the Black family structure, namely the Black mother's usurping of what would be otherwise the Black father's patriarchal position of power (Moynihan 1965, 29). The Moynihan Report, therefore, naturalizes patriarchy as the *structure* of family necessary not only for socioeconomic advancement but ultimately for normal existence and participation in civil society: "Ours is a society which presumes male leadership in private and public affairs" (1965, 29). By establishing patriarchy as the required structure for social normality, the report inscribes the dominance of the adult married man, as father, as ruling patriarch over the women, children, and other family members and the patrilineal transmission of this dominance from father to son as the internal domestic order for the nation-state. In doing so, the report ties masculinity to reproductive heterosexuality and patricentered descent and sociality.

The report's Black matriarch figures the Black family as the pathological antithesis of the cis-hetero-patriarchal structure of white civil society and attempts to erase and overwrite the trans and queer forms of embodiment, sexuality, and kinship lived and transmitted within Black womanhood, femmeness, masculinities, and genders outside of the lack and failure that the Black matriarch supposedly represents. As Hortense Spillers has argued, the myth of the African American matriarchate elides the histories through which African peoples were forcibly degendered and reduced to sensuous "flesh" and their kinship relationships destroyed, beginning with the fifteenth-century Atlantic slave trade (Spillers 2003, 203–29). While the Moynihan report refers to chattel slavery and Jim Crow, these histories are always subsumed within a concern for the weak Black male figure in the matrifocal Black household, which the report identifies as the only remaining sign and effect of structural racism in the post–civil rights era. Far from being a discrete policy proposal whose credibility could be merely discounted, Roderick Ferguson has identified the Moynihan Report as a "genealogical node" for new ideological alliances between liberalism, Black nationalism, civil rights, and neoconservatives consolidated through an attack on nonheteronormative Black female-headed households as depleting national culture and capital (2004, 110–37). The web of discourses and political and cultural consensus building that the report helped to create has continued to energize state rationales, cultural ideologies, and public debates under the Nixon administration in the 1970s and beyond, including the report's recent referencing in then-Senator Barack Obama's political biography *The Audacity of Hope* (Geary 2015, 1–12; Obama 2006, 254).

The flexible alliance of discourses and state and social blocs that the Moynihan Report helped to build converged around the internal diagnosis of the deviant gendering of families of color—and the queer social structures this engendering created—as the primary barrier to national racial assimilation as a potentially successful ethnic and economic class. The Moynihan Report drew from and validated anthropologist Oscar Lewis's "culture of poverty" thesis, which first appeared in Lewis's ethnographic reporting on the urban poor in Mexico in *Five Families: Mexican Case Studies in the Culture of Poverty* (1959). This thesis was further developed and circulated in Lewis's widely published studies in 1966 and 1967 on low-income Puerto Ricans in New York City and San Juan, funded partly by the University of Illinois and the Social Security and Welfare Administrations under President Lyndon B. Johnson (Lewis, *The Culture and La Vida* 1966; Motley 1967). For Lewis and his team of researchers, the culture of poverty describes strategies developed by urban poor communities under Western capitalism in response to the effects of rapid industrialization, including economic and social marginalization, the replacement of extended kinship and lineage systems with the nuclear reproductive family, and dominant upper-class individualistic values. These strategies, which are also described as symptoms that deter participation in national culture, include disengagement from dominant society and its institutions, social disorganization, unmarried mother–centered households, and individual fatalistic and inferiority complexes. Lewis's method of study focuses on the family because it is considered an intermediary "small social system" between national and class cultural values and between the community and the individual: "It helps us get beyond form and structure to the realities of human life, or . . . it puts flesh and blood on the skeleton (Lewis 1959, 3). In the studies of Mexican and Puerto Rican families, the family is what both houses and distorts the cultural strategies of the poor, especially the gender structures that produce "a high incidence of weak ego structure, orality, and confusion of sexual identification, all reflecting maternal deprivation," "widespread belief in male superiority," and "among the men a strong preoccupation with *machismo*, their masculinity" (Lewis 1966, 23).[3]

By identifying the cultural strategies used by Mexican and Puerto Rican urban underclasses, Lewis's studies treat poverty in Western capitalist nations as a feature of classed social inequality rather than a product of "natural" differences between "underdeveloped" indigenous or rural economies and urban modernity. Lewis argues that the culture of poverty cuts across racial, ethnic, national, and regional differences, countering the idea that the "high incidence of common-law marriage and of households headed by women" is somehow "distinctive of Negro [sic] family life in this country" (1959, 2; 1966, 19–20). He suggests that the culture of poverty may even host the potential of revolutionary change. Yet, what provides Lewis with a generalizable *culture* of poverty and class analysis are indigenous, racial, and ethnic systems of kinship, gender, and sexuality that exceed the patriarchal, heterosexual, and cismasculine social structures of Western capitalist nation-states. Lewis pathologizes these systems and positions them temporally as remnants of premodern life, even as he uses them to identify a subcultural class within Western capitalism and national cultures. In doing so, Lewis's culture of poverty ideology renaturalizes cisgender, heterosexuality, and patriarchy as the symbolic and material social order for modern life under Western capitalist nation-states, including the potential resistances described as entrapped within reactionary gender kinship relationships. It attempts to assimilate and further erase and displace the decolonial indigenous, racial, and ethnic temporalities of gender kinship that live outside and inside the social orders of the U.S. nation-state. Gloria Anzaldúa has used the myth of Coyolxauhqui, the dismembered Aztec goddess of the moon who symbolizes a conquered people, a sacrifice made to conquerors, and a traitor to her ruling mother and brothers, to remember the shifting gender positions and temporalities that underlie continuing histories of Anglo and Spanish colonization and hetero-patriarchal nationalism in the contemporary U.S. after 9/11 (Anzaldúa 2015; Blake 2008, 13–69; Umberger 1996, 85–108). These decolonial organizations of reality and sociality enable the translations and erasures that occur between local and transnational scales in Lewis's cultural class analysis. Examining the intimate dynamics of Puerto Rico's colonial occupation as an unincorporated territory and "domestic dependent" of the U.S., Juana María Rodríguez has argued for the possibility of mobilizing queer gestures of sovereignty that work through the inner spheres of psychic embodiment, sexuality, and kinship to produce social bonds that de-authorize the settler state (2014, 1–28, 69–98).

The now commonsense Asian model minority myth initiated by sociologist William Petersen's 1966 *New York Times* article, "Success Story, Japanese-American Style," continues the racially gendered pathologizing cultural strategies of the Moynihan Report and Lewis's culture of poverty—but with a positivist twist. Petersen argues that Japanese Americans are an exceptional "ethnic minority" that has overcome their historical experiences of discrimination, which at its extreme included forced relocation from the West Coast, internment, and labor during World War II, to become successful law-abiding middle-class citizens, in contrast to Black, Native, Mexican, Chinese, and Filipino Americans (1966, 40–41). He traces this success to the modern religious achievement-oriented ethic transmitted through the Japanese family, which he likens to the "Protestant ethic" (41). This cultural transmission relies especially on the "husband-father['s]" authority in the Japanese family, although his authority has no material support: "Each artificial restriction on the [first generation] issei—that they could not become citizens, could not own land, could not represent the camp population to the administrators—meant that the [second generation] nisei had to assume adult roles early in life, while yet remaining subject to parental control that by American standards was extremely onerous" (Petersen 1966, 41). Similar to the myths of the Black and Latinx matriarchal families, the myth of the model Japanese patriarchal family hosts a perverse racial gendering that distorts the *structure* of the self, family, and community. Whereas the Black matriarch's masculinized femininity displaces the dominance of Black men as heads of households, the purely symbolic or empty masculinity of first-generation Japanese men implicitly renders the Japanese women and the Japanese American children in the family passively compliant to authority, which for Petersen is a concern when it involves the nontransmission of power and resources (which have been stripped from the Japanese father) from father to son. Petersen's article repeats the Moynihan Report's description of the Black family as a "problem" minority, while newly placing Japanese Americans as the "model" counterpoint to Black Americans (1966, 43). Despite their attributed discipline and achievement, however, Japanese Americans remain foreign domestics preserving links to an "alien culture" that inhibits individual autonomy. On the other hand, Petersen claims Black Americans as native "daughter[s] of the American Revolution," if only to call attention to their orphan refugee dependency—marked as feminine—on white Americans for patronage (43). The 1966 *U.S. News and World Report*'s "Success Story of One Minority Group in U.S." and other public accounts extend Petersen's "model" analysis to other Asian groups. This report already begins to account for new waves of "alien Chinese from Hong Kong and Formosa [Taiwan]," whose immigration has been facilitated by the liberalized 1965 Immigration and Nationality Act.

As the least elaborated, least attuned to class differences, and seemingly least directly related to state policy of the three public accounts of racialized groups in the mid-1960s, the Asian model minority ideology relies the most explicitly on scientific positivism's claim to truth as self-verifying fact. Although Peterson and *U.S. News* base their arguments on the *figural* interpretation of statistics that are admittedly "not very satisfactory," their cultural production of scientific truth is occluded by the very symbols they supposedly report (rather than interpret): "Only four sansei were among the 779 arrested in the Berkeley student riots . . . One, the daughter of a man who 20 years ago was an officer of a Communist front, is no more a symbol of generational revolt than the more publicized Bettina Aptheker" (Peterson 1996). The numeric symbols must remain pure signifiers that do not transcend their instrumentalizing to signify insignificance, docility, and non-representability. The perversely positive coding of the Asian as a deracinated ethnic minority whose inherent ability to assimilate surpasses that of the European ethnic immigrant settler signals the neoliberal reorganization—rather than a reversal—of previous state and social regimes of anti-Asian racism. As Iyko Day has argued, the land dispossession, removal, incarceration, and forced labor of people of Japanese descent in Canada and the U.S. during World War II was not a final event that concluded the history of anti-Asian exclusion as much as a transition point in which Japanese North Americans were translated from their earlier personification as alien disembodied labor abstract value into ideal surplus laborers within domestic territories and racial hierarchies "native" to settler colonialism (2016, 1–40, 115–50). The Asian model minority myth accompanies the liberalization of immigration laws marked by the 1965 Immigration Act, 1975 Indochina Migration and Refugee Assistance Act, 1980 Refugee Act, 1982 Amerasian Immigration Act, and 1987 Amerasian Homecoming Act. Identifying continuities instead of departures between preliberalized immigration policies, such as the 1875 Page Law barring the entry of Chinese women (suspected of being prostitutes), and postliberalized immigration, Jodi Kim has read post-1965 legislation and immigration as "symptomatic of U.S. imperial Cold War presence in Asia and gendered racial formations both 'here' in the United States and over 'there' in Asia" (2010, 19–20). The positive representation of Asians by the mid-twentieth century produces a transparent visibility that screens out the possibility of perceiving the negating forms of state and social force that continue to secure the heterogeneous foreignness of Asians to define the boundaries of the U.S. nation-state. This positive screen also uses the migrant exteriority of Asians, as a racial grouping that has no native claim to the U.S. and the Americas, that has not been nativized within the national imaginary, and that did not gain the right of naturalized citizenry until the 1940s, to structure and mediate relations within the white settler colonial racial hierarchy.

The three state-sponsored myths not only divested the white settler U.S. state and civil society from responsibility for restorative justice, while transferring these responsibilities onto communities of color, indigenous peoples, women, migrants, LGBT people, people living with disabilities, and low-income people, during the moment when the state claimed to have abolished systemic subjugation through civil rights reforms. Beyond a more general leftist critique of neoliberalism, I want to suggest that these liberalized recodings renewed white supremacist settler colonial systems foundational to the nation-state through reformulated technologies of racial gendering. Through the pathologizing (mis)recognition of gender structures of kinship and sexuality in Black, Latinx, and Asian families within the terms of the cis-heteropatriarchal white social order, the state addresses communities of color anew as part of the national body, rather than absolutely alien to it. At the same time, the state establishes the gender and sexually normative middle-class family and the individuated collective form of subjectivity and sociality it reproduces as the social contract by which communities of color must abide to participate in white civil society.

Gender as a perception—or sensuous cultural interpretation—of bodily material at the threshold between the self and social world, is the target for policing, regulation, and rehabilitation in the negative and negating attempt to incorporate communities of color into the national body through cis-heterosexual social contract. The three myths use the unfixable identities of racial femininities and masculinities to assign affective hierarchies of social value including the criminal and civil, sick and productive, perverse and moral, and foreign and native. These affective orders help to mobilize state and social policies that create and intensify differentials in power between women and men and also gender differentiation itself based on naturalized binary female/male sex within communities of color. They entrench gender as socially prescribed structure, role, and identity, including establishing *cisgender* identity as the "natural" basis for subjectivity. Recognizing the changing, diverging, and sometimes contentious terms and definitions that continue to be created related to trans identities, I tenuously describe dominant cisgender identity as having a generally continuous subjective sense of gender embodiment stabilized through identification with gender assigned at birth (based on the interpretation of sex) and with the symbolic and social location provided by this identification.[4] This description attempts to highlight both the temporal subjective and spatial social dimensions that produce the ontological "I am a man (because I am perceived/assigned as male)" of cisgender identity, while signaling the fragility and ambivalence of cisgender identity as a structure of subjectivity. These racial gender myths and policies also reproduce internal power differentials that subjugate queers, survival or low-income people, migrants (especially undocumented and refugee), those with disabilities, and those who fail or refuse to perform respectable normality.

Trans Embodiments within/against
U.S. Racial Captivity and Settler Colonialism and Empire

The post–civil rights recoding of race and systemic white supremacy through the racial gender ideologies of Moynihan's Black matriarch, Lewis's Latinx culture of poverty, and Peterson's Asian model minority helped to activate the neoliberal restructuring of the settler U.S. state and civil society to minimally incorporate previously externalized communities within the national imaginary. This partial inclusion relied on the adoption of cis-hetero-patriarchal gender subject formation and social structures that would create and strengthen internal differentials in power and identity in ways that would diminish the possibility of material and symbolic social transformation. These power and identity differentials privatized within families and communities of color furthered the state's renewal of founding corporeal racial economies of anti-Black captivity, settler dispossession of Indigenous lands and nations, territorial occupation and control of Latinx Americas, and anti-Asian imperial expansion and containment under rationalized systems of rule that differentially distribute the necessities for survival, safety, livelihood, and social livability—or life and death themselves—in civil society (Haritaworn, Kuntsman, Posocco 2014; Spade 2011).

The prison industrial complex (PIC) that emerges by the early 1970s is a systemic continuation of the anti-Black chattel slavery and racial capitalism that enabled the establishment and development of the U.S. white settler political economy and its disembodied rights-bearing subject (Robinson 1983, 101–66). As Angela Davis and Michelle Alexander have argued, the PIC is a more recent incarnation of postslavery southern Black Codes and penal systems, including convict leasing, developed to reinstitutionalize slavery's conditions, ensure the incapacitated labor needed to modernize the American South and North, and restrict the possibilities of Black freedom to maintain white civil society (Davis 2003, 84–104; Alexander 2012, 20–58). Although convict leasing ended by the 1940s, a renewed era of anti-Black incarceration and policing was initiated by the Nixon administration's "law and order" regime by the late 1960s as a state response to movements for racial, gender, sexual, and decolonial justice. This regime of anti-Black criminalization, which Ruthie Gilmore has called the U.S. "domestic military state" or "military Keynesianism," harnessed the wealth and technologies developed through transnational military expansion and imperialism during World War II and the Cold War (2007, 87–127). Gilmore's analysis of the racial and militarized underpinnings of the welfare state and its war on poverty intervenes in critiques of neoliberalism that focus only on economic deregulation and the weakened state, state divestment from social needs, self-regulating individualism, and deindustrialized global capital. The PIC advances the neoliberal reconstruction of white supremacy through seemingly race and gender neutral, or even anti-racist and anti-sexist, value systems that rationalize the killing, policing, and containment of Black, Brown, and Native populations considered criminal, nonproductive, alien, and primitive—and therefore disposable (Melamed 2011, 1–49; Rodriguez 2005).

The necro/biopolitical administrative rule upheld by the PIC produces the racially, sexually, and gender differentiated distribution of death by targeting, exposure, and extraction of life-sustaining resources (Mbembe 2003; Puar 2007, 1–36). Dean Spade has situated the growth of the PIC within neoliberal policies and legal systems that criminalize to entrench the racial wealth divide, while also administering "care" through the unequal distribution of resources such as food, housing, transportation, employment, public safety, public health, education, and immigration (2011, 50–72, 73–93). The racialized, sexualized, and trans/homophobic targeting of survival- and low-income trans women of color by the police and the PIC for killing, sexual violence, and deadening in cages works alongside the withholding of resources from trans women of color through life-sustaining administrative systems, such as trans-affirming medical care, outside and within the PIC to increase the vulnerability of trans women of color to violence and death. Additionally, the maldistribution of death and life provide the differentially negating and/or sustaining bonds through which the state attempts to dematerialize social bodies and relationships and reconstitute them as groups or "populations" within hierarchies of social value and viability. The prioritizing of gay and lesbian marriage rights, protection for gay and lesbian military service, anti–gay and lesbian hate crime legislation, and corporate driven Pride celebrations by mainstream white upper-class-led organizations continues to pull resources and focus away from issues impacting LGBT communities of color and low-income LGBT communities, such as poverty, unemployment, homelessness, gentrification, state violence, sexual violence, health care, disability access, and community-based safety. It also continues to draw greater dividends of life-sustaining resources and protection from death and violence for privileged LGBT populations—and to participate in the maldistribution of death—through the (fragile and regulating) adoption of cis-homonormativity and cis-homonationalism in social contract with the state (Duggan 2003; Puar 2007, 2013). As Treva Ellison has suggested, legal reforms focused on gender and sexual injury and identity in the 1990s, such as the anti–gay and lesbian hate crimes and Violence against Women portions of the 1994 Violent Crime Control and Law Enforcement Act, participate in the neoliberal nation-state's "representational mode" of appropriating cultural difference while strengthening the anti-Black devaluation institutionalized through the PIC (2016, 323–45). Also, Jin Haritaworn has shored up the ways in which queer and transgender cultures and political organizing, even in their most progressive and radical forms, can make claims to injury, space, and protection through white structures of feeling that rely on the racialization and alienation of queer and trans people of color and communities of color (2015, 84–124). The brutal police arrest and jailing of Black trans and queer protesters, the Black Pride 4, during the June 2017 Pride march in Columbus, Ohio, highlights glaring differences in power and entitlement to state and community protection and safety within LGBT communities based on race, class, and gender identity. The Black Pride 4— Wriply Bennet, Kendall Denton, Ashley Braxton, and Deandre Miles—were part of a peaceful action involving ten protesters during the march to bring attention to the acquittal of the Minnesota police officer who killed Philando Castile, violence against and erasure of Black and Brown queer and trans people, and the fourteen reported murders of trans women of color by the first half of 2017. Yet they were targeted by the police and their attack was largely condoned and sometimes literally applauded by the predominantly white attenders and organizers of Columbus Pride. The Black Pride 4 together with Black Queer and Intersectional Coalition (BQIC), a coalition of Black queer, trans, and intersex people devoted to "fighting for a world where Black LGBTQ+ people from all backgrounds can thrive," are working to educate and mobilize communities on the ongoing local history of police violence and to call for accountability within the LGBT community for addressing racism, along with homophobia and transphobia.[5]

As a current manifestation of anti-Black captivity, the PIC is connected to the different systems of spatial and temporal control and containment effected by contemporary expansions of settler colonialism, imperialism, and racialization. The PIC's institutional location and criminalizing logic extend beyond corporate- and state-profiting prisons and jails to include what Eric Stanley and Nat Smith describe as a growing network of incarceration, policing, and surveillance that includes immigrant centers, juvenile justice facilities, county jails, military jails, holding rooms, courtrooms, sheriff's offices, and psychiatric institutions that enforce racial, sexual, and gender normalization (Stanley and Smith 2011). The era of Native self-determination announced by the Nixon administration in the 1970s reversed the U.S. government's 1953 termination policy, which withdrew federal recognition of tribes, converted tribal reservations from trust status to private ownership, and relocated tribal citizens from reservations to city centers, and the government's general drive toward terminating Native nations (Bruyneel 2007, 123–70; Rifkin 2012). As suggested by Mark Rifkin, this shift in state discourse toward recognition signals a transition into state-administered forms

FIGURES 1.2 – 1.5. Black Pride 4: Deandre Miles (*top left*), Wriply Bennet (*top right*), Ashley Braxton (*bottom left*), Kendall Denton (*bottom right*). Photos by Kendall Denton. Courtesy of Black Pride 4.

of self-determination that continue to deny, rather than support, the "changing force field of lived relations" of Native political sovereignty (2012). The granting of self-determination can be viewed as part of the settler state's cycle of connecting assimilative recognition with terminating annexation, as exemplified in the forcible removal of Natives from their lands in the 1820s and 1830s during a period of treaty-making that recognized Native nations as independent foreign nations based on their ability to conform to the political model of a centralized state (Rifkin 2015). Focusing on moral systems of ethnic cleansing aimed at assimilating Navajo cultures of matrilineal kinship, polygamy, and nonbinary gender following the military conquest of the Navajo in 1863, Jennifer Nez Denetdale calls attention to the heteropatriarchal force and violence of settler colonial tactics of assimilation (2017, 69–98).

Rather than overturning previous racial bans on immigration, the 1965 Immigration Act rationalized racialized immigration controls. Its categories of sanctioned migration based on family reunification, classes and sectors of work, and immigration status rely on the selection of cis-hetero-reproductive families, exceptional occupations, mind/body-abled workers in demand, and economically rational and moral immigrants (versus undocumented, refugee, sex workers, people who use drugs), instead of racialized categories of nationality and ethnicity. The 1965 Act's equal allotment of immigration slots to Western and Eastern Hemispheres actually placed restrictions on Western Hemisphere immigration for the first time, aimed at stemming Latinx immigration from the southern Americas and Caribbean (Ngai 2014). It relied on the infrastructure of policing, detention, and deportation established by U.S. Border Patrol at the U.S.-Mexico border facilitated by the U.S. government's Bracero Program from 1941 to 1964. The Bracero Program selectively recruited Mexican men for contractual seasonal agricultural labor while rendering other migrants, including women and children, and those without or falling out of contracts illegal. As Kelly Lytle Hernandez (2010) has discussed, state discourse and the Border Patrol's localized law enforcement during the program produced the figure of the alien worker as a state target in ways that retained connections to the figure of the enemy alien during World War II, which was shaped by perceptions of the Japanese Americans removed and interned by Border Patrol. The image of the Mexican alien worker also adopted aspects of the figure of Black criminal under new drug-related law enforcement mandates in the 1950s (Hernandez 2010). Moreover, as Jenna Loyd and Alison Mountz (2018) have argued, the current vast system of migrant detention and deportation by Immigration and Customs Enforcement (ICE), established as an agency within the Department of Homeland Security in 2002, and border deterrence by Border Patrol can be traced to U.S. Cold War efforts to contain Haitian and Cuban asylum seekers during the late 1970s and 1980s under the Carter and Reagan administrations. After 9/11, the second Bush administration's 2002 Homeland Security Act, following the Clinton administration's 1996 Antiterrorism and Effective Death Penalty Act, ties state counterterrorism measures targeting the figures of the Arab and Muslim alien terrorist to the federal and local anti- Black and Latinx police and carceral network (Macías-Rojas 2018).

The 1965 Immigration Act's positive image of immigration also indicated a higher level of rationalized control over Indigenous and Asian migration from the Pacific Islands and South, Southeast, and Northeast Asian regions. The U.S. Armed Forces is the largest and most richly funded, technologically equipped, and specialized military in the world. Its Pacific region Unified Combatant Command, which was established in 1947, is the oldest and vastest (in size and geographic area) of U.S. military commands. With its recent expansion and renaming to include the South Asian region under the Trump administration, the Indo-Pacific Command now covers over 50 percent of the Earth's surface spanning the east coast of Africa, through the Asian regions, to the west coasts of North, Central, and South America.[6] The enormous U.S. military presence in the Pacific is the result of the continued legacy of U.S. imperialism and colonial occupation, readapting the strategies of settler imperialism and colonialism and racial captivity developed within the contiguous continental territorial body of the U.S. nation-state. The overseas annexations of the Hawai'i islands (1898), the Philippines (1898), Guam (1898), Samoa (1899), and the Northern Mariana Islands (1947) in the Pacific and Puerto Rico (1898) and the Virgin Islands (1916) in the Atlantic and their divergent forms of administered governance (as incorporated, unincorporated, and trust territories), followed the white settler territorial incorporation of continental lands taken from Indigenous nations through conquest, removal, and allotment. These oceanic territories provided bases, resources, and models for U.S. military operations, economic extraction, and administrative rule during World War II and the Cold War, enabling the direct or indirect infiltration of Japan (after its final defeat through the use of nuclear weapons), Taiwan, Korea, Vietnam, Laos, Cambodia, Thailand, and Malaysia to contain communism and the then-U.S.S.R. and China. The Immigration Act's rationale controls, which allotted 6 percent of immigration slots per hemisphere to refugees, could not adequately account for the waves of migrants displaced by U.S.

wars in Vietnam, Laos, and Cambodia, who began to be held in U.S. military camps in Guam, the Philippines, and the U.S. in 1975, based on amendments to the 1965 Act. Mimi Thi Nguyen has described the temporal dimensions of the Vietnamese refugee's racialization within liberal U.S. state and dominant cultural discourses as a transitory figure of arrested development that necessarily produces war as rescue and refuge as rehabilitation (2012, 33–82).

The twenty-first century trans of color embodiments, subcultures, and social movements highlighted in *Trans Exploits* emerge through their displacement from the privatized internal affects and "public" social systems and ideologies of racial and settler colonial and imperial rule reproduced by the neoliberal U.S. nation-state. These subjective and social systems use racial (cis)gendering in particular to dematerialize and bind bodies and social relationships to the rationalized violence and power of the white supremacist state and civil society coestablished through ongoing anti-Black captivity, Indigenous dispossession through settlement, territorial occupation and containment of bordering Latinx Americas, and extraterritorial occupation of Asias, and expulsion of Asians. The book's methods and approaches draw most heavily on the socially and personally reflective intersectional analysis of women of color and transnational feminisms and the critical imaginations of queer feminist and queer of color, especially queer women and femme of color, cultural and literary theories and practices. These growing bodies of work shape my understandings of differentiated gradients of power and identity and the political possibilities of socially embodied feeling and affinities. I also engage with post-Marxist and psychoanalytic continental philosophy as it continues to be used in critical race and ethnic studies; gender and sexuality studies; and literary, film, performance, and digital media studies for contemporary theories of Western subject and nation-state formation.

In particular, I rely on Michel Foucault's biopolitical genealogies of state and social power under Western liberal democracies, as they energize his other genealogies of the state and civil society based on disciplinary and discursive normalization.[7] In *Security, Territory, Population* (2007), Foucault's description of the security power that enables the emergence of the modern state in the eighteenth century provides a theory of embodied collectivity through the biological or organismic concept of population, settlement through the concept of territory to which the population is spatially tied, and productive and reproductive civil society. The power of the state—and the state itself—are generated through rational management of the survival of the population at points of necessity where need and nature meet and respond to each other. In turn, population is created though its seemingly natural internal relationship to the state as necessity, which is the product of a form of rationalized (rather than overtly coercive) state force. Foucault briefly refers to state rule at the level of necessity as a kind of normalization: "we have here something that starts from the normal and makes use of certain distributions considered to be, if you like, more normal than the others, or at any rate more favorable than the others. These distributions will serve as the norm. The norm is an interplay of differential normalities (2007, 63)." The state tied to the population through security works through such a high degree of rationalization that it not only allows for deviations from the norm, or "differential normalities." It can make the "interplay" and "distribution," or the differential relationships between them, productive.

The deaths of Roxana Hernandez, who died under ICE detention in a private federal prison for men in New Mexico in May 2018; Jennifer Laude, who was killed in the Philippines by a U.S. Marine based there in October 2014; and Kayla Moore, who was killed by Berkeley police during a mental health crisis in California in February 2013 call for accountability from the officers and the police and military bodies to which they belong. They also call for responses to these acts of violence as expressions of state violence continuous with—and foundational to—the liberal democracy that is the U.S. settler nation-state. U.S. prison, federal and local policing, and military networks, which surpass all countries in size, brutality and lethality, funding, and mobility, are part of a state and social infrastructure that has made dematerializing, deadening, and confining racially gendered social bodies the precondition for the rights of white civil society. This same infrastructure forms the foundation of the cis-hetero-patriarchal family that represents the settled private body of the republic.

Although small in number, trans women of color and trans of color organizers, cultural workers, and communities living within differentials in power and identity that dispossess them and make them targets of state and interpersonal violence have been working to transform differentials into interdependent relationships and shared resources. Jennicet Gutiérrez and Familia: Trans Queer Liberation Movement, whose work I discuss in more detail in the conclusion, have called local and national attention to the detention, imprisonment, and deportation of undocumented Latinx LGBT immigrants, especially trans women, by ICE and the prison network. Gutiérrez and Familia intervene in more mainstream immigrant rights movements, which have focused primarily on legal reforms that divide communities be-

FIGURE I.6. TGI Justice family, San Francisco Trans March (June 23, 2017).
Photo by the author.

tween "good" immigrants viewed as deserving pathways to full citizenship
and "bad" immigrants seen as acceptable targets of immigration policing.
Using the model of the united "familia," they build alliances within and outside Latinx communities to make the criminalization and abuse faced by undocumented Latinx trans women and trans and queer liberation issues that
are integral to immigrant and racial justice movements.

TGI Justice Project and their Executive Director Janetta Johnson are
building a local and national movement for gender racial justice and self-
determination that centers on trans, gender variant, and intersex (TGI) sur-
vivors of prisons, jails, and detention centers, especially low-income trans
women of color. TGI Justice recognizes and elevates the leadership of currently and formerly incarcerated TGI people and takes seriously the need to
provide familial networks and resources for survival, resilience, and resistance. In addressing the growing reported number of trans women of color
murdered each year, most of them Black trans women, Johnson and TGI Justice call on community members to share responsibility for ending transphobia and violence against Black trans women:

FIGURE 1.7. Miss Major Griffin-Gracy from *MAJOR!* (2015). Film still courtesy of Annalise Ophelian and StormMiguel Florez.

Eliminating transphobia, and stopping the violence perpetrated against Black trans women in particular, requires each of us to be daring enough to reflect on how we have all contributed to it, and to be mindful of how we have, whether we are aware of it or not, given rise to an environment in which transgender people are in danger doing everyday activities like walking down the street, going to work, or having a cup of coffee. It requires educators to begin teaching lessons on the history of transgender people, for legislators to take seriously their job to protect every single person they claim to represent, and for everyday people to intervene when witnessing violence against trans people.[8]

Also, TGI Justice has asked the city of San Francisco, where the group is based in the Tenderloin, to begin giving some of the profits it reaps from LGBT-related cultural life and tourism back to the low-income trans communities responsible for making the city an LGBT haven. Trans movement mother and Stonewall 1969 veteran Miss Major Griffin-Gracy, who was the former Executive Director of TGI Justice, continues her forty years of organizing for gender and racial liberation and prisoner justice—one relationship and one conversation at a time—at age seventy-six.

Chapters Ahead

Chapter 1, "Cultures: Performing Racial Trans Senses," focuses on the aesthetics, cultural imaginings, and political potential of twenty-first-century trans Asian American multimedia performance. Yozmit's trans performance of femininity plays with the body's surfaces to deconstruct and rework binary cisgender and its relation to sex. Wu Tsang works across networked mediums and cultural economies to describe the tensions and affinities that enable trans solidarities in struggle. Zavé Martohardjono's performances stage their queer racial nonbinary embodiment as a nexus of displaced diasporic transmissions shaped by multiple histories of colonization and cultural consumption. The chapter describes and theorizes racially trans embodied practices, which intervene in state and social regimes of sense that have sought to extinguish and control the multiplicity of Asian American genders. It explores connections between emerging trans Asian American cultures and more established queer and feminist cultural critiques and histories.

Chapter 2, "Networks: TRANScoding Biogenetics and Orgasm in the Transnational Digital Economy," investigates the technological infrastructure that has networked different media, biological, and cultural forms in a transnational economy dominated by U.S. state capitalism. It focuses on the racially trans embodied digital art of Taiwan-born, gender queer digital nomad Cheang Shu Lea. In particular, the chapter engages with Cheang's postporn digital film *I.K.U.* (2000), which is a rip-off of Ridley Scott's analog film *Blade Runner* (1982), and *I.K.U.*'s sequel UKI (2009–14), a live video performance and online game. *I.K.U.* and UKI produce interactive experiences of the embodied racial, gendered, and sexed cultural labor that supports the digitally powered transnational economy.

Chapter 3, "Memory: The Times and Territories of Trans Woman of Color Becoming," addresses the literary, popular, and political impact of Janet Mock's first widely circulated trans woman of color memoir *Redefining Realness: My Path to Womanhood, Identity, Love and So Much More* (2014). The chapter discusses the potential interventions of popular literary memoir and memoir criticism on classed conceptions of literature in relationship to Mock's ambivalent repurposing of memoir and other dominant forms of cultural representation. It highlights Mock's embedding of her personal stories of trans self-realization within collective Black and Native Hawaiian cultural memory on the fortified Pacific and Atlantic borders of the U.S. state and national body.

Chapter 4, "Movement: Trans and Gender Nonconforming Digital Activisms and U.S. Transnational Empire," assembles three modes of trans and gender nonconforming cultural activism using digital technologies in different countries and regions of the world. Johannesburg-based lesbian, gay, bisexual, transgender, and intersex (LGBTI) human rights group Iranti-org uses digital media to document the intimate and state violence targeting Black South African gender nonconforming lesbians in Black townships. Bangkok-based Thai *kathoey* digital filmmaker Tanwarin Sukkhapisit produces independent and commercial films that feature kathoey storylines, characters, and actresses/actors. U.S. West Coast–based Latina queer transfemme media theorist, artist, and activist micha cárdenas mixes and repurposes digital media and virtual reality to address the survival needs and livelihoods of trans women of color and migrants of color in the Americas. Each of these trans and gender nonconforming activists exploit digital technologies against their dominant uses to intervene in transnational expansions of U.S. governance and finance, Hollywood, and state violence.

The concluding chapter, "Trans Voice in the House," revisits undocumented Chicanx/Latinx trans organizer Jennicet Gutiérrez's interruption of then president Barack Obama during his LGBT Pride speech at the White House in June 2015. As shown in the online YouTube videos documenting the event, Gutiérrez's presence and voice called attention to the daily torture, detention, and deportation of trans women, most of whom are Latinx women from Mexico and Central America, while revealing the racial gender and sexual histories of embodiment and sense that shape differential relationships to public/private U.S. citizenship and state rule. The chapter discusses the Trump and prior administrations' antimigrant policies and their fortification of the U.S.-Mexico and other national borders as attempts to control the multiple territories and identities that continue to survive and thrive within the colonial geographies of the Americas.

ONE. CULTURES

Performing Racial Trans Senses

Questions arising on the move, at the borders, in the encounter with the other, and when stranger meets stranger, all tend to intensify around the problem of the *other* foreigner—someone doubly strange, who doesn't *speak* or look like the rest of us, being paradoxically at once exotic guest and abhorred enemy. —TRINH T. MINH-HA, Elsewhere, Within Here: Immigration, Refugeeism and the Boundary Event (2011)

I refer to disidentification as a hermeneutic, a process of production, and a mode of performance. Disidentification can be understood as a way of shuffling back and forth between reception and production. For the critic, disidentification is the hermeneutical performance of decoding mass, high, or any other cultural field from the perspective of a minority subject who is disempowered in such a representational hierarchy. —JOSÉ ESTEBAN MUÑOZ, Disidentifications: Queers of Color and the Performance of Politics (1999)

In her documentary video "Transcending Stonewall" (2011), trans Korean American performance artist Yozmit evokes the 1969 Stonewall riots in New York City as the historical event that has made her art and existence possible. Against the increasingly gender, sexually, and racially normalized image of LGBT liberation, Yozmit (who alternates between feminine and masculine pronouns) reclaims this uprising for trans and gender nonconforming people, who continue to struggle with what she describes as the "stonewall inside." Her reclaiming of Stonewall makes it possible to remember the survival-income trans women of color and trans and gender nonconforming people of color, including Sylvia Rivera, Marsha P. Johnson, Miss Major Griffin-

Gracy, and Stormé DeLarverie, who have been written out of mainstream LGBT histories and whose organizing in the face of societal and state forms of criminalization, eviction, and violence sparked contemporary LGBT movements. Through a street performance just outside the landmark Stonewall Inn, documented by her video, Yozmit brings this submerged history to life through movement, costuming, and documentation.

Although Yozmit's performance documentary re-enlivens the history of Stonewall, it does not try to restore an image of Stonewall that will make the event more visible or transmittable. Her incrementally slow silent walk in outlandish polka-dotted costuming, which covers the entire surface of her body from head and face to toe, disaligns the iconic vision of Stonewall. Yozmit's voiceover description of the performance furthers another obstruction: "Just like our gender, male and female, there's no separation for me . . . But there's been so much conflict inside me as a human being. And I feel like I finally found harmony within. And without that energy, the fight, and struggle of Stonewall, I couldn't break that stone wall inside me. I think that's the Stonewall of 2011. That energy has transcended into something more harmonious and natural" (2011). If Yozmit's performance interrupts the view of Stonewall, the documentary's description reenergizes Stonewall as energy, fight, and struggle as it withdraws Stonewall from sight to refer to the ongoing struggle with the "stone wall inside," or internal conflict with—and potential transcendence of—the separation between genders. Her antivisual performance and narrative strategies intervene in what Che Gossett has described as the memorializing of Stonewall and other historical sites of queer and transgender resistance through a purging of criminalized racial, gender, and class undesirables that enables the production of a sanitized archive of queer memory (2013). Yozmit withdraws the image of Stonewall from the visible regime of the social world to reconstitute it within an internal world rife with struggle and utopian potential. Far from being apolitical or asocial, her antivisual aesthetics of interiority address, recode, and resist the colonization of embodied sense through racial gender histories of U.S. state and social rule, settlement, captivity, occupation, and containment.

This chapter focuses on the trans aesthetics, cultural imaginings, and political impacts of Asian American visual artists Yozmit, Wu Tsang, and Zavé Martohardjono. These cultural workers use multimedia performance and film/video to stage, disalign, and subvert the naturalized senses of binary cisgender embodiment that enforce the inside/outside boundaries of the white settler American subject, national body, and nation-state. In particular, the

FIGURE 1.1. Yozmit, *Transcending Stonewall* (2011). Courtesy of Yozmit.

piece describes and theorizes the ways in which their performed racially trans embodied practices intervene in U.S. state and social mind-body-sense regimes that have sought to extinguish, surveil, sequester, and control the multiplicity of Asian American genders—and the social and sensual relations this multiplicity engenders. The chapter builds connections between emerging twenty-first century trans Asian American art and activism and more established queer and feminist, especially Asian American queer and feminist, cultural critiques and histories.

Yozmit: Racial Trans Embodiments

Yozmit is a New York– and Los Angeles–based trans migrant Korean performance artist who draws from an eclectic mix of training and practices in costume design, traditional Korean singing (*pansori* and *gayageum byungchang*), modern dance, fashion, pop music and culture, corporeal mime (Étienne Decroux technique), Buddhist mythology and meditation, and shamanism. Her performance art brings together these interdisciplinary elements to create a multisensory experience of sound, spatial movement, and visual content that shifts between embodied and disembodied worlds. For Yozmit, who identifies as a trans woman who is both woman and man, feminine and masculine, performance expresses the "divine thing" that is "having both genders" (2011, 2014). If performance is a spatially and temporally bound cultural event that stages a collective encounter with the aesthetics and practices of the quotidian everyday through the body of the performer, Yozmit's performances so often produce an alienation from the performed self and from the live ecology of performance. As exemplified in the Stonewall street performance of *Transcending*, her bodily acts disrupt the familiar spatial and temporal continuities of seeing, moving, and producing meaning to provoke the body's internal senses. Beyond its confinement to the art event as a discrete moment of meaning-making or "speech acts," Diana Taylor has described performance as "doing," or as living gestures and actions that transmit knowledge, memory, and senses of belonging through repeated and new enactments (2016, 1–41). Performance works through and can also rework codified social practices embedded in the body through "imitation, repetition, and internalizing the actions of others" (Taylor 2016, 13). Yozmit uses her body as an expressive medium to transmit an understanding of the body's structuring through gender and the body's potential metamorphosis through gender.

In his live performance at the New Music Seminar's 2012 Opening Gala in New York City, Yozmit appears in a neo-Victorian gold-and-white monochrome dress propped by an enormous mesh skirt. His towering appearance draws us spatially upward and outward in a ritual of witnessing. Much like his Stonewall street performance, Yozmit's ornate costuming and routinized movements provide visual signals while dispelling the drive to see and read. The amorphous flow of his bulb-shaped bonnet and sleeves and the netted enclosure of his skirt invite more of an enfolding of sight where it meets the body than a gaze. Yet, the folds of Yozmit's costumed body also retain the rigid structure of their design so that the dress that absorbs our vision is also an exoskeleton that keeps us on the external surface of the body. Adding to his shrouded appearance, Yozmit chants and sings in an undecipherable language that vaguely resembles Korean, accompanied by electronic beats, streaming color lights, and dancers. This first part of the performance ends when the dancers open his mesh skirt outward into two split screens to reveal him at human scale standing on a platform just above electronica DJ Alek Sandar, who had been spinning music behind/within the mesh skirt. After

FIGURE 1.2. Yozmit, "Sound of New Pussy," with DJ Alek Sandar and dancers Trouve Belok and Joe Buffa, New Music Seminar Opening Gala performance, New York City (June 17, 2012). Courtesy of Yozmit.

a costume change behind the screens of the mesh skirt, Yozmit emerges for the second part of his performance, loudly singing the words he had chanted softly and indistinctly earlier—"sound of new pussy"—as the song chorus. Yozmit's staging of the interplay and tension between the surface and depth of the body continue the queer work of denaturalizing heteropatriachal gender/ sex while also highlighting the cisgender structures that continue to bind the materiality of bodily sense to binary essential sex.

The scene of drag performance continues to provide vital queer methods for deconstructing gender as a sign that "naturally" represents or correlates with the assigned sex of the body. In her groundbreaking work on gender performativity, which is situated distinctly from her more current focus on the precarious life of minoritized populations and the performative collective embodiment of political action, Judith Butler relied on drag as a subcultural practice and conceptual metaphor to show the "imitative structure of gender itself—as well as its contingency" (1990, 137; preface; politics of assembly). In *Gender Trouble: Feminism and the Subversion of Identity* (1990), Butler counters the perception of drag, cross-dressing, and butch/femme identities as imitations of "real" heterosexual masculinity and femininity by arguing that these supposed parodies of gender reveal the nonnatural parodic character of gender itself, which has no original to be copied. Butler draws on drag's particular association with performance to denaturalize the correlation between the sexed body and gender as performance or presentation and also between gender identity and gender performance or presentation:

> The performance of drag plays upon the distinction between the anatomy of the performer and the gender that is being performed. But we are actually in the presence of three contingent dimensions of significant corporeality: anatomical sex, gender identity, and gender performance. If the anatomy of the performer is already distinct from the gender of the performer, and both of those are distinct from the gender of the performance, then the performance suggests a dissonance not only between sex and performance, but sex and gender, and gender and performance (1990, 137).

The theatrical artifice attributed to drag as a "performance," especially femme drag, makes visible not only the socially constructed nature of gender but ultimately the production of the Western liberal subject's experience and knowledge of "being" as bodily individuated "felt" substance through the performance of gender. The repetitious acts (movement, gesture, utterances) that perform gender at the liminal external/internal surface of the body generate the imagined internal depth of gender identity and the binary differentiated boundaries of the gendered body unified through the concept of sex. Fusing queer subcultural styles with British speech act philosophy and French feminist psychoanalysis, phenomenology, and poststructuralism, Butler's gender performatives identify gender as an unstable assemblage that includes the surface of gender performance, the interiority of gender identity, and bodily containment unified by sex—produced under the coercion of the dominant social law of binary gendered reproductive heterosexuality.

In *Bodies That Matter* (1993), Butler further developed her theory of gender performatives through engagement with the racially and ethnically constituted gender performances and kinship systems of the Black and Latinx queer, trans, and gender nonconforming Harlem ballroom competitions documented in the film *Paris Is Burning* (1990), directed by Jennie Livingston. "Realness" in the film's ballroom culture, which is the main standard by which competitions are judged based on contestants' ability to authentically present as "real" heterosexual women and men across high/low socioeconomic classes in white and Black social contexts, provides Butler with a culturally specified description of the ambivalent structure of gender (as drag performance), established by a heterosexual discursive regime that enforces the reproduction of binary gender norms as real and natural while also producing gender's potential excess through parody, failure, recoding, and subversion. In particular, Butler reads Venus Xtravaganza, celebrated Puerto Rican trans "femme realness queen" in the balls, daughter in the House of Xtravaganza, and survival-income sex worker—and her murder—as illustrating the limitations of parody and the totality of discursive gender norms: "Venus, and *Paris Is Burning* more generally, calls into question whether parodying the dominant norms is enough to displace them; indeed, whether the denaturalization of gender cannot be the very vehicle for reconsolidation of hegemonic norms."

Despite her attention to some of the power differentials between the cisgay men in drag and Venus in the film's ballroom circuit and her strong critique of the gender laws that result in Venus's death, Butler treats Venus's trans desire to feel complete in her womanhood, which Venus also associates (sometimes hyperbolically) with the safety and comfort of being able to have a car, a man she loves, and a nice home, as a "tragic misreading of the social map of power" and "fatally unsubversive appropriation" (Butler 1993, 128, 131; Livingston 1990). In sync with the documentary's style of contrasting the imaginative desires of drag "realness" in the balls with narrated critical knowledge of the realities of the street for the ball's cisgay men, while emphasizing the nondifference between imaginative desire and the longing to be real according to dominant reality's gender standards for the ball's trans women (with Venus and Octavia Saint Laurent speaking to us much of the time from their private bedrooms), Butler reads Venus and her death as showing not only the symbolic rigidity and power of gender norms but also the (uncritical) incorporation and repetition of the gender norms that have dispossessed her—as pure imitation. Yet, can we understand Venus's murder not so much as socially enacted punishment for her failure (and desire) to make her body—her "remaining organs"—compliant with symbolic norms but rather as punishment for daring to exist at all as the woman she already was and would have continued to be if she had lived (with or without bottom surgery)—a woman differentially constituted by a transiting of racial gender that barred her from being "real" (Butler 1993, 131)?

As a trans artist who often performs in drag venues, Yozmit's performances play with the differences and connections between drag as a queer subcultural practice that makes the social imposition of gender and sex visible through gender expression; transgender as an internal gender identifica-

FIGURE 1.3. Yozmit, "Sound of New Pussy" music video (2012). Image design by Yvette Choy. Courtesy of Yozmit.

tion, disaligned with the gender assigned at birth, that may or may not be visible as or aligned with gender expression; and transsexual, a term that has not been politically repurposed (such as queer or transgender) while it continues to be used to describe those who undergo medically assisted hormonal and/or surgical gender transition away from gender assigned at birth, either as a subcategory of or distinguished from transgender. Yozmit's enclosed bodice, mesh screened skirt, and encoded chanting at the New Music Seminar stage femmeness as a surface with the promise of revealing the real (correlating or noncorrelating) gender and sex within and underneath. This suspended movement between gender as surface and depth is not resolved when Yozmit opens up her screened skirts. In part two of her performance, Yozmit appears from behind her skirts, stripped down to a bare Gothic-style gold metallic dress that exaggerates her breasts. She has a handheld screen strapped to her pelvis. Singing "sound of new pussy" mixed with familiar yet alien tones that mimic language, she strips away pieces of her dress, as if taking off metal armor, to reveal a sequin black dress. The blank screen between her legs begins to flash a pair of red lips as Yozmit dances out the rest of the song to DJ Sandar's electronic beats. By keeping viewers at the threshold between surface and depth, Yozmit's performance calls attention to the cisheterosexual discursive order of vision and desire that establishes differential social value between cismasculinity and cisfeminity by reading gender presentation as a binary sign for gender interiority and bodily essence in sex. Each stripping away of the femme surface only reveals another femme surface that suggests depth and substance.

Moreover, Yozmit's performance goes beyond staging the linguistic hierarchy of gender signs and meanings that normalize gender expression to provoke a *critical sense* of the self-referencing structure of internal presence and unified embodiment that enables the "I am the self that I am perceived to be and that I feel myself to be" of cisgender identity. Trans experience can not only be described as alienation from how one's gender has been perceived and assigned repetitiously at and after birth through social ideologies, institutions, and bodies. It can also be described as the experience of *sensing* the different interrelated spatial-temporalities that produce gendered being and their various degrees and contexts of disalignment and alignment, in contrast to the cisgender experience of relatively nondifferentiated spatial-temporal uniformity and cohesion. Butler's three layers of gender experience—the social surface of gender performance, the interiority of gender identity, and bodily containment unified by sex—powerfully denaturalize Western epistemologies of gender as essential soul or biological body by suggesting that the regulated social performance of gender produces inner experience and bodily substance. Yet, Butler's gender performativity relies on a linguistic conception of self-present speech that flattens the multiple spatial-temporalities, nonlinguistic gestures, and circuitries of internal sense and bodily material. These multiple spatial-temporalities, "languages," and relations of internal embodiment underlie and exceed what can be captured in the statement "I am a (trans)man," "I am finally the woman I have always felt myself to be," or what may sound only like the desire for gender conformity in Venus Xtravaganza's speech. With each performance of femininity, Yozmit evokes senses of interiority and embodiment in relationship to different styles of femme bodily enclosure, movement, and the familiar and alien sounds of his singing. "Sound of new pussy" gestures toward a different web of sensory relations between outer and inner life and body. Rather than recoding the meaning of the lowly name given to the feminine generally, to the sexual organ that continues to determine the assignment of female versus male gender, and to the imagined receptive interiority that gives language a reproductive body, Yozmit redistributes the bodily spatial-temporal fixity of the "pussy" through the sense of sound, which moves in-between and inside/outside of bodies, and his undecipherable singing. The live performance concludes with Yozmit emerging for a third time in a flowing black-and-white flower monochrome dress that masks his head, face, and body. He walks offstage to join the audience, with the long fabric of his dress extending outward like a parachute. Viewers gather under and within its folds to dance.

The multiple space-times of external/internal surface and embodiment made sensible and visible by Yozmit's performance transcend the normalized gender formation of Western liberal subjectivity—and its failures and subversions. They are shaped by the racial, colonial, and imperial histories of gendering that give rise to the white citizen subject of the U.S. nation-state. Karen Shimakawa has described Asian American racial formation as a state and process of abjection: "Asian Americanness . . . occupies a role both necessary to and mutually constitutive of national subject formation—*but it does not result in the formation of an Asian American subject or even an Asian American object*" (2002, 3; emphasis in original). Asian American performance brings into visibility the movement between visibility and invisibility and domestic incorporation and foreign expulsion initiated by U.S. state efforts to establish and manage Asianness as a frontier that unifies and purifies American national identity (Shimakawa 2002, 1–22). As shown in Yozmit's performance aesthetics, the ongoing effects of racial gendering produce a visual suspension between surface and depth, absence and presence, and mask and body when viewing and reading the gender of the Asian body. Yozmit makes this racial structure of suspension visible and palpable and transforms this suspension into moments for collectively sensing the other spatial-temporalities, modes, and relations of experience that exceed and constitute the mind-body-sense matrix of white Western liberal subjectivity.

Wu Tsang: Wild Affinities

In Wu Tsang's short digital film "Shape of a Right Statement" (2008), a multi- gender and racial Asian speaker addresses viewers directly through the screen of the film. But the act of speaking is mechanical. Words force their way out in spurts, interrupted by long pauses. The speaker is frozen in place, with their eyes locked in a permanent stare. The stage curtain in the background and front spotlighting further confuse our efforts to interpret the scene. The speaker's direct communication is also a staged performance. The last phrase spoken is "Only when the many shapes of personhood are recognized will justice and human rights be possible."

Los Angeles–based trans mixed-race second generation Chinese American visual artist and activist Wu Tsang is the speaker in the film and the film's director. She identifies as a trans guy and as trans feminine. Rather than producing single, discrete works of art, Tsang creates interlinked pieces across the cultural mediums of film, performance, installation, and digital media. "Shape of a Right Statement" itself is a transmission of the online digital video "In My Language" (2007) by autism rights activist Mel Baggs, who identifies as genderless and trans*.[1] The first segment of Baggs's video shows hir communicating in what ze calls hir "native language." Ze interacts with hir surroundings through high-pitched sound, waving movements, repetitive touch, and sight engaged with the objects ze touches. In the second part of the video, titled "A Translation," Baggs's sensory interactions are accompanied by verbal speech produced by hir typing on a computer program. This verbal speech, which also appears in subtitles, delivers a manifesto against the need to even translate hir ways of communicating and being into a language that viewers understand: "failure to learn your language is seen as a deficit but failure to learn my language is seen as so natural that people like me are officially described as mysterious and puzzling." The video addresses us directly as viewers who participate in hierarchies of communication, cognition, and ability that pathologize people with autism. Baggs's video went viral on YouTube. Tsang's "Shape" extends the viral reach of "In My Language" by becoming a copy. It retransmits verbatim Baggs's manifesto in the second part of her video "A Translation" and also the rhythm, intonations, and spacing of Baggs's technologically facilitated speaking. Tsang's copy does not just communicate Baggs's message but rather makes Baggs's differently embodied mind and inner life communicable as the medium's (other) message (McLuhan 1994, 7–21). In doing so, Tsang treats her own racially trans engendered body like a technological medium affected, or even instrumentalized, by the external force of Baggs's computerized voice. She blurs the lines between identification and miming to express solidarity with Baggs's manifesto. Tsang's "Shape," therefore, expands the impact of Baggs's "In My Language" by creating affinities between struggles to depathologize and liberate people with disabilities, transgender people, and trans people of color.

The most current version of the American Psychiatric Association's (APA) Diagnostic and Statistical Manual of Mental Disorders (DSM-5) (2013) introduced significant changes in the psych-medical diagnosis and cultural assessment of autism and transgender experience. The DSM-5's guidelines for autism collapse the DSM-4's five classifications for autism (Autistic Disorder, Asperger's Disorder, Rett's Disorder, Childhood Disintegrative Disorder, and Pervasive Development Disorder Not Otherwise Specified) under one umbrella diagnostic classification Autism Spectrum Disorder, with the exception of Rett's Disorder, which was reclassified as a genetic disorder and removed (*DSM-4* 1994, 2013).[2] Along with the subsuming of classifications, the DSM-5 shifts from diagnostic criteria for autism based largely on deficits in social interaction and communication, such as having "an interest in friendship but lack[ing] perceived understanding of the conventions of social interaction" (*DSM-4* 1994, 66), toward assessment that appears more objectively qualitative, such as the use of a table for specifying three levels of severity in deficit that would require different levels of support (*DSM-4* 2013). Although this shift seems to begin to destigmatize those deemed autistic by creating more quantitative measures for psych-medical and social diagnosis and "support," it continues to normalize both autism's status as a pathology and an internal hierarchy between those with autism based on a spectrum of functionality (Thomas and Boellstorff 2017). The spectrum ultimately provides a measure for degrees of defectiveness that Eli Clare has argued produces a justification for the ablest ideology of the cure and its systems of eradicating, imprisoning, and institutionalizing disabled people (Clare 2017, 4–20).

Changes in psych-medical diagnosis for transgender experience follow a similar pattern of destigmatization accompanied by more rationalized forms of pathologization. The DSM-5 replaces the DSM-4's diagnostic classification Gender Identity Disorder, which used "cross-gender identification" and "discomfort about one's assigned sex or a sense of inappropriateness in the gender role of that sex" (*DSM-4* 1994, 532–38) as two primary aspects of assessment, with Gender Dysphoria, defined generally as "an individual's affective/cognitive discontent with the assigned gender" and diagnostically as "a marked incongruence between one's experienced/expressed gender and assigned gender, of at least 6 months' duration" (*DSM-5* 2013). The DSM-5's entry for Gender Dysphoria is distinctive in that it defines its use of terms, including the differences between sex, sexual, and gender, before providing diagnostic guidelines. Its description of gender as "public lived role as boy or girl, man or woman" revises the DSM-4's understanding of gender within the confines of perceived binary biological sex, such that having a gender identity different from that assigned at birth was considered a "*cross-gender identification*" defined as the desire to be the "other sex" (*DSM-4* 1994, 532–38). The DSM-4 treats experiencing a gender identity different from one's assigned gender at birth itself as a disorder. In contrast, the DSM-5 takes care to identify gender dysphoria as a clinical problem, not gender identity, which it describes newly as a "category of social identity and refers to an individual's identification as male, female, or, occasionally, some category other than male or female," including transgender individuals who "transiently or persistently identify with a gender different from their natal gender" (DSM-5 2013). The term *transsexual* is used to describe someone who seeks or has undergone "social transition from male to female or female to male," sometimes involving "somatic transition" through hormone replacement and genital surgery (DSM-5 2013). The DSM-5 depathologizes gender identity and even recognizes gender identity as a form of social subjectivity. Yet, its focus on the experience of gender dysphoria or "incongruence" with one's assigned gender or one's "primary and/or secondary sex characteristics" further naturalizes socially prescribed binary gender expressions and roles and biological sex as inner feeling.[3] In the DSM-5, the problem is not enforced and naturalized (cis)gender as it continues to predetermine social value and relations and to shape the self-perception and embodied sense of trans and gender variant people. Rather, it is the disalignment that trans and gender variant children, adolescents, and adults feel internally with their assigned gender that is considered a mental illness. This dissonance can only be understood as it is expressed within the confines of a binary (cis)gender determinism described as the "desire to be the other gender" or the "desire for the primary and/or secondary sex characteristics of the other gender," instead of a disalignment with or opposition to the (cis)gender structure of social relations itself (DSM-5 2013). The DSM-5 continues to uphold dominant society's authority to produce perceptions of—and to assign a social location to—disabled and transgender and gender nonconforming people. The psych-medical discourse of "care" for socially deficient autistic and internally dysphoric gender variant selves rationalizes the colonization of body, mind, and inner sense; forced institutionalization and psych-medical treatment; and the gatekeeping of psych-medical resources and services. Both autism and gender identity disorder first appeared in the DSM-3, which shifted away from the psychological paradigms of earlier DSMs toward symptom-driven arguments (Drescher 2013). While homosexuality was removed from the DSM-2 in 1973, the new classification Ego-dystonic Homosexuality appeared in the DSM-3 to diagnose "homosexuals for whom changing sexual orientations is a persistent concern" (DSM-3 1980, 281).[4]

By miming Baggs's video manifesto "In My Language," Tsang's "Shape of a Right Statement" links Baggs's indictment of the pathologizing of body-mind-sense interactions and communication outside of what is considered natural social language to the perceptual confinement of racial trans bodies. The words typed and spoken by Baggs on computer in the second portion of hir video are a translation only so much as they use the dominant form of language familiar to viewers. Baggs uses words in our language to call attention to the limitations of our conceptions of language and the social interaction language enables: "My language is not about designing words or even visual symbols for people to interpret. It is about being in a constant conversation with every aspect of my environment" (Baggs 2007). These words are spoken and seen alongside images of hir moving hir fingers under running faucet water in a sink: "In this part of the video the water doesn't symbolize anything. I am just interacting with the water as the water interacts with me" (Baggs 2007). Baggs uses our language to call attention to the ways in which our naturalized language actually involves the imposition of concepts onto the world through symbolism and interpretation. Rather than using words and images to instrumentalize the world into thought-things, ze interacts with hir surroundings through multiple mind-body-senses. In both parts of hir video, Baggs turns images and words away from decipherable representation to make hir video message an experience of communicability. In "Shape," Tsang repeats the spoken manifesto-translation from the second part of Baggs video, including the artificial sound, rhythm, and tone of the computerized speech used by Baggs. By copying Baggs's technologically communicated speech exactly, Tsang rejects the attempt to rehabilitate a naturalized language and voice for Baggs. Instead, she retains and intensifies the artifice of Baggs's translation of hir embodied interactions into dominant spoken language. Although Tsang speaks Baggs's computerized words from her own mouth, her performance of speaking conveys an alienness that disaligns her speech from any sense of natural embodiment or interiority. Tsang calls her performance style in "Shape" and other artwork "full body quotation": "Full body quotation is a performance technique I've been working on, but the name could change as it evolves. The performer has a hidden audio source and she respeaks voices mimetically—not just the text but tone, breath, accent, idiom, etc. The idea is to question the authenticity and intention of the speaker, and understand content differently, out of its original context. . . . The full body quotation technique is a way to perform our ambivalences" (Wyma 2012). "Full body quotation" deauthenticates and interrupts the linguistic aim of speech and its home in the speaking social subject. The performed respeaking voice retains and marks the externality of the original source it is repeating and the source's other body and context. Yet, the respoken speech and context occupy a new body and context that also affects the original. If Baggs's video manifesto counters ablest society's claim to thought, communication, and social interaction, Tsang's film performance denaturalizes the alignment between expression, body, and essence in the dominant cisgender imagination. The "incongruence" between assigned social self, body, and inner feeling attributed to transgender and gender nonconforming people is staged visibly and viscerally as an effect of socially and technologically mediated perception that privatizes and confines the gender variant mind-body-sense to an inner world of struggle considered asocial and apolitical. Rather than opposing this dominant social diagnosis of transgender and gender nonconforming people by claiming normality, Tsang uses differently constituted gender variant senses of embodiment to create a mimetic affinity with other mind-body-sense relations perceived as asocial and to perform disidentification with dominant social sense.

The gender variant senses of embodiment that shape Tsang's sensibilities and politics of mimetic performance are also racial senses. I want to argue that her mimetic aesthetics have been shaped by ongoing histories of anti-Asian racialization, colonialism, and imperialism that have operated through gendering. Both before and after the liberalization of U.S. immigration policies beginning in the mid-twentieth century, the assignment of gender based on white cis-hetero-patriarchal ideals has enabled state and societal control of Asian bodies, social relations, and movement for the purposes of socioeconomic extraction and securing racialized Asianness as the external/internal boundary for the settler nation-state. As documented in the more widely known historical accounts of Chinese, Filipino, Indian, Korean, and Japanese men in the U.S., Asian men were recruited as laborers for rapidly developing agricultural, fishing, railroad, mining, lumber, factory, and service (restaurant, laundry, domestic work, etc.) industries before World War II. Federal immigration and citizenship bans; local state antimiscegenation and alien land laws; and individual state and city health, housing, labor, and crime policies worked together to selectively exact the exploitable and disposable masculinized productivity of Asian men, while attempting to contain the perceived sexual, moral, and social corruption embodied by Asian men through spatial policing and enforced temporal transience. Revising more prevalent Asian American histories focused on the "bachelorization" of Asian men through labor recruitment and bars on immigration, which tend to reinforce the "settled" racially homogenous heterosexual couple and family unit as the most significant forms of social kinship, Nayan Shah has tracked the sexual and social intimacies between South Asian men and the interracial relationships between South Asian men and Mexican and white women in western North America and Canada during the first decades of the twentieth century (Shah 2011). South Asian migrant men in the Pacific Northwest and Northern California were a subset of the eighty thousand Punjabi, Sindhi, Gujarati, and Afghani merchants, former soldiers, and laborers who left British colonial India to travel through Southeast Asia to Canada, the U.S., Australia, Hawai'i, Mexico, Panama, and Argentina between 1834 and 1930 (Shah 2011, 1–18). The adaptive and transient homosocial bonds and domestic living arrangements, nonbinary (homo/hetero) sexual practices, and nonnormative gender comportment of South Asian men were identified as threats to the settled white heterosexual family and normative white masculinity and femininity by white mob violence, corporations, populist and labor groups, and federal and local government (Shah 2011, 19–89).

While feminized Chinese, Filipino, Asian Indian, Korean, and Japanese women were also considered dangerously immoral and contagious in their sexual and social embodiments and practices, they were viewed as economically nonproductive. Rather than being selectively recruited as transient laborers, the white settler state and society sought to almost entirely absent, externalize, and immobilize Asian women. Asian women were the first group ever barred from immigration to the U.S. by federal law, laying the foundations for the subsequent barring of Asian immigration in 1882 (Chinese), 1917 ("Asiatic Barred Zone" including India, Indochina, Afghanistan, Arabia, and the East Indies), 1924 (Korea, Japan, and all "aliens ineligible for citizenship"), and 1934 (Philippines), and for the transfer of immigration control from states to the federal government by 1891 (Espiritu 2008, 19–48; Kang 2002, 114–63; Luibhéid 2002, 1–54). The Page Law of 1875 was used specifically to target women from "China, Japan, or any Oriental country" perceived by state officials as being sex workers, intending to do sex work, or entering the country for "lewd and immoral purposes," especially Chinese women (U.S. Congress 1875; Luibhéid 2002, 31–54). As Eithne Luibhéid has suggested, the Page Law did not so much selectively distinguish between "respectable" Chinese wives (to be) and "immoral" Chinese women sex workers (to be) as enforce the state practice of policing *all* Chinese and Asian women's sexualities and bodies as morally and legally suspect. It produced and naturalized presumably identifiable visual differences between good and bad, high and low socially classed Asian women and arguably established the first state biometrics for classifying immigrants at the national border through biographical data and photographs, before the systematic use of passports by 1915 (Luibhéid 2002, 31–54). Overturning the rule of women's derivative citizenship based on the citizen or noncitizen status of their husbands, the Cable Act of 1922 granted independent, reproductively transmittable U.S. citizenship rights to white and Black women, except when they married Asian men, or "alien[s] ineligible to citizenship," in which case they lost their citizenship status and became denationalized and deportable.[5] The Cable Act, however, further weakened rather than strengthening the social power and independence of Asian women, as they could neither obtain marriage-derived citizenship status nor independent citizenship because they were "aliens" ineligible for citizenship. At a moment when married white women were gaining citizenship, land ownership, and labor rights independent from their husbands, this law retained the derivative status of married Asian women's rights from their Asian or other "alien" husbands when it would ensure the denaturalization of U.S.-born Asian women and nonnaturalization of migrant Asian women and enabled the independent status of married Asian migrant women when it would ensure their ineligibility for naturalized citizenship. Together with confinement to informal domestic, service, and sexual segments of the economy and through federal and local state immigration, antimiscegenation, alien land, and housing, health, labor, and crime policies, citizenship laws targeting Asian women sought to altogether sequester the spatial movement, socioeconomic relations and resources, and temporal presence of Asian women outside/inside the U.S. national body. The Chinese War Brides Act of 1946 and the amended War Brides Act of 1947 enabled the first mass migration of Asian women to the U.S. and can be considered the originator of the family reunification paradigm used to liberalize nearly a century of explicitly anti-Asian immigration policies (U.S. Congress 1946; Kang 2002, 114–63; Espiritu 2008, 49–70). Yet, these laws continued rather than departing from the engendering, surveillance, and control of Asian women initiated by earlier anti-Asian women/femme state practices. They bound the migration, embodied identity, sexuality, and sociality of Asian women to marriage with U.S. military personnel, especially those who were part of U.S. occupations in Japan following World War II and in Korea during and following the Korean War from 1950 to 1953. This regulated structure of "inclusive" and "free" migration depended on and strengthened differentials in socioeconomic and interpersonal power between Asian women who immigrated to the U.S. as alien "war brides" and the American citizen and noncitizen men who were their husbands.

As shown especially by the confining of Asian women by the state, anti-Asian racism and white nationalism has also relied on assigning and regulating gender to select, control, and contain the bodies and body types, movements, sexualities, and social relations of Asians. The settler nation-state's racially gendering differentiation of Asian women from Asian men and from white women (and also other racialized women) has helped to secure and reproductively transmit the naturalized nativity, social power, and wealth of white citizen cismen and their family units. This racial engendering based on Euro-American cis-hetero-patriarchal norms has attempted to use and restrict the multiplicity of embodiments and expressions by Asian women and men—a multiplicity considered dangerous, unstable, foreign, and perverse. Wu Tsang's mimetic multimedia performance in "Shape" makes visible and sensible the external contexts that constrain, externalize, and alienate the visibility and embodiment of racially gendered Asian bodies. At the same time, she retains the indeterminate wildness of Asian femininities and masculinities that ongoing histories of anti-Asian racism attempt to control—an ambivalent indeterminacy without essential or authentic identity. Tsang's visually and viscerally "incongruent" image, sound, and movement call attention to—and create solidarities between—the differentially embodied social histories that circumscribe the constrained scene of mimesis between copy and original, sameness and difference, and natural sense and its artificial reproduction.[6] The image of the mimetic performance stage in "Shape" also appears in Tsang's digital feature documentary *Wildness* (2012).

Wildness tells the story of a local Los Angeles bar, the Silver Platter, which has been a refuge for Latinx trans and gay communities since the 1960s. A weekly performance party called "Wildness" organized by Tsang and collaborating artists DJ Total Freedom (Ashland Mines) and NGUZUNGUZU (Daniel Pineda and Asma Maroof) at the Silver Platter brings multiracial, mostly American-born queer cultural workers in their twenties and thirties into the same space as the older Latinx immigrants who are part of the bar's community. This encounter creates possibilities for intergenerational, cross-racial and ethnic community and inspires the opening of a free legal clinic next door to serve trans people and immigrants. But the "Wildness" party risks exposing the Silver Platter to the gentrification already underway in MacArthur Park and other low-income East LA neighborhoods. When the

LA *Weekly* begins listing the performance party as a local attraction, more people come to "Wildness," threatening to displace the trans and gay Latinxs who have made the Silver Platter their home for more than forty years. Although the general arc of the film centers on the possibilities, risks, and complicities introduced in the Silver Platter community by "Wildness," Tsang's documentary style keeps viewers in a transitional space and time just outside the storyline. Most of the documentary alternates between expository strategies such as interviews and evidentiary footage, self-reflexive elements of cinéma vérité that implicate the filmmaker in the world being filmed, and performative or poetic modes that provide a visceral experience of the space of the bar and the lives inside it. But the film also breaks away from documentary realism altogether by positioning the Silver Platter itself as the narrator of the film and of its own life. Dreamlike segments that show the bar's transitions between multiple communities and types of cultural expression align viewers with points of view outside the filmmaker and film subjects, while staying inside the scope of the film. *Wildness*'s documentary magical or hyperrealism gives the Silver Platter a spaciousness and timelessness that can host the divided communities there and the complex histories and social identities they bring.

Through the liminal positioning of the bar, Tsang's *Wildness* produces a trans space and time between the bar's trans and gay Latinx immigrants and multiracial, American-born trans and queer people, which highlights social differences based on immigration status; race, ethnicity, nationality; language; age; and educational privilege. In particular, this trans space-time calls attention to class differences beyond income, wealth, or job type. The "Wildness" community has access to secondary or "soft" economic sectors, including art, media, and NGO worlds. In contrast, the bar's Latinx immigrants provide what is considered secondary *service* to the formal economy, including sex, domestic, and "unskilled" work or underemployed "reserve" labor that boosts wages and employment for workers with more access. Whereas the work of the "Wildness" community is given cultural or creative value, the work of the bar's Latinx migrants is perceived as having no cultural or social value, despite providing the basis for the normative political economy. This difference in cultural class translates into greater social mobility and protection for those in the "Wildness" community and greater social confinement and vulnerability for the bar's Latinx immigrants. By making these differences visible, Tsang's *Wildness* also produces the possibility of solidarities between groups. The Silver Platter's Latinx and "Wildness" community members are gender and sexually nonconforming people who have been expelled from dominant national communities and marginalized racial and ethnic communities through direct and "technical" forms of state violence and cis-hetero-patriarchal cultures. Their alienation from dominant and marginalized communities heightens their vulnerability as workers within devalued contingent economies that are unpredictable in stability, pay, and recognized value. *Wildness*, therefore, documents the differences that both divide and potentially connect the bar's communities. The Silver Platter's position just outside the documentary invites viewers to remain critical of gentrification's displacement of low-income communities of color and immigrants. It also broadens our understanding of gentrification to take into account a deindustrialized U.S. transnational political economy that works through the segregation and hierarchy of labors of the mind, sense, and body. This contemporary political economy brings differently classed communities in close, tense contact in urban spaces of work and leisure. As shown in Tsang's *Wildness*, the effects of this political economy also produce a longing for home that creates affinities between classes in a local bar in East LA.

Zavé Martohardjono: Transcultural Diasporic Gesture

In their "Untitled (Balinese Dance Study)" (2016) presented at Movement Research at Judson Church in their home city of New York, nonbinary mixed-race Indonesian Italian American queer nonbinary multimedia artist Zavé Martohardjono blends elements of Balinese dance with Black and Latinx queer trans House and Ball cultures. The performance opens in darkness with the sounds of gongs, metallophones, and drums, remixed by Ava Omega Jarden, from the gamelan gong kebjar classic "Hudan Mas," or "Golden Rain." When the music ends and the lights go on, Martohardjono appears wearing a black veil that covers their body down to the bottom of their high heels, except for their outstretched bare hands. The black fabric accentuates the angular postures of their arms, back, and legs in contrast to their pulsating fingers and rotating hands, head, and hips. The staunchness of their poses falls away when they peel away the veil to show regions of their body engaged in different gestures. The fingers on both hands move in concerted trembling, pointing, and bending, while the hands twist and wave in synchronized and asynchronized motions. The eyes dart left to right, stare, blink, and widen, and facial expressions alternate between frozen, relaxed, smiling, and intense. The head and neck shift left and right, up and down,

FIGURE 1.4. Zavé Martohardjono, *Untitled (Balinese Dance Study)* (May 2, 2016). Photo by Scott Shaw. Courtesy of Zavé Martohardjono.

or stay still, whereas the shoulders and arms twist and glide up and down, left and right, extended and locked. The hips sway and the legs pivot left and right, but the back remains straight, even when bending. The veiled body initially perceived and surveilled within the dominant national and transnational imagination as a racially gendered figure for terror, sacrifice, primitivism, and exoticism has been revealed to be a collection of disarticulated yet connected gestures that convey oscillating feelings, intimate and unknown, rapid and still, forceful and playful, changing and repetitious. Martohardjono's gender transiting body features and dress, which include a black Balinese men's head cloth; eye makeup; facial hair; a sleeveless sheer tan kurta without pants, showing the outlines of their body; and black thigh-high stockings provide yet another layer of coding. Their Balinese dance gestures flow seamlessly into the low poses, shoulder locks and rolls, and sashaying hips of House and Ball dancing, and the performance concludes with Kecak-style chants "kidi-kidi-kidi-cak-cak-cak" as Martohardjono walks around the room, untying their head cloth to let down their long hair.

Martohardjono has developed the aesthetics of racial and colonial transcultural transmission performed in "Untitled (Balinese Dance Study)" over a growing visual repertoire of performances, documentaries, installations, and videos. Along with "Untitled," performances such as "Territory" (2018), "Disco Permiso" (2017), "General Dynamics" (2017), and "Brother Lovers" (2014) intermix gender, racial, ethnic, national, regional, and religious cultural material drawn from Javanese, Balinese, Butoh, and House and Ball dance and performance; Hindu, Muslim, and Buddhist symbols, rituals, and mythologies; and transnational popular and political cultures.[7] Their hybrid uses of veiling, gesture, movement, masking, and doubling stage the gendered structures of visibility and embodiment that drive American and European Orientalist fantasies about the Middle East and South, Southeast, and Northeast Asian while also reenlivening gender shifting bodily practices shaped by colonial, nationalist, and neoliberal/neocolonial histories and desires. In "Untitled" and other performances, the partial or full veiling of Martohardjono's face and/or body calls attention to the anti- Arab, Middle Eastern, Asian, and Muslim colonial histories that have rendered the veil a feminized spectacle for exotic savage sexuality, irrational religious fundamentalism, and premodern social primitivism. As argued by Ella Shohat in her discussion of Hollywood cinema, the figure of the veiled woman is a "metaphor for the mystery of the Orient itself, which requires a process of Western unveiling for comprehension" (1990). Films such as *Thief in Damascus* (1952) and *Ishtar* (1989) align spectators with the male gaze of the Western heroic "discoverer," who exposes the veiled female Other to conquer her and the backward Arab and Third World lands and societies that she allegorizes (Shohat 1990). Martohardjono's performances draw the masculinized gaze of viewers through the aesthetics of veiling and unveiling, while allowing veiling to convey its own gestural meaning as a deflection of the Orientalist drive to fix the veil as a static symbol. Their uses of veiling echo growing multivocal practices of the veil, or *jilbab*, in Indonesia, which is home to the world's largest Muslim population. Young, university educated, urban middle-class Muslim women in Java, in particular, have recoded the meanings and styles of veiling to embody public political activism, social mobility, and religious piety, counter to the veil's feminized privatizing as a symbol for traditional domesticity within Western Orientalist and nationalist state conceptions of modernization (Smith-Hefner 2007). Moreover, Martohardjono's performed veiling exploits and intensifies the gender uncertainty produced by Orientalism's aesthetics of visibility. If the veil is a visible symbol for a primitively feminized and sexualized foreign body bound and hidden from view (and in need of discovery, rescue, and conquest) within Orientalist fantasies, this same fantastical emblem fails to contain Arab, Middle Eastern,

Asian, and Muslim femininities through its own fraught interplay between the visible and invisible. Martohardjono's practices of unveiling only reveal more gender shifting and threat.

Western Orientalist regimes of visibility have also sought to constrict South, Southeast, and Northeast Asian bodily senses through the perverse assignment of hyper-(hetero)sexualized femininity and de-(hetero)sexualized "feminized" masculinity. Through close engagement with representations of Asian American women in American cinema, theater, and pornography, Celine Parreñas Shimizu has suggested that the dominant cultural inscription of nonnormative hypersexuality onto/into Asian women's bodies has encoded racial difference as sexual difference (2007, 1–57; 102–39). Drawing on early twentieth-century heterosexual stag films made for illegal private viewing by white men featuring white women performers in yellowface, Parreñas Shimizu has tracked the visual projection of phenotypically racialized Asianness onto the sexual interiority and sexed body of Asian women: "The Asian woman's face, as the site of the visible identification of her racial difference in [the] heterosexual interracial scene, becomes the sign of her genitalia" (117).[8] While scenes on white to white sex in the stag films focused on bodily and genital contact, the scenes on (yellowface) Asian to white sex used shots of the face, hair, and full body (without genitalia) instead of shots of genital contact to explicitly mark the (white) woman's body as Asian. Building on Parreñas Shimizu's work, one might contend that the porn's codified substitution of the Asian woman's face for genitalia can be read not only as a response to antimiscegenation laws and practices in effect or as an aesthetic method that compensates for the inability to visually exact racial essence from sexed (or any) body parts, including those of the white women performers in yellowface. The very exchangeability of the face for sexed parts indicates that the excessive racial engendering of Asian femininity produces the equation, beyond just correlation, of feminine gender with heterosexual hypersexuality and the gender assigned "female" sex—so much so that multiple body features associated with femininity can stand in for the "female" sex organs.

Examining the psychic and material feminization of Asian American masculinity within dominant U.S. national culture, David Eng has argued that Asian American masculinity is read on the gender assigned male body as lacking a proper sexuality and sex. Eng has built on the visual analysis and artwork of Richard Fung, who has stated strikingly "Asian and anus are conflated" to describe the (passively positioned) homosexuality attributed to Asian American men generally (Eng 2001, 1–2; see also Fung 1991, 153).

Furthering this critique, Tan Hoang Nguyen reconceives racialized Asian male effeminacy through a concept of "bottomhood" that refuses to remasculinize Asian manhood at the cost of degrading femininity: "Posed as a sexual practice and a worldview, . . . bottomhood articulates a novel model for coalition politics by affirming an ethical mode of relationality. Instead of shoring up our sovereignty by conflating agency with mastery, adopting a view from the bottom reveals an inescapable exposure, vulnerability, and receptiveness in our reaching out to other people" (2014, 2). Each of these compelling analyses emphasizes the queerness constituting racialized Asian American sexuality as it is embodied in Asian American women and men and femininity and masculinity and refuses the desire to rehabilitate queerness toward "normal" sexuality and gender. The critiques also directly and indirectly address the dislodging of Asian American gender from its naturalized "origin" in the sexed body. Within white symbolic imaginings about the Asian engendered body, the vagina overtakes other body features in Asian womanhood, and the anus displaces the penis in Asian manhood. Each argument describes the racial severing of normalized connections between sexuality, gender, and sex as visual occurrences involving the interplay between hypervisibility (seeing everywhere or in place of) and invisibility (not seeing what is there or seeing as hidden or distorted). The racialized disconnection between sexuality, gender, and sex also produces slippages, conflations, substitutions, disappearances, and multiplications between and within embodied categories in white Orientalist imaginations, for example between Asian American masculinity and femininity; Asian American masculinity, heterosexuality-homosexuality, and penis-anus-vagina; and Asian American femininity, vagina-anus-penis-clitoris-. . . , etc. These visual and virtual ruptures in Western colonial regimes of sexuality, gender, and sex assigned to Asian American bodies are the products of attempts to pathologize, police, and contain spatial-temporal senses of embodiment that surpass the naturalized correlations and differentiations between surface gender presentation, the sensory inner depth of gender identity, and the sexed essence of the body in embodied white subject formation.

The trans Asian American embodied practices performed by Martohardjono recognize and energize the excess gender potential contained in the queer cultural and historical constitution of racialized Arab, Middle Eastern, and Asian American sexualities and genders. The multiplicity of their gender expressions and embodiments draws from their transcultural experiences and memories as a mixed-race Indonesian American diasporic migrant.

In addition to veiling, hybrid gestures, movements, masking, and shadowing in many of Martohardjono's performances revitalize the slippery senses of gender that continue to live in Indonesian Balinese and Javanese performance. In "Untitled," they blend wider, stiffer, angular stances and walking considered masculine with tighter, energetic, swaying poses and walking considered feminine in Balinese dance (Dibia and Ballinger 2012). Eye and head movements and facial expressions accompany these body postures and movements to inspire emotional, animal, mythical, and spiritual states beyond representational language. The inclusion of Kecak chanting, usually performed by Balinese men imitating monkey-like creatures from the Sanskrit Indian epic *Ramayana*, furthers the gender hybridity of "Untitled." In the experimental play, "Brother Lovers," performed as part of the 2014 New York City LGBTQ Fresh Fruit Festival, Martohardjono draws from elements of Javanese shadow puppet, or wayang kulit, theater and courtly dance to give a trans and queer retelling of the story of exile, rivalry, and unacknowledged kinship between warrior half-brothers Arjuna and Karna from the Sanskrit Indian epic *Mahabharata* (Kina 2016). The opening ritual that shows Martohardjono as the play's storyteller muse initiating collaborating performers, who are wearing black veils, into characters in their story; the blue and gold masks worn by the four performers (nyx zierhut, Mieke D, G. J. Dowding, and Zachary Frater) who play different incarnations of Karna and Arjuna; and the image screen in the background that captures the shadows of the onstage performers all indicate that the play's storytelling is impressionistic rather than representational. Instead of following a linear or cohesive storyline with central and secondary figures, "Brother Lovers" asks viewers to move with changes in scenes that convey synchronous yet different senses of the blue-masked Arjuna's exile from homeland and the gold-masked Karna's exile from family and community, Arjuna's dispossessed yet celebrated social status and Karna's materially wealthy yet outcast social position, and Arjuna's heroic masculinity and Karna's wounded masculinity. We also transition between diverging yet coexisting embodiments of Karna and Arjuna through the different trans, gender nonconforming, and gender queer embodiments and presentations of the four performers of the two brothers, who periodically reveal their full faces underneath the masks. Additionally, erotic and romantic relationships unfold between the two Arjuna doubles with the two Karna doubles, resulting in four differently embodied, sexually charged masculinities that complicate binary notions of heterosexual homosocial and gay homosexual brotherly love. The play guides viewers through these layers of metamorphosis and nonidentical miming through coordinated, exaggerated, and slow body movements between the Karna and Arjuna doubles. "Brother Lovers" illuminates the subtextual gender and sexual pluralism of the *Mahabharata* through its blending with the gender and sexual multiplicity of Javanese dance and theater.

Martohardjono's shape shifting performances are transcultural creations assembled through the partial and imaginative practices of diasporic recollection. After viewers have been introduced to Arjuna and Karna in "Brother Lovers," Martohardjono appears onstage as storyteller to describe how the story of the *Mahabharata* was transmitted to them:

> (Martohardjono speaking while standing on darkly lit stage with their shadow cast on image screen in background, holding two different sets of masks in their right and left hands.) I'm here to tell the story. It came to me by incredible chance. Five thousand years ago, it went from ear to mouth to written word. And it came to my family probably between the seventh and thirteen centuries when the Hindus conquered Java, which means it survived the Muslims, then the Dutch, then the Japanese occupation. There was independence in 1949 but then sixteen years later there was the coup. And then there was dictatorship, which seems to have unfolded in perpetuity. (Sound of firm footsteps on the stage floor. Performers walk onstage with faces unveiled and unmasked and with black veils wrapped around the upper half of their bodies in a single line circling Martohardjono as they continue speaking.) I was born thirty years ago and four years ago I found the translation. And now here we all are together. There's a second way to start the story. There was once two half-brothers who didn't know that they were brothers.

"Brother Lovers" is not just a transmission of the Javanese reenactment of the *Mahabharata* for American viewers. The play shows and ritualizes the disruptions and reimaginings that shape cultural memory and transmission for the temporally and spatially dislocated diasporic Indonesian migrant. The chance discovery of a translated (English) version of the Javanese *Mahabharata* by Martohardjono, whose mother is a first-generation Indigenous Javanese migrant in Canada, in their thirties reflects the unstable discontinuous transmission of cultural material and history between diaspora and homeland. Yet, as highlighted in the play, cultural transmission was already displaced and episodic within the Indonesian nation of origin based on centuries of Hindu, Muslim, Dutch, and Japanese conquest, colonization, occupation, and intermixing, followed by the establishment of the independent nation-state of Indonesia in 1949 and then the overtaking of the first government of Indonesia by a dictatorship.

The art forms used in Martohardjono's "Brother Lovers," "Untitled," and other performances to remember and embody multigender gestures of Indonesian culture and history are forms overlaid with indigenous, migrant, settler colonial, nationalist, and neocolonial histories and aesthetic influences. Eng-Beng Lim has traced the ongoing Western fascination with the sensuous masculinity displayed in Balinese Kecak performance to its encoding as a magical trope for Bali's preserved exotic cultural nativism under Dutch colonization beginning in 1908 (2013, 41–89). This fascination is structured through an ethnographic colonial dyad between gazing white man and engendered and sexualized brown woman or "boy" that includes an unacknowledged queer aesthetics and erotics that also reproduces the colonial encounter (Lim 2013, 41–89). Christina Sunardi has studied state and societal efforts to control Indonesian women's social, martial, spiritual, and sexual power and gender embodiment using Javanese performance, following the Japanese military occupation of Indonesia (1942–45), the Indonesian revolution against the Dutch empire (1945–49), and the proclaiming of the archipelago republic of Indonesia beginning in 1945. State, military, and police practices such as ethical codes sponsored by first president Sukarno's regime (1945–66) prescribing "proper" behavior, movements, songs, and dress for women performers; and murder, rape, violence, and surveillance against women artists suspected of being leftists during second president General Suharto's "New Order" regime (1966–98) sought to contain and extinguish the subversive potential of "female masculinity" in women's gender crossing performances (Sunardi 2015, 1–62). The Reformation era after the dissolving of Suharto's regime has brought greater democratization, including the leadership of the country's first woman president Megawati Soekarnoputri (2001–4). Yet, the postauthoritarian Indonesian state has also adopted neoliberal cultural pluralist policies that have reproduced binary gender and heterosexual orders of national identity and respectability; consumable notions of nativity and hybridity that further dispossess indigenous and rural communities while heightening xenophobia against migrant populations and appealing to transnational cultural economies; and increasing economic instability and impoverishment through deregulation and decentralization guided by the World Bank and International Monetary Fund (Kusno 2013, 3–27;

FIGURE 1.5. Zavé Martohardjono, "Brother Lovers" (July 18, 2014). *Left to right*: Mieke D., nyx zierhut, Zavé Martohardjono. Photo by Bridget de Gersigny. Courtesy of Zavé Martohardjono.

FIGURE 1.6. Zavé Martohardjono, "Brother Lovers" (July 11, 2014). *Left to right*: G. J. Dowding, Zachary Frater, nyx zierhut, Mieke D. Photo by Bridget de Gersigny. Courtesy of Zavé Martohardjono.

Lim 2013, 41–89; Sunardi 2015, 1–62). Martohardjono's artwork evokes Javanese and Balinese performance practices in their gender, indigenous, racial, ethnic, religious, and mystical hybridity, rather than national or local purity. The cultural hybridity of Javanese and Balinese performance is the product of layered ongoing histories and regimes of settler colonialism, nation-state building, neoliberalism, and neocolonialism that have attempted to annihilate, repress, assimilate, and hierarchize the indigenous, racial, ethnic, and religious communities and geographies composing the Indonesian archipelago—and also the product of the survival and re-creation of these communities and geographies. Martohardjono's performances blend these Indonesian art forms with other hybrid, historically overlayered cultural forms from the transcultural perspective of a second-generation, gender nonbinary, mixed-race Indonesian American. "Brother Lovers" melds Javanese theater and dance with the low slow movements of Japanese Butoh to magnify the gestural possibilities for transforming the disciplined binary masculine/feminine, hetero/homosexual, and human/nonhuman form of the body (Baird and Candelario 2019; Kina 2017). "Untitled" combines the gender recoding and alternating angular and swaying body poses of Balinese dance and Black and Latinx American House and Ball performance to rework racial regimes of visibility that attempt to confine gender's potential as a practice of spatial-temporal remembering, movement, and transformation.[9]

TWO. NETWORKS

TRANScoding Biogenetics and Orgasm
in the Transnational Digital Economy

Building on the previous chapter's discussion of the technically managed image of Asian American gender embodiment as a means for delimiting the inside/outside of the U.S. national body, this chapter focuses on the projection and recoding of American imaginaries of racial gender in the Asia-Pacific as a region defined as a laboratory for U.S. imperialism and capitalism through technological and cultural prosthetics. In particular, this chapter focuses on the racially trans embodied, transnational digital media of Cheang Shu Lea. For more than thirty years, Taiwan-born queer digital nomad Cheang has produced new media art that highlights and plays with the boundaries of gender, racial ethnicity, sexuality, nationality, cultural genre, and technological medium. In particular, I look at her postporn digital film *I.K.U.* (2000), which rips off Ridley Scott's analog film *Blade Runner* (1982), and *I.K.U.*'s sequel UKI (2009–14), a live video performance and online game.[1] These coupled pieces, along with Cheang's other work in the first decade of the twenty-first century, make visible the digital technologies that had linked cultural mediums, media technologies, and media industries (film, television, newspapers, books, radio, performance, games, photography) nationally, regionally, and globally by the conclusion of the twentieth century. Using *I.K.U.* and UKI as examples of her larger body of work at the turn of the century, I argue that Cheang's attention to networked media technologies and their new interfaces with viewers, who become users and players, urges us toward an investigation of the structural and institutional impact of digital technologies in mediating transnational neoliberal capitalism. As a crucial part of this argument, I show how Cheang's work compels us to think about and experience racially gendered/sexed embodiment and biogenetics as motive forces in the restructuring and globalizing of political economies of the United States, Western Europe, and the Global North.

The chapter begins with a discussion of Ridley Scott's *Blade Runner* and the kinds of racialized anxieties that shape the film's nostalgia for the human and American liberal society in the urban rubble of high-tech deindustrialization. It follows with a focus on *I.K.U.*'s playful trans recoding and subversion of *Blade Runner*. Cheang's digital film *I.K.U.* highlights and embodies the racial and binary gender/sex/sexual cultural economies that underpin *Blade Runner*'s postapocalyptic vision of high tech, which the 35mm film projects at a moment when the U.S.-based Hollywood film industry is undergoing transformation by a new, digitally powered global economy. While *I.K.U.* intervenes in the representational politics of *Blade Runner* and dominant visions of high tech, *I.K.U.*'s sequel performance and game UKI breaks away from the representational politics of visibility and viewing by wiring us to the invisible off-sites of the digital economy, including electronic and biogenetic dumping sites that give birth to live trans genetic, species, and media forms. Against neoliberal accounts of the digital economy driven by technological, economic, and social determinisms, *I.K.U.* and UKI suggest that *racially* binary systems of gender, sex, *and sexuality* fundamentally structure this new political economy.

Nostalgia for the Human "Race" in Ridley Scott's Blade Runner

Ridley Scott's *Blade Runner* (1982) opens with the radioactive landscape of 2019 Los Angeles. Rising high above this landscape of fiery ethers, acid rain, and blinking electromagnetic surfaces, we are given a view of Tyrell Corporation's pyramid headquarters. Wide shots of the LA cityscape are intercut with close shots of a disembodied eye that mirrors an image of the city on its surface. Moments later we associate this early shot of an eye with the interrogation tool developed by the Tyrell Corporation to distinguish between real humans and human clones, called Replicants. The tool is used by Blade Runners, or human police agents trained to kill Replicants, to measure the eye movement and other involuntary bodily reactions (or lack thereof) of suspected clones as they are asked emotionally charged questions. In *Blade*

Runner's 2019 LA, the Tyrell Corporation's genetic engineering of Replicants represents the final frontier of high tech's encroachment on nature, divine creation, and human society. The human clones were originally produced to explore and colonize planets beyond Earth as slave laborers. But when a more intelligently designed Nexus 6 generation of Replicants starts a revolt on an off-planet colony, Replicants are banned from returning to Earth under threat of death. Scott's film follows weathered Blade Runner Deckard (Harrison Ford) as he is forced out of retirement to hunt down a group of Replicants who have returned illegally to Earth to confront their creators at the Tyrell Corporation. As Deckard terminates these illegal Replicants one by one, his ambivalent identification with the human clones grows. He "falls in love" with Rachael (Sean Young), a Nexus 6 female Replicant employed by the Tyrell Corporation, and his life is saved by the prized leader of the renegade Replicants, Roy (Rutger Hauer). Deckard's identification with the Replicants is secured by the conclusion of the film when he escapes with Rachael. Viewers are left questioning Deckard's status as human or clone.

As argued by neo- or post-Marxist social critics, *Blade Runner* gives a visually and narratively engrossing indictment of the degrading effects of high-tech-ruled postindustrial global society. Postmodern geographer David Harvey mourns the loss of the human exemplified by Deckard's falling in love with Replicant Rachael (1990, 313–14). Feminist film scholar Vivian Sobchack emphasizes the film's spatial excess, which displays the decay and allure of postconsumer materials that have lost their use-value (2001, 262–63). These social critiques tend to match *Blade Runner*'s own suspension between melancholia and erotic awe, except that the film has no memory of human life before the intrusion of biotech.[2] For Harvey and Sobchack, new intimacies between humans, enslaved clones, and perhaps also the discarded refuse that is the city signal humanity's degradation by a high-tech corporate state that has remade humans into exploitable, consumable "things." These critiques, however, fail to address the racial politics of the film's vision of 2019 Los Angeles.

Blade Runner's dystopian view of postindustrial techno-bio-science relies on the racialized imagining of Los Angeles as a transnational capital of the future. As racial theorist and media scholar Adilifu Nama suggests, "the historical model of black-white binary race relations symbolized by the Replicant 'other' is juxtaposed against the impending multicultural future signaled by the Asian iconography that has displaced all that is 'American'" (2008, 58). Nama situates the film's anxiety about the human within the racialized crisis of American national identity and global dominance in the 1980s, following the Black Power and women's movements and defeat in the Vietnam War and newly facing the growing economic power of the Pacific Rim. I would add that the human-clone relationship in *Blade Runner* is not only premised on the historical model of binary race relations between Blacks and whites but also displaces *the cultural memory* of embodied racial communities affected by histories of systematic captivity, racism, and forced migration through the analogy of social class. Replicants (who are all white, it seems) are coded as the enslaved and exploited "Black" and migrant underclasses of the future. To be clear, I am not arguing that Hollywood films need to mirror social histories and experiences of violently imposed inequality. Rather, I am arguing that *Blade Runner*, like most films in the conventional science fiction Hollywood genre, participates in the cultural encoding of whiteness as a race at risk of becoming an underclass and, ultimately, an extinct species (standing for the human). This encoding of whiteness borrows from histories of dispossession, exploitation, and violence experienced by nonwhite social groups, even as it displaces the possibility of remembering the histories borrowed. In *Blade Runner*'s exchange between race and social class, Black Americans and the African diaspora are disappeared from all social positions within the global landscape of 2019 LA. This emphatically white-to-white alliance between human and clone is then juxtaposed with Asian-styled market multiculturalism, the liminal mestizo figure of police agent Gaff, and the high-tech corporate state rulers of the city-state-world.

Blade Runner's iconography of Asianness signals not only what Nama identifies as the rival threat of an Asian-inflected global multicultural economy in the heart of LA but also the decline of an American mass industrial society equated with rational pragmatism. In its place is a street market of sensory delights that includes bazaar vendors who sell rare or synthetically made animals, a subcontracted genetic engineer who makes human eyes, and a bar that features female performers with snakes. The commodities exchanged in this postindustrial market are severed from "proper" productivity and use, as they return to their neoprimitive or technologically induced "natural" state. The wild market replacing the rational geography and public life of America's metropolis for mass industrial capitalism is racially coded as ethnic Asian. Contributing to Hollywood's Orientalist archive, Asianness itself is perceived as a collection of ethnic surface-substances compliant with the demands of the primal market or state.[3]

Despite the floating signifiers of Asian-centered multiculturalism, the only visible human embodiment of multicultural hybridity in Scott's *Blade Runner* is the blue-eyed Mexican European Japanese cop Gaff (Edward James Olmos), who is charged with looking after Deckard (Ford). Although he speaks the Spanish German Japanese hybrid "Cityspeak" of the street market, Gaff is a liminal character who also occupies the corporate and police offices above the street. He appears to be the only nonwhite human or clone that crosses into above-street LA in *Blade Runner*. Gaff's embodied hybridity builds on the racialization of Latinx Americans as mestiza/o, with its overdetermined dimensions (Anzaldúa 2012, 99–113; Fiol-Matta 2002, 7–15). Considered native to the precolonial Americas and, at the same time, fundamentally mixed with "Old World" Spanish (Hispanic) ancestry prior to British colonial settlement, Latinx Americans are claimed by the white-dominant American nation in envisioning a multiracial hybridity original to U.S. territories (especially in the Southwest), while retaining ties to Western European empires. This racial hybridity, however, must always be policed and managed by the nation-state (Anzaldúa 2012, 99–113; Fiol-Matta 2002, 7–15). It poses the threat of an irretrievable, unmeasurable Western European ancestry mixed irreducibly with Indigenous peoples—and other peoples colonized by Western European and American empires—to form modern Chicanx and Latinx racial identities, communities, and nationalities with indigenous ties to the U.S. landmass and social histories. In *Blade Runner*, therefore, Gaff appears as an "authentic" embodiment of racial and ethnic hybridity. But his hybridity and border-crossing between street market and corporate state towers remain hermetically sealed in his lone, vanishing presence in the future city-world of 2019 LA.

Blade Runner's racialized geography of disappeared Blacks, Asianness equated with the neoprimitive market, and policed Latinxs provides the visual and visceral detail through which the film delivers its dystopian commentary on high-tech twenty-first-century dictatorship. Within this racial geography, the white European American humans in the film are placed in the ambivalent position of risking substitution or even extinction by human clones while also identifying and finding kinship with the cloned image of themselves—however artificial. Blade Runner Deckard's "romantic" escape with Replicant Rachael at the conclusion of the film represents an ambivalent tactic for racial (coded as human) survival in a world imagined to be relentlessly globalized, denatured, and un-(white) American. Although the technocratic rulers in *Blade Runner* are also white, Dr. Tyrell and the Tyrell Corporation are already hopelessly transnational and transhistorical. The palatial design of the Tyrell Corporation headquarters and the aristocratic extravagance of Dr. Tyrell's bedroom mimic the style of Western European monarchies, intermixed with pyramid structures associated with early Egyptian civilization.

Racial Trans Embodiment and Cultural Labor
in Cheang Shu Lea's I.K.U.

Described as a riff-porn-sequel to Ridley Scott's *Blade Runner* (1982) and set in the near future 20xx (approximately 2030), Cheang Shu Lea's digital film *I.K.U.* begins where *Blade Runner* ends. We find a human male Blade Runner and a clone female Replicant getting inside an elevator. But *I.K.U.* is not at all about human and clone falling in love and fighting to survive in a hostile new world under techno-corporate dictatorship. *I.K.U.* trades love for sex and sex for sexual simulation, and human and clone remain within the confines of high-tech corporate-ruled systems, if only to exploit them toward other aims. Cheang's rip-off exposes and remembers the racially gendered/sexed bodies and histories that have made transnational postindustrial cultures, technologies, and capital possible.

In *I.K.U.*'s opening scene, sex between the masculine human Runner and the feminine human clone—called the Coder—programs the clone to obtain "ecstasy data" through sex with humans of all genders and sexual desires:

RUNNER: Say kiss me.

CLONE: Kiss me.

RUNNER: I want you.

CLONE: I want you.

Activated, the Coder moves through different scenarios that make up the film's futurist urban landscape in search of sexual transactions. These scenarios located in a subway, strip club, highway overpass and underpass, theater bar, underground parking lot, and sushi bar never provide a complete cinematic mise-en-scène of the cityscape. Instead, they revisualize the city as a series of decontextualized internal window-worlds that could be anyplace. In each of *I.K.U.*'s scenarios, the feminine Coder's body and sexual practices

FIGURE 2.1. Cheang Shu Lea, *I.K.U.* (2000). *Left to right*: Dizzy (Zachery Nataf) and Reiko #4 (Miho Ariga). Film still courtesy of Cheang Shu Lea.

mutate to match the sexual desires and bodies of its human sexual partners. The Coder's arm turns into a virtual prosthetic phallus that penetrates both male and female human partners.

While clone-human interactions in *I.K.U.* could be described as playfully pansexual and pangender, the commands that flash onscreen to direct the Coder to "her," "their," or even "its" (referring to the Coder's status as "non-human" clone) next sexual assignment suggest otherwise. The Coder's sexual interactions and polymorphous sexual body have less to do with agency, desire, and diversity than with command, programming, and modulation. Both Coder and human Runner are agents of the Genom Corporation, which has combined IT and genome technology to produce and mass market "ecstacy" [*sic*] data that provides "sexual excitement without sexual friction." Users of different sexualities and genders plug into this audiovisual sexual data with an *I.K.U.* chip and wearable computer. The Coder, human Runner, Genom Corporation, and humans who provide raw sexual experience simulate positions within an informalized economy of sex work (sex worker, pimp, TRANSNATIONAL CORPORATIONS, and johns). Yet the technological enframing of *I.K.U.*'s future world overrides what might otherwise be a representation of exploitation within an advanced capitalist economy that has made sex, de-

FIGURE 2.2. Tokyo Rose (Aja) in Cheang Shu Lea, *I.K.U.* Film still courtesy of Cheang Shu Lea.

sire, and intimacy into commodities. *I.K.U.* does not presume that sex and sexuality *ever* were expressions and measures of individual self-possession, freedom, and choice. Neither utopian nor dystopian in tone, Cheang's film operates on the flat, smooth techno-scientific register of the pregiven, where capital and its exploits are preprogrammed as natural impulse, biology, and genetics. Resistance, conflict, and contradiction exist only through mutation and modulation. The lone outlaw in *I.K.U.*'s world, the Tokyo Rose virus, operates *internally within* the system produced and circumscribed by the Genom Corporation. As mutated code and sexual performer, Tokyo Rose turns the Genom Corporation's networks of data transmission into a literally embodied "net," used in performance to seduce and hack into the only male Coder in *I.K.U.*

In Cheang's *I.K.U.*, the neoliberal ideology of the Internet as the meta-network of networks becomes the object of play, exploitation, and subversion. The film makes it impossible to interpret the internet and the IT networks it enables in the objective, rational, and neutral terms of technology as pure mediator; *I.K.U.* "worlds" the Internet and networked technologies by embodying them through the representational orders shaped by "real" world sexual, racial, and colonial histories. The sexual mutability of *I.K.U.*'s inhabitants remains confined to racially gendered forms of embodiment, imagined within colonial fantasies. Humans who provide raw, predata sexual experience are unchanging in their binary gender expression as biologically culturally sexed males and females. Their sexual practices are tied to the heterosexual or homosexual coding of binary gendered sexualities, except when they have sex with the human clone Coder.

While the feminine Coder and masculine human Runner also seem to take binary gender forms, their binary gender expressions are in a constant state of deconstruction and reconstruction through the redistribution of biological signs for sex into "secondary" cultural expressions of gender and sexuality.[4] The femininity of the Coder does not rely on "female" sexual organs to sex gender but rather displaces the overvaluation of the vagina and breasts in their sexual (and reproductive) "function" and gender representation of femaleness. The Coder's virtual prosthetic phallus-arm, other erogenous body parts, and the entire body provide multiple gender/sexual surfaces. The Coder's femininity is a disarticulated mix of female and male gender signs and sexual practices that remain suspended in relay between binary genders and sexualities, never able to wholly symbolize one or the other sex or sexuality. The masculinity of the Runner similarly displaces the overvaluation of the "male" sexual organs in representing sexual (and reproductive) "function" and engendering maleness. The Runner's mixed gender signs and sexual practices, which include the use of a dildo-gun for downloading sexual data from the Coder, denaturalizes not only the presumed correspondences between sex, gender, and sexuality but the *differences between* sex as nature or biology, gender as social construction, and sexuality as cultural expression. Sex, gender, and sexuality become delinked, ungrounded, and mixed in the crossing of the bio-social-cultural.

The trans gender/sex/sexual embodiments and sexual practices of *I.K.U.*'s Coder and Runner are far from pure expressions of freedom, fluidity, or choice. Their bodies and interactions remain under command and control of the networked technologies of the Genom Corporation, which has incorporated not only sex/gender/sexuality but also race and ethnicity as technologies for extracting information capital. The trans mutability of the human clone Coder draws on her coding as racially ethnic Asian. Within an increasingly transnational American Orientalist imaginary, the racialization of Asianness continues to work through attributing ethnic detail and gendered sexual deviance, while generalizing racially. Ethnic racialization authenticates a fantasy of particularized ethnic "foreignness" based on a cultural location elsewhere. Simultaneously, it deauthenticates this specificity through a joint fantasy of the departicularized multitude, displaced from any delimited culture, history, or geographic place. Within this relay of racial ethnic fantasies, gender and sexuality become viral signs without material substance in what is perceived as the "normally" binary white sexed body and its sexual practices. In *I.K.U.*, the Coder's Japanese-sounding techno-jibberish and morphing Asian features express forms of Orientalist racial ethnic coding that disarticulate gender/sex signs and sexual practices from anything like "normal" subjectivity with interior depth and agency. The Coder's femininity and sexuality are merely plastic, surface expressions that respond elastically (though unpredictably) to the desires of desirers. *I.K.U.*'s clone Coder is the embodied image of racialized Asian femininity.[5]

As a codependent prototype, the human *I.K.U.* Runner is coded as a racially ethnic Black American within the transnational imaginary of American neoliberal multiculturalism. Speaking in clearly identifiable American English (in contrast to the speech fragments of the Coder), the Runner as Genom agent with a dildo-gun embodies the image of militarized Black hypermasculinity produced by the U.S. state and American dominant culture. Racialized blackness is coded as an assimilating ethnic who "belongs" to America, thus being capable of representing an exportable multicultural American national identity made for global circulation. Simultaneously, racialized blackness is coded as an unassimilable ethnic, bearing the everpresent threat to overturn the veneer of multiculturalism based on erased histories of racism, apartheid, enslavement, and forced migration. The anxiety between "inside" and "outside" produced by racial ethnic fantasies of blackness is expressed and managed through gendering and sexuality. Black bodies are attributed with liminal or ambiguous sexual features in excess or failure of "properly" sexed white American subjects (Mercer 1994, 131–70).

Yet Cheang's *I.K.U.* does not attempt to break from these American racial fantasies in order to recuperate humanized subjects with "normal" racial gender and sexual embodiment. Instead, the film shows that the cultural and biologically encrypted *relationship between* sex, gender, and sexuality is shaped—or even enframed—by racial imaginaries. The encoding of sex, gender, and sexuality within transnationally circulating white Euro-American culture relies on hetero- and homo-binary logics of male/female sex, masculine/feminine gender, and opposite-sex/same-sex sexuality. On the other hand, different expressions of sex, gender, and sexuality—and of their relationship with one another—within subjugated nonwhite racial cultures remain displaced from any naturalized sense of binary origins. Non-Western expressions of sex, gender, and sexuality are perceived as inauthentic, substituted, failed, excessive, or without origins, except in relationship to naturalized whiteness as the primary origin from which one is always already displaced. Thus, racial trans embodiment in Cheang's *I.K.U.* does not merely expose and play with the Western binary gender/sex/sexuality system. The film highlights the primacy of binary conceptions of gender, sex, and sexuality as products of dominant global racial imaginaries that shape worlds, bodies, and experiences through digital technologies and programming at the genetic molecular level. Black American masculine human Runner and Asian feminine clone Coder both transgress binary gender, sex, and sexual boundaries, but their transgressions remain constrained by techno-biologically programmed dominant culture, managed by the Genom Corporation. Nevertheless, the trans bodies of *I.K.U.* derive pleasure, connection, experience, and productivity in the pockets of autonomy enabled precisely by the corporation's reliance on transnational technological networks for control and management.

In sharp contrast to the nostalgic tone of Scott's *Blade Runner*, Cheang's *I.K.U.* has the flat yet live feel of viewing an information feed that becomes interactive. As viewers watch the Coder extract, store, and transmit sexual data in different scenarios, we become implicated in these communicative acts as if we are intercepting the scenarios and data as live performances. For example, viewers are given a virtual "internal" view of the Coder's prosthetic phallus-arm as it penetrates different humans and extracts orgasmic data. The thrill or shock of getting this impossible view is undercut by the informational representation of the internal body as a grid-surface and the viewers' alignment with the biotechnological apparatus of the Genom Corporation. In the absence of any feeling of loss, rage, or fulfillment, Cheang's *I.K.U.* does not engage in *Blade Runner*'s depth-models of cinematic narrative, identification, and interpretation. While *I.K.U.* shows the penetration of biotech capitalism into the innermost recesses of the human body and subjectivity (the cell, sexual organs, desire, agency), it also shows the pleasures and potential of the autonomous experiences, relationships, and subversions enabled by transnational high-tech corporations' overreliance on technological networks. With the Genom Corporation nowhere to be seen in *I.K.U.*'s world, the Coders, Runner, Virus, and humans who do all the work (and anti-work) of sexual data extraction play with and run astray from their bio-tech programming to use digital technologies of command, control, and communication in unintended ways. *I.K.U.* remakes the technologically facilitated globalization that *Blade Runner* mourns as the loss of the American nation-state, liberal society, and the human.

It is striking that, in *I.K.U.*, resistance and subversion always remain circumscribed by the Genom Corporation's dislocated yet controlling presence. Their absence in the form of pure transgression speaks less to their impossibility than to the urgency—or what *I.K.U.* presents as flat, living fact—of understanding and responding to the new material conditions that frame and shape the politics of cultural representation by the conclusion of the twentieth century. Cheang's *I.K.U.* not only exposes, intensifies, and modulates the racially binary gender/sex/sexual Euro-American imaginaries produced by Scott's *Blade Runner* but, just as important, also shows how these imaginaries newly relate to mediated political economies at the historical moment of their transition from the cultural form of analog film to digital information. Following more than two decades of unprecedented social mobilization for racial, gender, sexual, and economic justice, decolonization, and an end to war, the American culture wars of the late 1970s highlighted the centrality of culture to politics in the post–civil rights era. In particular, the debates on sexual morality that were part of the culture wars illustrated the ability of the formal state apparatus and corporations to co-opt and manage the sexual and racial countercultures produced as part of 1960s and 1970s social movements (Everett 1996; Hunter 2006; Rubin 2011, 137–81). They also exemplified the partial entry of previously barred and segregated racial, gender, and sexual communities into a new "multicultural" public sphere of cultural contention, restructured in response to mass movements.[6] Countercultural and leftist critical strategies shaped by post–World War II and post–Civil Rights American neoliberalism and empire, including cultural studies, poststructuralism, and postmodernism, have tracked the increasingly decentralized forms of dominant ideological production within a political economy newly mediated by culture and dislodged from institutional foundations. Yet these cultural and critical strategies have only barely addressed the cultural technologies and economies that mediated the American culture wars and that have continued to transform the industrial foundations of the formal political economy by the end of the 1990s.

I.K.U. documents the transition from the analog film Hollywood industry that produced Scott's *Blade Runner* to the digital technologies that enable Cheang's irreverent sequel. Without nostalgia, it shows the shift from the cumulative storytelling (montage) of narrative analog film to the dispersed composite images of computerized digital media.[7] This shift also moves viewing practices away from the more passive depth perception and consumption of the industrial film complex (Fordist Hollywood production, distribution, and theatrical reception) toward the personalized, interactive use of perceived images as windows for information, communication, and action. Without sentimentalizing, *I.K.U.* reminds us that these transitions remain tied to cross-sector corporate, state, military, and bio-techno-science institutions that have created and continue to manage and profit from a decentralized transnational Internet-based economy. Counter to utopian and dystopian sentiments about the digital economy, *I.K.U.* shows us that there is nothing "new," "postindustrial," or "global" about the IT economy. The Internet-based economy builds on and expands the *cultural modes* of economic development that gave Third World countries marginal, unequal entry into transnational economies dominated by Western European and Japanese empires before World War II and by the United States and the USSR after World War II. These informally organized "Third" cultural economies exacerbated the violence, displacement, and structural inequalities of colonization, war, poverty, and cis-hetero-patriarchal nationalisms. They also offered contingent work and mobility, especially to low-income gender and sexually nonconforming people, girls, and women, through service, leisure, entertainment, and sex industries that provided "secondary" intimate labor to formal industrial state economies in First and Second World countries and to formal economic development in Third World countries.[8]

For instance, Cheang's *I.K.U.* poses connections between the Internet-based digital economy and Japanese and American militarized corporate sex, service, entertainment, and leisure industries in Northeast and Southeast Asia during World War II and the Cold War (Shigematsu and Camacho 2010). *I.K.U.*'s feminine Asian Coders were originally nursing robots. They were then recruited to work in a twenty-four-hour live porn show on Internet TV before becoming sexual data collectors. *I.K.U.* also links the high-tech economy to the pre-1990s analog American film and media industry through the image of the masculine Black American human Runner. The Runner documents the co-optation of the militarized masculine image of the Black Power movement by American mainstream media and policymakers starting in the mid-1960s (Ferguson 2003, 1–29; Keeling 2007, 95–117). This co-optation culminated in Hollywood's Blaxploitation in the 1970s and then transnational Hollywood's mainstay images of Black urban life by the end of the 1990s (Harris 2006, 63–78; Keeling 2007, 95–117). Both Coders and Runner perform forms of cultural labor considered tangential to the "hard" political economy. Yet Cheang's film suggests that these disavowed cultural modes of labor not only sustain formal political economies but *drive* the material foundations of political economies.[9] Rather than trying to undo these images of exploitation, *I.K.U.* resituates these images within their cultural economies of production and poses the possibility of autonomy, pleasure, relationship, and subversion at the very edges of overextended, technologically facilitated transnational networks.[10]

Trans Genetics, Species, and Media in Cheang Shu Lea's UKI

UKI (2009–14) is Cheang's inverted sequel to *I.K.U.* While *I.K.U.* followed the clone Coder as she collected sexual data according to the Genom Corporation's programming, *UKI* focuses on the viral by-products of Genom's intensified efforts to harness human sexual experience as data for profit. In *UKI*, the Internet-based biotech and media networks used to extract, store, and transmit sexual data crash and are abandoned by Genom. The corporation bypasses the embodied world of *I.K.U.* Coders, Runner, humans, digital technologies, and urban scenarios for programming at the micro-cellular level. Genom creates BioNet, a network of microcomputing cells that recode human orgasm into "self-sustaining pleasure" (Cheang 2000). In the transition from embodied to intracellular networks, outdated *I.K.U.* Coders and networked digital technologies are dumped at electronic trash sites, off the visible urban grid. In these e-dumps, junked *I.K.U.* Coders, Genom agents and Runners, UKI viral mutations, and their offspring and cohabitants steal, swap, inject, lick, suck, and ejaculate bits of code and bio-parts to form trans genetic mutants such as part-human clone, part-fly UKI Mosca and the code junkie Coder XQ. This wasteland orgy of viral coding gives "birth" to the UKI virus, which tries to overtake the city and the human body, infiltrate the Genom Corporation's BioNet, and sabotage and reclaim its cellular orgasm data.

Together, *I.K.U.* and *UKI* have something to say about the so-called global civil societies or public spheres facilitated by networked high-tech economies in the twenty-first century.[11] *I.K.U.* envisioned a future controlled by a biotech-media conglomerate and populated by the conglomerate's agents, workers, raw material for extraction, and markets. In *I.K.U.*'s totalized networks of extraction, viewers are situated as interactive users positioned both inside and outside *I.K.U.*'s worlds. This inside/outside position does not just amplify the pleasurable "liveness" of the digital film. It implicates viewer-

FIGURE 2.3. Trash Mistress (Radíe Manssour) in Cheang Shu Lea, *UKI* (2009–14). Photo by Rocio Campana. Courtesy of Cheang Shu Lea.

users in the conglomerate's processes of extraction as interceptors of data transmitted between conglomerate and workers and, ultimately, as "secondary" consumers of digital imagery simulating the work of producing simulated experience. Against conceptions of digital civil societies or public spheres that view high tech as inherently democratizing or dehumanizing, *I.K.U.*'s viewer-users experience our interactivity with new media as itself a mode of capitalist extraction—extraction that produces pleasurable yet confining cross-embodiment with the clone and human workers, agents, raw material, and markets of *I.K.U.* In *UKI*, the new media interface shifts from the multiple screens (theater, TV, computer, installation surface) of *I.K.U.* to the embedded kinesthetic and viewing technologies of networked performance and gaming. Part 1 of *UKI* is a "live code live spam" performance featuring an off-site junkyard inhabited by post-*I.K.U.* trans genetic viral mutants and electronic trash. Each permutation of this performance in different locations centers around a video recording that seems to be feeding live from the e-junkyard.[12] This video feed–recording is played onscreen while being patched together with other audiovisual media objects (including DNA and virus imaging) by on-site artists and programmers who work collaboratively to create, mix, control, and show the performance as data flows. Each performance provides a site-specific sensory experience of what appears to be "live" communication from the trans genetic viral inhabitants of an e-wasteland off-the-grid.

Part 2 of *UKI* is a "viral coding viral orgasm" game with two levels. The first level, "Infect the City," invites us (the public) to sign on as UKI viral agents using a Google Maps Geolocation interface that pinpoints our geographic location using cell towers and WiFi nodes. Once we are geographically embedded, we can infect our city "gesturally" based on the relationship between our bodily location and surroundings. Zooming out from our city, we can view red blots that signal the spreading virus across multiple cities on the world map. After collecting enough points from spreading the UKI virus, we move to the second level, "Enter the BioNet." This part of the *UKI* viral game allows the inner biochemical worlds of UKI agent-players to infiltrate the microcomputing cells of the Genom Corporation's BioNet. Here, multiple UKI agent-players occupy a dark room together wearing biosensors that detect the skin's responses to internal emotion, thought, and motion. Sensory data based on skin responses is sent wirelessly from each agent-player to a computer that uses the data to change the pattern, speed, and rhythm of moving red laser lights and the low base pulsing of subwoofers in the room. When agent-players' bio-sensory data levels synchronize, one red laser beam in the likeness of one Genom microcomputing blood cell (representing one unit of millions of blood cells) goes out. The elimination of one laser beam or blood cell changes the level of self-sustaining orgasm produced by the engineered cell, which changes the pulsating rhythm of the subwoofers. Once all laser beams or cells are destroyed, the subwoofers also cease.

As the counterpart to *I.K.U.*'s world of embodied biological and media technologies, Cheang's *UKI* makes visible and "felt" the disembodied off-world sites that are the new frontiers colonized by transnational high-tech conglomerate states. The high-tech-initiated dematerialization of the human and her/his productivity (across biological, social, and political economic spheres of life) during the postindustrial turn of the twenty-first century is further intensified by biomolecular and electromagnetic technologies that penetrate divisions between surface and depth, outside and inside, above and below, self and other, and subject and object. The Genom Corporation bypasses the use of human clones for mass sexual entertainment in order to directly capitalize on intracellular life through genetically engineered cells that self-reproduce orgasm. Part 1 of *UKI* shows the fallout from this shift in the junked body parts that have been evicted from *I.K.U.*'s world. This electronic waste remains off-site and invisible in the transition to micro- and macroscopic scales of technologically facilitated capitalism. Making the junkyard visible, UKI's viral performance calls attention to the exploitative social ecologies produced by what is considered officially to be the clean and equalizing high-tech global economy. Electronic pollution in Ghana's global dumping grounds, cassiterite mining in the Congo, semiconductor sweat-shops in Northeast and Southeast Asia, and undervalued creative labor in the Global North highlight the new forms of extraction, exploitation, and labor that occupy the invisible edges of the networked transnational high-tech economy.[13] Instead of arguing for the inclusion of these off-sites into the formal political economy, UKI sees these wayward sites as sites of trans gen-esis where rejected bodies reuse, revalue, reassemble, and transform refuse parts into trans genetic, species, and media forms.

Cheang's work ends where it begins, with the almost naturalized premise that the human never was pure or exempt from the exploitative operations of social institutions. In this way, Cheang's networked art focuses on the embodied perspectives of gender, racial, sexual, and class deviants pushed to edges of Euro-American liberal political economies of the human, even as their/our bodies, cultures, and experiences are made objects of extraction. Without investment in late twentieth-/early twenty-first-century utopian or dystopian views on the human in relationship to technology, Cheang's work calls for a reclaiming of biological, communications, and media technologies from their control and management by transnational corporate states. By us-ing the very high-tech networks created and used by dominant institutions, Cheang's trans media generates the possibility of autonomous, collaborative, and subversive play, pleasure, relation, and coordination.[14] In UKI and I.K.U. in particular, trans gender/sex/sexual, genetic, and species counterhumans create and transform the under- and off-sites of the twenty-first-century new global economy.

THREE. MEMORY

The Times and Territories of Trans Woman of Color Becoming

I have always wanted to be both man and woman, to incorporate the strongest and richest parts of my mother and father within/into me—to share valleys and mountains upon my body the way the earth does in hills and peaks. —AUDRE LORDE, *Zami: A New Spelling of My Name* (1982)

For many years our sovereigns had welcomed the advice of, and given full representations in their government and councils to, American residents who had cast in their lot with our people, and established industries on the Islands. As they became wealthy, and acquired titles to lands through the simplicity of our people and their ignorance of values and of the new land laws, their greed and their love of power proportionately increased . . . So the mercantile element, . . . the sugar planters, and the proprietors of the "missionary" stores, formed a distinct political party, . . . whose purpose was to minimize or entirely subvert other interests, and especially the prerogatives of the crown, which, based upon ancient custom and the authority of the island chiefs, were the sole guaranty of our nationality . . . It may be true that they really believed us unfit to be trusted to administer the growing wealth of the Islands in a safe and proper way. But if we manifested any incompetency, it was in not foreseeing that *they* would be bound by no obligations, by honor, or by oath of allegiance, should an opportunity arise for seizing our country, and bringing it under the authority of the United States. —LILIUOKALANI, *Hawaii's Story by Hawaii's Queen* (1898)

The significance of Janet Mock's first memoir *Redefining Realness: My Path to Womanhood, Identity, Love and So Much More* cannot be overstated. It is the first memoir by and about a trans woman of color within the marginalized literary body of transgender popular memoirs to have crossed into wide readership and discussion within U.S. civil society, becoming a *New York Times* Bestseller just a few weeks after the book's hardcover publication on February 1, 2014. *Redefining Realness* is a collection of memory-stories recounting Mock's coming-of-age as a Black Native Hawaiian trans girl moving between families, sisterly friendships, and geographies in her Hawai'i birthplace, California, Texas, and New York. Departing from predominately white authored transgender memoirs that often pivot on moments of gender transition, Mock's childhood stories convey her processes of trans adaption, self-realization, and reconstruction as they unfold within and between intimate and social relationships and environments. Her liminal storytelling across multiple times and spaces at the borders between internal reflection and external address anticipates and generates multiple forms of popular engagement. For trans women of color and transgender communities, Mock's first memoir provided new decolonized language and imagery through which to imagine and affirm the experiences of trans women of color and transgender people, apart from the state and psych-medical and social institutions that have attempted to criminalize, pathologize, and assimilate their inner lives, bodies, and social practices. It also emphasized the differential racial gender histories and power shaping different transgender and gender nonconforming communities. For cisgender communities encountering transgender literature for the first time, Mock's book provided an unapologetic, strategic, and accessible introduction to transgender issues that aimed especially to build connections between Black trans women and trans women of color *and* Black and women of color feminisms. Along with Mock's burgeoning media activism and production, *Redefining Realness* attempted to produce an intermediary mode of internal/external and personal/public interaction on transgender issues that would have a mass impact through its particular Black and Indigenous trans woman of color worldview. Mock's current status as one of the most outspoken, recognized, and culturally prolific leaders within contemporary transgender justice movements attests to the widespread effects of her first memoir.

This chapter shifts from the previous chapter's discussion of Cheang Shu Lea's networked imagining of the Asia-Pacific region to focus on Janet Mock's first trans woman of color memoir, assembled through the vestiges of Native Hawaiian and Black cultural memory on the fortified Pacific and Atlantic borders of the U.S. state and national body. The first section assesses the potential interventions of popular literary memoir and memoir criticism on classed conceptions of literature, followed by an analysis of Mock's much more restricted and ambivalent repurposing of memoir and dominant forms of cultural representation more generally in section two. Section three discusses Mock's embedding of her personal stories of trans self-realization within collective histories of Black and Indigenous genocide, enslavement, and occupation in ways that deprive transgender narratives.

Memoir's Potentials

Mock's *Redefining Realness* joins the small number of trans women of color and gender nonconforming and people of color writing in the wildly diverging forms of memory-based life literature tentatively gathered under the label "memoir," including Deborah Miranda, Lovemme Corazón, Leah Lakshmi Piepzna-Samarasinha, Ceyenne Doroshow, Toni Newman, Kai Cheng Thom, and Lady Chablis. These memoirs contribute to what literary and cultural critics Sidonie Smith and Julia Watson have described as the memoir boom across literary, visual, and virtual genres in the first decades of the twenty-first century. Smith and Watson provide a transnational survey of the types of contemporary memoir written in English, especially those authored by women, that trouble what can be described through a more unified and generic disciplinary understanding of autobiography literature. Memoir includes new adaptations of more traditional autobiographical forms, such as the late eighteenth-century bildungsroman or developmental coming-of-age novel (Michelle Cliff's *Abeng* and *No Telephone to Heaven*, Nawal El Saadawi's *Woman at Point Zero*), as well as post- or anticolonial national autobiographies of political leaders (Benazir Bhutto's *Benazir Bhutto*, Shirin Ebadi's *Iran Awakening: A Memoir of Revolution and Hope*), narratives of witnessing (Rigoberta Menchú's *I, Rigoberta Menchú*, Assata Shakur's *Assata: An Autobiography*), narratives of loss and mourning (Paul Monette's *Borrowed Time: An AIDS Memoir*, Joan Didion's *The Year of Magical Thinking*), narratives of illness and disability (Audre Lorde's *The Cancer Journals* and *A Burst of Light*, Jean-Dominique Bauby's *The Diving Bell and the Butterfly*), narratives of embodiment (Esmeralda Santiago's *When I Was Puerto Rican*, Christine Jorgensen's *Christine Jorgensen: A Personal Biography*), and narratives of familial displacement (Sally Morgan's *My Place*, Barack Obama's *Dreams of My Father*) (Smith and Watson 2010, 127–66). By adopting the meanings *self-life-writing* from autobiography's Greek roots *autos-bios-graphe*, Smith and Watson render autobiography just one mode of (self) *life writing* or autobiographical practice that now also includes—or is overpopulated by—memoir. They refer to all writing that "takes a life, one's own or another's, as its subject" as life writing, including the explicitly self-referential writing of memoir and autobiography and also biographical, novelistic, and historical writing (2010, 1–4). In response to the explosion of twenty-first-century self-referential life writing described mostly as memoir, they revise and diminish the elevated genre specificity of autobiography, which has been established as the dominant canonical nonfiction literary form by literary studies and criticism, to incorporate and to be incorporated by memoir. Smith and Watson also implicitly privilege *life* and *writing* over the *self* of autobiography, which originates in its modern form in eighteenth-century cultures of Western Enlightenment and its universal private subject of civil society.

While Smith and Watson retain and use memoir's ambiguous relationship to autobiography, Julie Rak argues for popular memoir's unincorporable difference from autobiography despite the new attention given to memoir by autobiography literary studies. Rak describes the slipperiness of memoir's meanings:

> [Memoir's] gender and number are inconsistent, reflecting its multiple meanings as a document note or a record, a record of historic events based on the writer's personal knowledge or experience, an autobiography or a biography, an essay, or a memory kept of someone (*OED Online*) . . . It is both finished and unfinished, unofficial and official, a collection of reminiscences of an occasional character, but also a record of historic events where the events, not the person who records them, is emphasized. It is about the self in relation to others, or even just about "others" without being biography or history. (2004, 495).

Using Jacques Derrida's deconstructive strategy of the "supplement" as it was developed through a reading of Jean-Jacques Rousseau's "Essay on the Origin of Languages," Rak identifies memoir as an unstable form and body of writing that poses a threat or "dangerous supplement" to autobiography because of what is considered memoir's inferior, inauthentic, and unliterary status in comparison to autobiography. Her use of Derrida's critique of Rousseau's economy of speech over writing is pointed, given that Rousseau is considered a forefather of modern autobiography. Rak contends that memoir's excess to the genre of autobiography, including its fluctuating gender, makes it particularly adaptable for writing by women, people of color, and other oppressed peoples. Memoir's blending of private and public, interior and exterior, and feminine and masculine assigned spheres counters autobiography's entrenchment of these divides based on the high principles of (pre)Romantic thought (Rak 2004).

Additionally, G. Thomas Couser provides a historical account of memoir broadly conceived as life writing that further questions not only autobiography's status and discreteness as a canonical nonfictional literary genre but also the distinction between nonfiction life writing and the fictional novel in literature. According to Couser, most novels imitated memoir life writing, especially the "inside" first-person narration of autobiographies and the "outside" third-person narration of biographies, from the emergence of the English novel in the eighteenth century to the beginning of the twentieth century (2012, 54–78). The introduction of "interior monologue," or narrative without a narrator, in the novel around 1900 interrupted the novel's simulation of memoir (2012, 54–78). Moreover, Couser argues that the contemporary renaissance of memoir as a recognized art form in its own right draws from this longer, even originating, history of life writing literature. In particular, the boom relies on memoir's flexible capacity to relay both the life stories of those who are well-known public figures and those who are not known publicly and must earn their readerships by telling an "extraordinary story" (Couser 2012, 145). Couser argues that memoirs by unknown writers, especially the disability memoirs that he highlights, have contributed greatly to democratizing the memoir form.

These compelling examples of emergent memoir criticism harness the current popular burst of life writing forms tentatively called memoir to democratize the institutional and disciplinary boundaries of literature and literary art and value. They identify a renewed set of popular narrative practices and aesthetics created and adapted especially by women; indigenous peoples, people of color, and colonized peoples; lesbian, gay, bisexual, transgender communities; low-income people; and people living with disabilities through memoir. They also give broader historical context to memoir in ways that identify memoir in continuation and excess of the Enlightenment cultures and structures of rational individual subjectivity (and conventional Romantic reactions against rationality) that found American and Western European nation-states. Even as I align myself with these democratizing approaches to memoir that include or center marginalized communities, I want to argue that the popular or even populist aesthetics that they enliven have yet to address contradictions at the heart of American and Western European liberal democracies. These contradictions include not only liberal orders of civil society and governance founded on abstract universal evocations of the rights and sovereignty of "the people" that effectively dematerialize and confine the power and participation of "the people." They also include the founding of the liberal principles of "the people" on bodily and territorial senses of sovereignty exacted through settler colonization of Indigenous peoples and lands considered part of U.S. territories, anti-Black enslavement, and occupation and imperialism in Latin America, the Middle East, and Asia. All three interpretations of memoir position memoir not only as what precedes and overtakes autobiography as it has been solidified as a modern literary genre but as what is ultimately at the cultural origins of a distinctly American literature:

> Unlike the literary genres flourishing in English . . . life-writing genres were vital to American experience from the start. So although anthologies of colonial American literature rarely acknowledge it explicitly, they traffic heavily in life writing: not only the aforementioned letters, diaries, and journals, but also narratives of exploration, settlement, Indian captivity, and more. The reasons for the prominence of life writing in early American literature are not far to seek. For one thing, the European institutions—monarchy, aristocracy, the Church—that served as the patrons of the arts in the Old World did not function the same way in the New World. Here, their patronage applied to writing only insofar as the colonial enterprise required communication and documentation (Couser 110–11).

According to Couser, the American roots of memoir engaged in communicating and documenting the material details of "American experience from the start," in contrast to memoir's artistic patronage within the European system of "monarchy, aristocracy, and the Church." The approaches of Couser, Rak, and Smith and Watson invest memoir retrospectively with a populism that exceeds and predates the late eighteenth-century establishment of the U.S. nation-state and its rational forms of subjectivity and governance—an original life materialism that the twenty-first century memoir boom revitalizes. Their championing of the populism within memoir's contradictory history presents possibilities for overturning higher social classes of life writing, like the genre of autobiography, and literature more broadly. Yet, I would argue that Mock's uses of memoir offer interventions in this emerging memoir analysis and, more broadly, in the cultural and political imaginings of American populism that pervade the representational forms of the state and civil society.

Realness and the Limits of Representation

The three prefatory chapters that introduce and frame Mock's memoir-stories in *Redefining Realness* stage Mock's navigating of the exploitative effects of representational systems. While memoir, along with documentary film/video, has offered perhaps the most accessible cultural form for transgender expression, memoir's anti-formal, mimetic, and self-reflexive aesthetics belie the codified orders of sentiment that structure memoir's interaction with readers. Within an emblematic memoir like Henry David Thoreau's *Walden* (1854), the initial chapter authenticates Thoreau's internally reflective discourse as a private extension of his socially established public persona so that he may connect personally with his readers through common emotions and experiences: "I should not obtrude my affairs so much on the notice of my readers if very particular inquiries had not been made of my townsmen concerning my mode of life . . . Some have asked what I got to eat; if I did not feel lonesome; if I was not afraid; and the like . . . I will therefore ask those of my readers who feel no particular interest in me to pardon me if I undertake to answer some of these questions in this book" (1995, 3). Thoreau remembers and narrates his time alone in the woods of Walden Pond, Massachusetts, as part of an imagined continuing conversation between his "townsmen" and himself, allowing him to journey into the racially figured sensuousness of nature to recover the tempered inner nature of Western man against industrial bondage. In contrast, Harriet Ann Jacobs (Linda Brent) must not only verify the truthfulness of her recounting of her experiences as an enslaved Black girl in *Incidents in the Life of a Slave Girl* (1861). She must also authenticate her own status as a narrator, fit enough to address the white public: "READER, be assured this narrative is no fiction. I am aware that some of my adventures may seem incredible; but they are, nevertheless, strictly true. I have not exaggerated the wrongs inflicted by Slavery; on the contrary, my descriptions fall far short of the facts. I have concealed the names of places, and given persons fictitious names. I had no motive for secrecy on my own account, but I deemed it kind and considerate towards others to pursue this course." While Thoreau's introductory musings ask readers apologetically to act like his townsmen in indulging the mundane details of his private life, Jacobs's preface attempts to establish a "real" relationship with readers beyond the fictional realm of the imaginary, outside of both the private and public spheres of the republic, to which she has been confined. An editor's introduction by white feminist abolitionist L. Maria Child follows Jacobs's preface in *Incidents* to reconfirm Jacobs's legitimacy and character as a narrator.

In *Redefining Realness*, Mock's prefatory chapters go beyond authenticating the "realness" of her personal stories and herself as narrator to create and define "real" relationships between readers and her life stories. The "author's note" establishes personal truth and history drawn from memory as the basis for her stories: "This book is my truth and personal history. I have recalled facts, from events to people, to the best of my ability. When memory failed me, I did not seek answers in imagination. I sought clarity through conversations with those who've shared experiences with me. When my recollection of events varied from theirs, I sided with my memory and used their voice, often direct quotes, to contextualize events" (2014, xii). Mock's memoir-stories are neither subjective recollections of events and people, infused with imagination where memory gaps occur, nor objective or universal representations of trans women's experiences: "Though I highlight some of the shared experiences of trans women and trans women of color throughout this book, it was not written with the intent of representation. There is no universal women's experience. We all have stories, and this is one personal narrative of untold thousands, and I am aware of the privilege I hold in telling *my* story" (2014, xii). In these opening paragraphs, Mock orients readers, especially anticipated cisgender readers with differential power, toward an engagement with personally mediated and materialized memories that document and transmit her truth and history in ways that will affect readers in the social world, while refusing the potential reading of her experiences as purely subjective or as representational. As conveyed in the "introduction" that follows the "author's note," she navigates these dynamics of interpretation and representation with an understanding of dominant culture's prevalent reduction of trans women's life stories into "plot devices": "from Venus Xtravaganza's unsolved and underexplored murder in *Paris Is Burning*, to the characters of Lois Einhorn (played by Sean Young) in *Ace Ventura: Pet Detective*, and Dil (played by Jaye Davidson) in *The Crying Game*, to numerous women exploited as modern-day freak shows on *Jerry Springer* and *Maury*. Let's not forget the "tranny hooker" credits seen everywhere from *Sex and the City* to every *Law & Order* and *CSI* franchise" (2014, xvi–ii). The appearances of these trans women figures within popular culture have been scripted so that they disrupt gender stability just enough to titillate and to ultimately reentrench binary cisgender's social and biological naturalness and superiority. In addition to these popular spectacles produced about trans women, she identifies a more permissible narrative for trans women that allows for their own storytelling under a different structure of dehumanization and negation. Mock identifies media attention on Christine Jorgensen's "sex change" story in 1952 as the moment that introduces a new model for trans representation with tight controls: "On the one hand, there are through lines, common elements in our journeys as trans women, that are undeniable. At the same time, plugging people into the "transition" narrative (which I have been subjected to) erases the nuance of experience, the murkiness of identity, and the undeniable influence of race, class, and gender. It's no coincidence that the genre of memoir from trans people has been dominated by those with access, mainly white trans men and women, and these types of disparities greeted me head-on when I stepped forward publicly" (2014, 255–56). Mock describes the new appearance of trans self-narrating through a web of popular mediums and forms that includes televisual, photographic, and print news; film; and memoir literature, beginning with Christine Jorgensen. While this emergence enables a moment of public and self recognition, she notes that it also reproduces the "cis gaze" and power disparities between trans people (Mock 2014, 255–56). She suggests a connection between greater access to the memoir genre by white trans men and women and the codification of a diminished trans self-narration centered on psych-medically assisted transition. Mock's *Redefining Realness* itself is an attempt to redress the confining image of her projected in the 2011 *Marie Claire* article, "I Was Born a Boy," which first introduced aspects of her life story (2014, xiv). This brief piece distills the complexities of her life down to an exposé on one "secret" aspect of her identity: "Janet Mock has an enviable career, a supportive man, and a fabulous head of hair. But she's also got a remarkable secret that she's kept from almost everyone she knows. Now, she breaks her silence."[1]

Even as Mock repurposes memoir for a more complex rendering of her life stories, she explicitly addresses the limitations of memoir and any cultural form in its ability to adequately capture and represent the experiences of trans women of color. As long as the state and the social institutions comprising civil society continue to bar and restrict the survival and livelihoods of trans women of color, the cultural visibility enabled by dominant representational systems will continue to legitimate if not feed the rationalized dispossession of trans women of color. Thus, Mock asks readers to do more than read and consume her stories. She asks us to "deconstruct these stories and contextualize them and shed a light on the many barriers that face trans women, specifically those of color and those from low-income communities, who aim to reach the not-so-extraordinary things I have grasped: living freely and without threat or notice as I am, making a safe, healthy living, and finding love" (2014, xvii). Throughout her book, Mock uses the perceptual surface of the story's cultural form to unfold the layers of experience, identity, and history that she lives and to create a different relation between readers and her embodied stories. By countering the dominant representational demands made on her memoirs and her Black and Indigenous transfemme embodied storytelling, Mock attempts to dehabituate readers from what Kara Keeling has described as common sense perceptions and ways of feeling embodied in affected relationship to engendered Blackness, based on the entrenchment of devaluing and assimilated images of racialized Blackness within dominant individual and collective memory (Keeling 2007, 11–44). Keeling analyzes the new cinematic, televisual, photographic, and print imagery of Black masculinities, femininities, and sexualities introduced into the common sensorium by the post-1965 Black Power movement, Hollywood film industry, and independent Black cinemas to track the underlying potential of a Black femme imagination and social reality, displaced by white supremacy and Black nationalism. I want to argue that the yet-to-be realized perception, senses of embodiment, and social relations marked by Keeling's theorizing of the "Black femme function" allow for understandings of mass-mediated culture that address the racial gender and sexual surplus extracted from captive Black bodies to reproduce the individual and collective senses of whiteness constituting "the people" and polity of the U.S. nation-state (Keeling 2007, 118–58).

Set in 2009 in New York City when Mock is in her twenties, the book's third prefatory chapter uses the common image of heterosexual cisgender romance to open up the layers of history and identity that she embodies. Readers become intimately aligned with Aaron, the man of her dreams, when Mock suspends and unravels their romantic scene to share her coming-of-age stories with Aaron and us: "I have to tell you something" (Mock 2014, 11). Mock's storytelling is less of an autobiographical narrating of the self than a transmission that seeks to mobilize a different form, archive, and worldview of the self. As Noenoe K. Silva argues, white settler colonial methods and practices of documenting history have not only suppressed native histories and knowledges, they justify the continued occupation of Hawai'i by the U.S. today. By focusing on stories, editorials, essays, songs, and poetry produced in the Hawaiian language, Silva retrieves a counterarchive of Native Hawaiian anticolonial resistance and resilience that defies the "persistent and pernicious myth . . . that the Kanaka Maoli (Native Hawaiians) passively accepted the erosion of their culture and the loss of their nation" (2004, 1). This counterhistory includes a return to an original account of British Captain James Cook's arrival in Hawai'i by Samuel Manaiakalani Kamakau in 1866–67, which diminishes the godlike importance attributed to Cook in Western histories to just one event within a much longer genealogy of Kanaka voyages and foreign encounters from a nineteenth-century Kanaka worldview (Silva 2004, 15–44). The opening chapters of *Redefining Realness* not only authenticate Mock's stories and her status as storyteller but also deconstruct and transform readers' perceptual and bodily relationship to her trans woman of color embodied storytelling. They ask readers to mobilize oppositional senses of subjective and collective relation attuned with the Black and Indigenous disavowals and differentials that have enabled the establishment of white elite and populist cultural forms and mass affinities.

Black and Native Hawaiian Cultural Memory

By the time Mock introduces her first childhood memory in Chapter 1, *Redefining Realness* has already multiplied our senses of time as readers. The prefatory chapters have established Mock's storytelling as a future retelling that enlivens scenes from Mock's adolescent pasts in the present-tense and that continually approach the future marked by Mock's romance with Aaron as an adult—a future romance that is also part of a (more recent) past enlivened in the present-tense from an even further future. The exponentially doubled times of Mock's storytelling surpass the rational linear subjectivity and stability of the coming-of-age narrative and the narrator relation in dominant and subdominant autobiographies and nationalist novels.[2] They allow her to convey past experiences from a liminal space and time that is both outside and inside memory:

> I was certain that the sun's rays would filter through the legs of the table under which I slept and Grandma Pearl would wake me from my fold-up mattress with the scents of margarine-drenched toast and hot chocolate. I knew my sister Cheraine and her best friend Rene, a towering Samoan girl with waves flowing down her broad back like lava, would walk me to school, the heels of our rubber slippers smacking the warm cement. I was certain my first-grade teacher would part her coral-lacquered lips to greet me with a smile as I carefully placed my

slippers in the blue cubbyhole labeled Charles. I was certain that when it was time for recess or bathroom breaks, we would divide into two lines: one for boys, and the other for girls (Mock 2014, 15).

In this first shared memory of childhood set in her birthplace Honolulu in 1989, we find first-grade-aged Mock waking up groggily to the warm rays of the sun and smells of "margarine-drenched toast and hot chocolate," nestled underneath her grandmother's table. In this state between sleeping and awakening, she feels comfort in the daily routines that have become so familiar, they have internally imprinted rhythms. Her sister and her sister's best friend will walk her to school, with the "heels of [their] rubber slippers smacking the warm cement." Her school teacher will greet her with a smile while she puts her slippers in the gender color-coded cubbyhole labeled with her gender assigned birth name. In this opening adolescent memory, Mock's storytelling eludes the developmental schema of the child within the "normal" white cisgender heterosexual upper-class family, who moves from the primal innocence of an undifferentiated nature aligned with the imagined plenitude of private maternal sense toward their more restricted gender differentiated public image in the paternal social order.

The multiple futures-pasts-presents of Mock's storytelling show that the Indigenous and Black child is already "prenatally" inscribed within social histories that override the possibility of a private sense of familial childhood and developing self untouched by the racial gender hierarchies of public life. Her memoir narration lingers at the threshold between the internally felt and externally perceived to highlight the senses of self radically excluded from legibility through the (pre)natal assignment of Western gender at birth:

> I was certain I was a boy, just as I was certain of the winding texture of my hair and the deep bronze of my skin. It was the first thing I'd learned about myself as I grew aware that I existed. There was evidence proving it: the pronouns, the penis, the Ninja Turtle pajamas, the pictures of hours-old me wrapped in a blue blanket with my eyes closed to the world. When they opened and I began learning the world, my desire to step across the chasm that separated me from the girls—the ones who put their sandals in the red cubbyholes labeled *Kawehi, Darlene,* and *Sasha*—rose inside me. (Mock 2014, 16)

In this passage, Mock describes her "male" engendering as an embalming field of force that has imprinted her from the outside and inside even before her first moments of self-awareness. It was the first thing she learned about her existing self through "the pronouns, the penis, the Ninja Turtle pajamas, the pictures of hours-old me wrapped in a blue blanket with my eyes closed to the world" as evidence. The "faint desire" to "step across the chasm that separated me from the girls" arose at the same elusive moment of her self-sensing, when she opened her eyes to look outward and inward at the gender cues she had been assigned in the world. Departing from more codified transgender narratives that may reproduce the notion of gender as internal essence or biological prescription, Mock's remembering of her earliest moments of gender self-recognition describe and theorize trans "feeling" as something that emerges at the interplay between assigned social embodiment, social location, and mode of sociality *and* desires—affected by and in excess of this assignment—for another social embodiment, social location, and mode of sociality. Mock's moments of gender sense between internal and external worlds and between the socially assigned and its excess are also moments of racial sense when she feels "certain of the winding texture of [her] hair and the deep bronze of [her] skin" through a kind of self-recognition that already understands (and defies) the bodily marking of racial value within colonial regimes.

The surplus spaces and times of Mock's storytelling enact practices of Black cultural memory made otherwise impossible by the disavowal and continuation of legacies of slavery and genocide by the U.S. state, civil society, and national body. As suggested in Saidiya Hartman's memoir *Lose Your Mother: A Journey Along the Atlantic Slave Route* (2007), the fragments that compose Black cultural memory attempt to address the ongoing workings of slavery's past within the present and future of the Black diaspora in the U.S., despite the state's declarations of racial progress beyond slavery as past, including nineteenth-century emancipation and twentieth-century civil rights (Hartman 2002). Her literary memoir documents her journey to the forts of Ghana (Gold Coast), where African slaves were imprisoned after their kidnapping and deported by Portuguese, English, Dutch, French, Danes, Swedes, and Brandenburgers (Germans) merchant colonists beginning in the late fifteenth century at the densest origin point of the transatlantic slave trade (Hartman 2007). By remembering the incalculable enormity of the violence and loss (of mother, home, kin, and community) suffered by Black slaves, beginning at the original site of their capture, Hartman's memoir calls for the public mourning and responsibility denied by the state's failed liberal gestures toward racial equality (2002): "If the past is another country, then I am its citizen. I am the relic of an experience most preferred not to remember, as if the sheer will to forget could settle or decide the matter of history. I am a reminder that twelve million crossed the Atlantic Ocean and the past is not yet over. I am the progeny of the captives. I am the vestige of the dead. And history is how the secular world attends to the dead" (2007, 17). Her refusal to forget the terror at the genesis of the Black diaspora remembers the assignment of death-in-life that has enabled the extraction (and enjoyment) of the racial supremacy binding together white Western national bodies and the circulation of capital. It also recalls the vast reservoir of humanity, strength, and imagination that created Black kinship within the captive dungeons of the transatlantic land and water borders of U.S. and West African colonial national territories. In *Redefining Realness*, Mock's memoirs provide a personal and collective witnessing of the alienation in emergence that defines her coming-of-age. The trans feeling of social dislocation described in Mock's natal scene of gender-assigned birth is overdetermined by the ongoing history of assigned Black death-in-life that continues to exact the bonds and entitlements of white social futurity through the poverty; barred access to employment, education, and social resources; criminalization; sexual and state violence; and imprisonment survived by Black communities. Mock describes the repeated displacement of her transfeminine self from her earliest moments of self-awareness onward as part of a larger network of Black family and community that has also endured foreclosed emergences as part of everyday life: "As a kid, I had no idea that we were poor because our friends looked like us" (2007, 57). Her stories remember her divorced single Black father's devoted love despite his defeated sense of self in the face of cyclical poverty, unemployment, and addiction. Her father's lover, Janine, who helped to take care of Mock and her younger brother Chad, and the other single Black mothers who lived in Oakland, where Mock lived with her father and brother in the early 1990s from age seven to nine, struggled with these same conditions. Mock's coming-of-age as a trans woman is less an individual narrative of growing into normal racial and national gender subjectivity than a collection of collectively embedded personal memories about the fugitive practices of reconstructing self and kin on the outskirts within and outside the U.S. civil society and national body.

Native Hawaiian lineages of cultural memory also determine Mock's processes of trans becoming within persisting colonial histories of genocide and occupation. Her coming-of-age occurs within indigenous cosmologies of belonging that white settler colonialism has attempted to extinguish:

> Ages before Hawaii's sugar boom, voyagers from Tahiti left their home to see what was beyond the horizon. Navigating the seas in handcrafted canoes with the mere guidance of the stars, they arrived in Hawaii and created new lives. Centuries later, I landed in 1995, and it was here, on the island of Oahu, that I would mirror my ancestors on my own voyage, one guided through a system of whispers, to reveal the person I was meant to be. I will forever be indebted to Hawaii for being the home I needed. There is no me without Hawaii. (2014, 88)

Beyond dominant culture's reduction of trans experience to moments of state and medical assisted transition from one sex to the other, Mock understands her experiences of trans self-realization as mirroring her Polynesian ancestors' legacy of navigation. This transmitted Oceanic history and technology of navigation, which treats the ocean as a dynamic entity interconnected with—rather than bordering—land, is guided by the stars and a "system of whispers." Mock's own process of trans self-actualization is a voyage that navigates already interrelated internal and external worlds and past, present, and future selves. This dynamic view of nature as knowledgeable technology with ancestral ties to the Native Hawaiian people runs counter to the white settler conception of land as raw material for annexation, ownership, and cultivation and ocean as a natural boundary to be crossed and fortified. As Haunani-Kay Trask has recounted in her collection of political memoirs in *From a Native Daughter: Colonialism and Sovereignty in Hawai'i* (1999), the arrival of British military explorer James Cook in the Hawaiian archipelago in 1778, followed by American capitalists and missionaries in the 1820s, disrupted two millennia of Hawaiian civilization based on interdependency and caring for the land. By the 1840s, the diseases introduced by white foreigners had destroyed nearly 90 percent of the indigenous Hawaiian population. The remaining 100,000 Native Hawaiians were converted to Christianity. By the 1850s, Native Hawaiians had been dispossessed of their communal birth lands, which were divided by European and American powers to be owned as private property and developed into sugar plantations. White foreign planters began attempts to annex Hawai'i to avoid U.S. sugar tariffs, which were stalled by reciprocity treaties that the Native government hoped would protect the independent sovereignty of Hawai'i. But these treaties were used by the United States and white planters, who were the descendants of missionaries, to further force the cession of Hawaiian lands and resources and to expand the sugar industry. European and American settler encroachments culminated in the cession of the Pearl River Lagoon to the United States and the imposition of a supposedly democratized system of government that effectively allowed white property owners to dominate the legislature. Soon thereafter, the Hawaiian Kingdom governed by Queen Lili'uokalani was overthrown in 1893 and the white-ruled Republic of Hawai'i established.[3] The founding of the Republic of Hawai'i secured Hawai'i as a colonized frontier ready for incorporation into the U.S. settler nation-state through annexation as territory and then statehood in 1959. The admission of Hawai'i as the fiftieth state further occludes Hawai'i history and identity as an Indigenous nation under active U.S. occupation. The shift from unequal treaty-making with the "foreign" sovereign kingdom of Hawai'i to the domestic incorporation of Hawai'i as a state within the U.S. extends the colonial strategies of conquest and guardianship used by the U.S. government to externalize, terminate, and assimilate the sovereignty, lands, and tribes of Native Americans (Bruyneel 2007: 1–96). In *Redefining Realness*, the impact of Hawai'i's history of genocide and dispossession appear in the severed and ephemeral geographies of belonging where Mock builds family and home from age four to seven and twelve to eighteen with her divorced single Native Hawaiian mother, older sisters Cori and Cheraine, and younger brothers Chad and Jeff. These geographies include her grandmother's place in Ka'ahumanu Public Housing, her mother's low-income rented house in the mixed- race and class neighborhood of Kalihi, and a residential motel near the airport, where Mock witnesses her mother's struggles with poverty; restricted access to education, employment, and social resources; addiction; unstable and inadequate housing; and domestic violence and abuse.

Trans Woman of Color Becoming

Mock concludes her childhood memoir-stories in *Redefining Realness* with a description of her genital reconstruction surgery at age eighteen, following the beginning of hormone replacement therapy at age fifteen. Her account addresses dominant culture's reduction of transgender and transsexual experience to the privatized narrative of "incongruent" body, mind, and inner sense seeking alignment and unity by crossing over to the opposite gender role and/or bodily sex (American Psychiatric Association 1994, 532–38; American Psychiatric Association 2013):

People often describe the journey of transsexual people as a passage from the sexes, from manhood to womanhood, from male to female, from boy to girl. That simplifies a complicated journey of self-discovery that goes way beyond gender and genitalia. My passage was an evolution from me to closer-to-me-ness. It's a journey of self-revelation. Undergoing hormone therapy and genital reconstruction surgery and traveling sixty-six hundred miles from Hawaii to Thailand are the titillating details that cis people love to hear. They're deeply personal steps to become closer to me, and I choose to share them. I didn't hustle those streets and fight the maturation of my body merely to get a vagina. I sought something grander than the changing of genitalia. I was seeking reconciliation with myself. (2014, 227)

Rather than a passage from one sex and gender to the other, Mock defines her gender affirming bottom surgery as part of a more complex journey of "self-discovery," "closer-to-me-ness," "self-revelation," and "reconciliation," beyond "gender and genitalia." The process of self-realization that she has undergone exceeds the racially "normal" cisgender, heterosexual, ablest ordering of bodily time and space, in which the body matures in linear progression with a private, relatively stable inner feeling of being embodied that is secured and reflected in an external public world that, for the most part, only perceives and values (unequally) two genders reducible to two biological interpretations of sex. For Mock, genital reconstruction offers another gender practice, out of the many she has created and used (dress, makeup, hairstyle, self-naming, preferred pronouns, etc.), that will cue and affect the dominant social world to perceive and interact with her in the ways she has already felt, known, and recognized herself to be. This self is not an unchanging, timeless private essence untouched by the social world:

When I look back at my childhood, I often say *I always knew I was a girl* since the age of three or four . . . No one—not my mother, my grandmother, my father, or my siblings—gave me any reason to believe I was anything other than my parents' firstborn son, my father's namesake. But it was my very first conviction . . . When I say *I always knew I was a girl* with such certainty, I erase all the nuances, the work, the process of self-discovery. I've adapted to saying *I always knew I was a girl* as a defense against the louder world, which has told me . . . that my girlhood was imaginary, something made up that needed to be fixed (Mock 2014, 16).

Instead, it is a sense of self that has grown into self-certainty in response to social structures that have made her existence as a girl/woman virtually impossible as someone assigned male at birth.

I want to argue that Mock's voyage toward gender and sexually reconstructed self-certainty draws from the surplus reservoir of racial gender and sexual senses targeted for annihilation by the white settler colonial imposition of Western cisgender heterosexuality and patriarchy. Deborah A. Miranda (Ohlone-Costanoan Esselen Nation, Chumash) has uncovered the missing archives that document the survival and reemergence of the indigenous California third-gender joyas in contemporary Two-Spirit people (2010). The joyas, whose gender and sexual liminality positioned them as guides in the passage from life to death in their communities, were explicit targets of gendercide, or the "killing of a particular gender because of their gender," by Spanish colonizers in California territory beginning in the late eighteenth century (Miranda 2010, 259). Miranda suggests that the strategic colonial extermination of third-gender Natives destroyed a segment of Native communities devoted to ensuring Native vitality, with the added effect of pushing surviving joyas underground and setting a precedent within indigenous communities for the persecution and sacrifice of third-gender people. Also tracing the gendered and sexual dimensions of settler colonialism, Andrea Smith has argued that sexual violence against Native women has been based on the perception of Native bodies as inherently impure and sexually perverse and, therefore, available for violation (2005). Sexual violence has been a primary technology of white settler society, enabling the disappearance of Native peoples and the installing of heteropatriarchy internally within Native communities (Smith 2005, 7–33). Within the context of Hawai'i, J. Kēhaulani Kauanui (2008) has analyzed the U.S. state's use of blood quantum classification as a settler colonial strategy of assimilation that continues the genocide against Natives and the dispossession of Natives from lands and sovereignty, following European imperial war and conquest. The U.S. Congress's 1921 Hawaiian Homes Commission Act (HHCA) established a fifty-percent blood rule by which native Hawaiianness must be measured as a qualification for leasing 200,000 acres of land allotted to eligible native Hawaiians and held in trust by the U.S. government—land originally belonging communally to Kānaka Maoli, or Native Hawaiians (Kauanui 2008, 1–66). Furthering the logic of blood quantum imposed on Native Americans, the fifty-percent rule in Hawai'i seeks to uproot the self-sovereignty of Kānaka Maoli through a racialization of blood that translates indigeneity into a quantifiable, dilutable, and assimilable racial minority. The blood quantum attempts to overturn Kānaka Maoli genealogies of land and kinship that rely broadly on bilateral (maternal and paternal) descent and that embrace relationships with outsiders, including interracial marriage (Kauanui 2008, 1–66). It installs racial purity as a cultural and biological qualification for Kānaka Maoli identity and land access in ways that penalize Natives for their inclusiveness of outsiders and that exploit the diminishing of the Native population by state-sponsored genocide and forced assimilation (Kauanui 2008, 1–66). Moreover, the blood quantum's evaluation of racial authenticity often hinged on policing the sexual and reproductive practices of Kanaka Maoli women, who supposedly diluted Hawaiian "full-bloodedness" through interracial relationships (Kauanui 2008, 121–44). The unattainable (and unmeasurable) blood quantum ultimately allows for the reconfiscating of Kanaka Maoli sovereignty and lands through the state administered "return" of natives to the land. Kauanui calls attention to the participation of Kanaka Maoli elites and the local Hawaiian state in establishing and enforcing the fifty-percent rule as a way to re- nativize and ruralize Kanaka Maoli away from urban slums in ways that accommodate the U.S. federal state's incorporation of Natives. The indigenous Hawaiian sovereignty movement, which began to take shape in the late 1960s, continues to contest the (neo)colonial undermining of Kānaka Maoli sovereignty and genealogies of kinship and land.

The Native invisibility affected by settler colonial strategies of Native disappearance and forced assimilation differs from the white supremacist hyper-visualization of racialized Blackness as a state and social practice that claims utter entitlement to the enslaved and free Black body. Christine Sharpe has described the ruptured historical, social, and "human" conditions that give (non)birth to Black (non)being through the terror of slavery as primal scenes that continue to reproduce the death and shackling of Black people as preconditions for the life of the state and society (2010; 2016). The slave ship in the Middle Passage is the womb that births blackness: "Reading together the Middle Passage, the coffle, and . . . the birth canal, we can see how each has functioned separately and collectively over time to dis/figure Black maternity, to turn the womb into a factory producing blackness as abjection much like the slave ship's hold and the prison, and turning the birth canal into another domestic Middle Passage with Black mothers, after the end of legal hypodescent, still ushering their children into their condition" (Sharpe 2016, 74). The lawless and noneconomic nature of the slaveowner state and society's proclaimed absolute right over Black bodies has exerted itself through the disfiguring and expropriation of the maternally and materially embodied scene of birth itself. The Atlantic Middle Passage becomes the maternal womb, or birth origin, and birth canal for reproducing blackness, conceived in terror and captivity and severed from familial, social, and human origins. Slavery dispossesses the Black woman of her gendered, sexual, reproductive, and familial body, capacity, and relation, including the relation to her own sense of embodiment. It inducts the Black woman into the anguished impossible labor of black slave making by "turning the birth canal into another domestic Middle Passage" that will continue to transmit the nonhuman status of the black slave to her children, even after the formal end of hypodescent (Harris 1964).

Sharpe's remembering of the state and society's founding on the non-representable labor and body of the captive Black woman extends the work of Black feminist scholars such as Sylvia Wynter, Angela Davis, Hortense Spillers, Saidiya Hartman, and Jennifer Morgan. In particular, Spillers has provided a Black countermemory—otherwise made unspeakable within the symbolic laws of American grammar—that traces the creation of the New World's white patriarchal social order to the destruction of African social personhood and kinship relations through the systematic reduction of the African captive body to "flesh" in the transatlantic slave trade: "Under these conditions, one is neither female, nor male, as both subjects are taken into 'account' as *quantities*. The female in 'Middle Passage,' as the apparently smaller physical mass, occupies 'less room' in a directly translatable money economy. But she is, nevertheless, quantifiable by the same rules of accounting as her male counterpart" (1987, 72; emphasis in original). The mass objectification of the enslaved Black body is executed through an "ungendering" that destroys the gender differentiation between female and male, including the "displacement of the genitalia," that engenders familial maternal/paternal kinship and also heterosexual reproductive lineage and futurity (Spillers 1987, 72–73). The degendering of the Black captive woman in particular is an enactment of the slaveowning state and society's unrelenting disposal and rapture of the Black body. She is not only stripped of her gendered social positions and relations as woman and mother and exploited, tortured, and killed without gender distinction from Black captive men. Her embodied sense of self in relationship to gender, sexuality, and sex is forcibly infiltrated and confiscated to reproduce the slave population and the surplus racial sense, value, and capital that provides white heteropatriarchal household with its gender differentiated senses of private interiority, family in domesticity, and public bonds (Hartman 2016; Sharpe 2010; Spillers 1987). This labor of Black womanhood exacted through gender and sexual violence and forced intimacy ruptures rational understandings of labor and its reproduction; the division between private and public; and the unity of the mind/body/inner life (Hartman 2016; Sharpe 2010; Spillers 1987). This captive surplus gender and sexual labor constitutes the birth scene of racial blackness and the mass affinities and social bonds of racial whiteness (Sharpe 2010). The survival and insurgency of Black womanhood, however, has also enabled a reclaiming of this surplus labor for potential embodiments of gender, sexuality, sex, kinship, domesticity, and sociality that surpass the social order and state of the white heteropatriarchal family during and after slavery (Hartman 2016; Sharpe 2010; Spillers 1987). Matt Richardson has identified a cultural archive of vibrant Black gender and sexual nonconformity within contemporary Black lesbian literature. This archive, which has been submerged within dominant white cultural memory and also Black countermemory, remembers and catalyzes the queerness and transness that constitute racial Blackness: "The Black female body has historically been irreconcilable to white society in relation to notions of womanhood. Even as Black women reconstructed the category to reflect their own needs, they were simultaneously subject to brutal scrutiny under the scientists' knife . . . The Black becomes the aporia between sex and gender such that the two never meet in any fashion that would satisfy the dictates of normative heterosexuality" (Richardson 2013, 7). Richardson's expanded Black literary historiography provides an analysis of the collectively unwitnessed and unmourned deaths of Black queer, trans, and intersex people at the hands of the police and other state entities, including the deaths of Logan Smith in Chicago in 1996; Tyra Hunter in Washington, D.C., in 1995; and Duanna Johnson in 2008 in Memphis, Tennessee (2013, 159–67).

In the final chapter of Mock's childhood memory-stories in *Redefining Realness*, her description of her gender and sexual reconstruction as a moment of self-realization, beyond mere genital surgery, marks a culmination in the present, with surplus potentials yet-to-be revealed in the future, and a reconciliation with the past. This event is not so much an arrival as a remembering and redistribution of the multiple times and relations of racial gender disappeared, deadened, and assimilated by the white settler state and social order. This moment when Mock states, "After eighteen years, my body mirrored me," is also the moment when she finds herself mirrored in her father and her mother through a reconciling return to memories of feeling unreflected and misrecognized during her childhood. Her first thoughts after surgery were about her Dad's determination to raise her to be a strong, self-assured, and independent person: "I thought of my father because I knew that though he would be uneasy about the surgery, he'd respect my independence. I thought about his way of doing things, how he'd taught us to ride our bikes without training wheels, and how he'd thrown me in a pool to teach me to swim" (Mock 2014, 232). This renewed memory of her father as an eighteen-year-old adds another dimension to Mock's earlier narrating of a younger impression of her father:

> The expectations my father had of me had nothing to do with me and all to do with how he understood masculinity, what it meant to be a man, a strong black man. My father welcomed two sons into the world, and one was feminine and needed fixing. Using my childlike lens, I felt Dad was against me, consistently monitoring me and policing my gender. I've come to realize that he simply loved me and wanted to protect me, even from myself . . . My adult understanding of my childhood with my father doesn't erase the effects of his policing. I felt his gaze always following me, making me feel isolated as I quietly grappled with my identity. The loneliness and self-consciousness from these exchanges made me vulnerable in a way I wasn't able to recognize until decades later. (39)

In this earlier passage, Mock remembers her father's policing gaze, which attempted to contain, control, and "fix" her femininity. Rather than reflecting and affirming her femme gender, her father expected her to mirror his masculinity, or "what it meant to be a man, a strong black man." In retrospect, Mock attributes her father's gender monitoring to fear for her vulnerability as a feminine, gender nonconforming person assigned male at birth, while noting that it was actually her father's gaze that isolated her and made her vulnerable. In the lines following this passage, Mock links her feelings of loneliness from these exchanges with her father to her heightened vulnerability to the sexual abuse that she experienced, inflicted by Derek, the teenage son of her father's girlfriend Janine. Similarly, Mock's self-realized gender and sexual reconstruction also initiates a revised return to memories of her mother: "I had faulted Mom for not living up to the image that I had projected onto her, the image of the perfect mother I felt she should've been for me. No one was able to live up to that ideal because that woman did not exist. What I appreciate now is that my mother never projected such an image of the perfect child onto me. She never made me feel bad about being feminine" (2014, 239). This new relationship with the image of her mother seeks to repair a younger Mock's experiences of abandonment, when her mother's dependency on her abusive boyfriend Rick (which echoed Mock's grandmother's relationship with her grandfather) put Mock and her brothers in danger of violence and homelessness: "The woman I had dreamed about as a child, the woman with the perfume, long dark hair and shelves of books, did not exist. Mom was no longer my dream girl. I had to become that dream. My vulnerability, resentment, and desperation to survive were the backdrop of my first nights at Merchant Street in downtown Honolulu" (2014, 167). The desperate conditions that shattered Mock's childhood dream of her mother further jeopardized Mock's sense of safety, stability, and survival, including her ability to continue with her gender transition through medically supervised hormone replacement therapy (2014, 166–67). These conditions shaped Mock's decision to begin the sex work on Merchant Street that provided her with the funds to undergo bottom surgery and to help her mother pay bills.

Mock's reunion with these younger memories of her parents following her bottom surgery is literalized by her return to Honolulu, "wrapped in [an] airline's blue blanket," to recover with her mother's care on the twin mattress on their apartment floor (2014, 239–41). Her body's mirroring of her also enables the recovered mirroring between her parents and her. The redistributed remembering that produces Mock's reconciled mirroring suggest that gender and sexual reconstruction is a process that cannot be reduced to the idea of transitioning from one gender and sex assigned at birth to the opposite gender/sex. Gender and sexual transformation in its multiplicity of experiences, identities, expressions, and practices struggles to move from dislocated and foreclosed senses of gender embodiment and social location toward gender embodiments and social locations that can find material survival and expression within, against, and beyond the constitutively white settler binary cisgender symbolic and social order. As shown in Mock's reconstructive process, her lifelong passage into becoming the trans woman of color she has sensed herself to be was a journey shaped by a felt understanding of the differential power relations that shaped and overdetermined her nonreflection and nonrecognition by her parents and other figures of social authority within the racially gendered and sexed symbolic order of the social world. Mock identifies and holds responsible her father's performance of cisheterosexual masculinity through the devaluation of femininity and gender nonconformity and also her mother's enactment of cisheterosexual femininity through the overvaluation of cisheterosexual masculinity. At the same time, she understands these racial gender performances as strategies for dealing with real dislocation from white cisheterosexual social normalcy and power. Mock's multiple times and spaces of reconciled memory, self, and family draw from the exuberant surplus of racial gender and sexual embodiment and relations that remain despite the white setter state and society's destruction, theft, and incorporation of Black and Native worlds. She derives her reconciled self- and familial images through gender and sexual reconstruction that remembers the power differentials, superimposed histories, and remaining potentials that determine the limits and possibilities of the internal and external mirroring of the racial gender shifting self within the social order. The forcible removal of father, mother, and other kin from "mimetic view as a partner in the prevailing social fiction of the Father's name, the Father's law" (Spillers 1987, 80) has also generated insurgent kinship practices of "world enlargement" (Hau'ofa 1995; Kauanui 2008, 11–12) and "promiscuous sociality" (Hartman 2016). Many other kin have appeared within Mock's mimetic view to perform the labor of co-imagining and reflecting Mock's unfolding trans woman of color worldviews, including Grandma Pearl; older sisters Cori and Cheraine; younger brothers Chad and Jeff; Native Hawaiian Filipina first childhood friend Marilyn; transfemme Filipina best friend Wendi; Rebecca, Heather, Angela, Shayna, and Kahlúa, the trans women who did sex work alongside Mock on Merchant Street, in Honolulu; her father's girlfriend Janine in Oakland; her Grandma Shellie, Auntie Linda Gail, Auntie Joyce, and Makayla, the daughter of her father's girlfriend Denise in Dallas; and Black women writers Audre Lorde, Maya Angelou, and Zora Neale Hurston.

This expanded field of mimetic kinship implodes the privately bounded notions of self, family, household, and territory that found and bind the white settler state and society. The different scenes of porous domesticity that have provided Mock with care, mirroring, and insurgency in the kitchens of the Mock women in Dallas and her Grandma Pearl's and mother's apartments in Honolulu demonstrate practices of affinity that exceed the mutually constituting public and private, social and internal, foreign and domestic boundaries that establish the U.S. national body, nation-state, and empire. Although not addressed explicitly in Mock's memoirs, these domestic scenes that move between the heavily militarized Pacific cities of Honolulu, Long Beach, and Oakland and the equally fortified Dallas, near the Gulf of Mexico, mark the settlement and potential unsettling of Native lands, Black bodies, and alternate world relations claimed as territory by the white settler republics that underlie the state and civil society. Hawai'i's occupation, annexation, and forced domestic incorporation into the U.S. as an overseas sovereign kingdom in 1898 coincides with the confiscation of the Philippines (1898), Guam (1898), and Samoa (1899), followed by the Northern Mariana Islands (1947), in the Pacific and Puerto Rico (1898) and then the Virgin Islands (1916) in the Atlantic. These oceanic territories in the Pacific and Atlantic establish the northwestern hemisphere as the sovereign domain of the U.S. state through modes of colonization, militarization, and administrative rule that extend the forms of conquest, genocide, captivity, and imposed assimilation developed through the settler colonial annexation and slaveholding industrialization of the continental lands of the U.S., including the later territories of Louisiana (1803), Florida (1821), Texas (1845), Oregon (1846), the Southwest (1848 and 1853), and Alaska (1867). Mock's memoir-stories in *Refining Realness* do not conclude following her gender and sexual reconstruction surgery at age eighteen. Mock, the storyteller located outside/inside and across the times and spaces of her memories, begins a new chapter in her adult life in 2009 in Manhattan island on the Atlantic seaboard, which was part of Native Lenape lands before seventeenth century Dutch colonization. This final chapter brings all the layers of memory composing her womanhood into her unfolding relationship with Aaron and with the differentiated publics and outcast populations amassed through engagement with her memoirs: "Though you may not perceive me as trans, I am trans, and being trans—as is being black, Hawaiian, young, and a woman—is an integral part of my experience, one that I have no investment in erasing. All of these parts of myself coexist in *my* body, a representation of evolution and migration and truth" (2014, 258; emphasis in original). The trans Black Native Hawaiian woman of color senses of being, belonging, and migrating transmitted in Mock's personal collective memory catalyze potential mass affinities that remember the territories and bodies that make the private and public bonds of the subject, family, and state possible.

FOUR. MOVEMENT

Trans and Gender Nonconforming Digital Activisms

and U.S. Transnational Empire

In 1950 the United Nations (UN) declared December 10 to be Human Rights Day "to bring to the attention 'of the peoples of the world' the Universal Declaration of Human Rights as the common standard of achievement for all peoples and all nations."[1] On Human Rights Day 2014, online reporting company the *Daily Beast* invited more than twenty-five LGBT activists from around the world to New York City to share their stories and struggles. This event, called "Quorum: Global LGBT Voices," was reported live on social media and also video recorded to be released later online for the *Daily Beast*'s readers.[2] With the goal of "reversing the megaphone" of the U.S.-global LGBT conversation, featured activists such as Bisi Alimi (Nigeria), Anastasia Smirnova (Russia), Maurice Tomlinson (Jamaica), Meena Seshu (India), Alice Nkom (Cameroon), Nisha Ayub (Malaysia), Kenita Placide (St. Lucia), Parvez Sharma (*A Jihad for Love*, 2007), Xiaogang Wei (China), and Jabu Pereira (South Africa) gave TED-style inspirational talks to a small live audience.[3] The audience was made up of members of international LGBT organizations that cosponsored the event, including U.S.-based organizations Astraea Lesbian Foundation for Justice, American Jewish World Service, All Out, International Gay and Lesbian Human Rights Commission, Human Rights Campaign, GLAAD, 76Crimes.com, and Muslims for Progressive Values, as well as Geneva-based ILGA-Europe. Additional audience members included representatives from event cosponsors the New York Public Library,

Delta Airlines, and HBO; media technicians and social media gurus; guests of invited speakers; and people who found out about the event through its targeted publicity. With audience members and cameras focused on the stage where activists gave their talks, the event had the look of a live performance and broadcast television show. Yet the *internalized* framing of the space of performance and viewing signaled that this media event's representational effects went beyond the now common-sense expectations and experiences of mass-mediated culture.

Invited speakers were encouraged to give talks that were personal, reflective, and impactful rather than informative or narrative in style and content. The stage was a bare minimalist setup with only a screen for projecting images and text as background for activist speakers. The audience remained a dimly lit presence, kept for the most part outside the recorded images and video of the speakers onstage. Instead of speaking to the audience in the space or the audiences imagined beyond photo and video cameras, speakers' talks addressed virtual elsewheres already instantaneously and yet-to-be-materialized digitally in other times and spaces. The event was constructed to translate speakers' talks into personalized thought and image bytes that would transmit easily and quickly—without the burden of representing social contexts—through cell phones, cameras, and audience members that acted as transmitters of the event. During an intermission, the emcees announced that it had/would reach twenty million people, further reminding us that the event addressed spaces and times that were not here and now.

Against the digital event's emphasis on speedy transmission, unburdened by social context, mixed-race transmasculine South African activist Jabu Pereira of Iranti-org redirected the event's attention toward the broad social histories and connections that shape the experiences of lesbian, gay, bisexual, transgender, and intersex (LGBTI) South Africans in the present. South Africa is considered the most democratic and wealthy country in southern Africa. The nation's postapartheid constitution is the first in the world to explicitly protect diverse sexual orientations against discrimination, and same-sex marriage has been legalized nationally. Yet, during his talk, Pereira stated, "We have great laws. . . . Laws don't feed people. They don't make you sleep better, and they don't protect you from being raped and killed because of sexual orientation and gender identity." South Africa's legislated rights for sexual minorities have mostly benefited white gay and lesbian South Africans in practice. Even after the formal end of racial apartheid, according to Pereira, racial dominance and wealth allows white gays and lesbians to "safely hold hands, kiss in public, and drink cocktails in bars securely designed for them." LGBTI Black South Africans who continue to live in the townships created by the apartheid state to segregate out and dispossess nonwhites face poverty, violence, rape, HIV infection, and exclusion from housing, employment, education, and health systems. Pereira called on the audience in the here and elsewheres of the event to remember the legacy of those who fought against racial apartheid and to view the current struggles of LGBTI Black South Africans as part of the struggle against the "extension of apartheid into our democracy." He also connected the Black LGBTI South African struggle against racism, poverty, violence, and dispossession to the American-based Movement for Black Lives against anti-Black state violence and the societal devaluation of Black lives. Pereira's call to make visible and feel the racial and economic apartheid of the present in South Africa—and in connection with racial struggles in the United States—works against the digitally fragmenting technologies, times, and spaces of American transnational empire.

This chapter builds on the previous chapter's exploration of the porous intimate and social economies and histories of U.S. empire, racism, and cishetero-patriarchy embodied, survived, and transformed by Janet Mock and trans women and girls of color who may share experiences like those documented in Mock's memoirs. The chapter continues to question and contest the inside/outside borders of the U.S. nation-state as they have been established through different cycles and technologies of imperial conquest, colonization, and incorporation behind the screen of U.S. liberal exceptionalism. The first section focuses on South African LGBTI rights group Iranti-org's overturning of top-down narratives and data on LGBTI lives by the transnational U.S.-led human rights complex through documentary media activism. The second section discusses gender nonconforming kathoey Thai filmmaker Tanwarin Sukkhapisit's deft navigation of the growing entanglements between transnational, regional, and national film cultural economies to produce semi-independent films that center the complexity, vulnerability, and transformative power of kathoey lives and relationships. The final section returns to the internal transnational territories of the U.S. nation-state to highlight the media activism, art, and theory of Latinx queer trans femme micha cárdenas, whose media projects usurp the networked digital infrastructure created to further the interests of the U.S. state, military, corporations, and universities toward building solidarities and safety for and between criminalized and targeted migrants, trans and queer people, and Black and brown communities living in the borderlands of U.S. empire.

Perhaps more than any other chapter, this chapter calls for more explicit reflection on the limits of my use of *trans* both in connection to and disruption of the term *transgender*, even when I have described *trans* and *trans of color* as analytics creating provision, potential solidarities based on interrelated experiences and histories of displacement from the white Western binary gender/sex system. I use *trans* only when *transgender* and/or *trans* are repurposed explicitly by the groups and individuals discussed. Otherwise, I use the same English or English-translated terms used by the activists, such as *gender nonconforming*, *lesbian*, or *kathoey*, to identify themselves and the communities with which they are involved. Additionally, I use *gender nonconforming* to describe forms of gender/sex embodiment and expression outcast within social and geopolitical contexts outside the United States, knowing that this term is also an imposition given the U.S. and Western histories and systems of psycho-bio-medicine, state capitalism, and civil society within which "gender" as an organizing concept emerges (Meyerowitz 2004, 98–129; Preciado 2013, 99–129). Similarly, I do not use *trans of color*, *trans women of color*, *women of color*, or *people of color* unless they are already mobilized by the activists in the chapter in connection with larger histories of coalitional repurposing. While signaling the limits of *trans*, *trans of color*, *and other terms* and the limitations of my strategies for dealing with these limits, I also want to emphasize that each of the activists discussed interrupts U.S. and Western dominance and exploitation by transnational institutions, networks, and technologies to readapt, localize, and even exploit the transnational.

Iranti-org and Transnational Human Rights

Iranti-org was founded in 2012 in Johannesburg, South Africa, by human rights activist and visual artist Jabu Pereira. Iranti-org uses digital media to document the stories of LGBTI South Africans in their local vernaculars and to build movements for LGBTI justice in South Africa and the southern Africa region. The organization gives particular attention to the experiences of Black gender nonconforming, trans, and queer South Africans who have been exposed to violence, discrimination, and poverty as structural effects of racial apartheid and postapartheid nation-building within the U.S.-dominated global economy. The organization's media team, which has included organizers Kokeletso "Kay" Legoete, Itumeleng "Tumi" Thandeka Mkhuma, Zikhona Gqozo, Ayanda Msiza, and Gugu Mandla from the Black

FIGURE 4.1. Iranti-org team (2017). *Back row*: Gugu Mandla, Jabu Pereira, Nomsa Manzini, Joshua Sehoole, Kanyanta Kakana. *Front row*: Zikhona Gqozo, Zethu Gqozo, Sandi Dlamini, Kellyn Botha. Courtesy of Jabu Pereira.

FIGURE 4.2. Iranti-org team (2012). *Back row*: Rethabile Gamede, Betesta Segale, Tumi Mkhuma, Jabu Pereira, Neo Musangi. *Front row*: Ayanda Msiza, Gugu Mandla, Zikhona Gqozo, Dolar Vasani. Courtesy of Jabu Pereira.

townships outside Johannesburg and director and founder Pereira, translates the local stories of LGBTI South Africans into collaboratively produced, circulated, and archived visual narratives and documentaries. These visual "documents" provide the basis for dialogue and information sharing with community members, technological skills building within the organization and with communities, and movement building and advocacy across communities locally, nationally, regionally, and transnationally. Iranti-org uses these visual productions as both evidence and cultural reimaginings that work strategically "alongside and outside" international human rights frameworks for LGBTI racial, gender, and sexual justice.

The strategic use of neoliberal human rights frameworks was an important part of the anti-apartheid struggle in South Africa. Describing racial apartheid as a gross violation of human rights, anti-apartheid activists called on codes of governance and ethics that exceeded those defined, legislated, and enforced by the apartheid South African government for the benefit of white South Africans. Anti-apartheid activists appropriated the universal humanist concepts used by Western neoliberal states and international governing bodies, such as the United Nations and World Bank, to provide a collective category of belonging and valuing that countered apartheid's systematic racial violence, dispossession, and devaluation. Appropriated human rights frameworks also helped to galvanize mass international support and to revise the Eurocentric conception and application of human rights and humanism for only white subjects of Western European descent. Anti-apartheid human rights activism was only effective when paired with grassroots mobilizing that put direct pressure on the apartheid regime and on governments, corporations, and universities internationally to divest from supporting the apartheid South African state. Throughout the 1980s, the Reagan administration, the World Bank (WB), and the International Monetary Fund (IMF) continued to provide political legitimacy and economic support to the apartheid South African government, often under the mantle of human rights and human development (Bond 2003). Anti-apartheid uses of human rights frameworks helped to materialize protections for "fundamental human rights" in the first postapartheid South African Constitution of 1996, which was established after the first general election to include nonwhite voters in 1994. They also enabled the postapartheid South African nation-state to become a member of a global economy mediated by the human rights frameworks of transnational institutions like the UN, the IMF, and the WB. As Pereira and other South African community-based activists point out, however, Black low-income South

Africans, especially those who are gender and sexually nonconforming, continue to experience the nonmaterializing of rights, protections, and livelihoods under the postapartheid state. To date, the postcolonial South African state has not redistributed the economic wealth, land, and political and social authority amassed by white South Africans over more than three centuries of colonization, genocide, and formal and informal racial apartheid.

The twenty-first-century "free" market and neocolonial logics driving Western European– and U.S.-dominated international human rights economies have become even more difficult to navigate for communities in the Global South, including the Black low-income rural and urban LGBTI South Africans participating in and represented by Iranti-org. Human rights have become tied even more tightly to the expansion of transnational capitalism and the neoliberal state structures that accompany capitalist accumulation and circulation. Since the 1990s, the UN has advocated for a shift away from the infrastructural (1960s–70s) and structural adjustment-based development (1980s) it once initiated and coordinated with the WB and the IMF. Instead, the UN has reestablished itself as a leader in reforming the macroeconomic developmental ideologies and policies of the WB and the IMF to embrace a human development approach, or "people-centered" economics (United Nations General Assembly 2000; United Nations 2015).[4]

The UN's human development approach has given communities and activists some avenues for calling attention to the persistence of colonial dispossession in the late twentieth century and to the exploitative impacts of globalization through economic instruments like structural adjustment policies. However, this approach also activates the new incorporation of "minority" and "marginalized" populations into neoliberal transnational regimes of governance and finance. By 2000, the UN's humanist turn has been adopted by the WB and the IMF, with encouragement from the Organisation for Economic Co-operation and Development. The UN's Millennium Goals for the global reduction of poverty by 2015 have become core and coordinating objectives for international development, thereby replacing the macroeconomic goals of structural development with the microeconomic targeting of social issues and populations. The eight Millennium Development Goals set by the UN aim to eradicate extreme poverty and hunger; achieve universal primary education; promote gender equality and empower women; reduce child mortality; improve maternal health; combat HIV/AIDS, malaria, and other diseases; ensure environmental sustainability; and develop a global partnership for development (United Nations General Assembly 2000; United Nations

2015). Reflecting this shift in developmental frameworks, both the wb and the imf have shed the language and aims of structural development or even development at large.[5] Since 2015, UN Millennium Goals have been reassessed and readapted into seventeen Sustainable Development Goals to be met within the next fifteen years, with greater emphasis on environmental issues and social equality (United Nations General Assembly 2015).[6]

The wb and the imf were created in 1944 just before the conclusion of World War II, when older imperial global divisions gave way to a landscape polarized between the U.S.-led First World and the USSR-led Second World in the Cold War.[7] The wb was created to reconstruct and promote economic growth in war-damaged European nations, while the imf was charged with ensuring unrestricted world trade by overseeing the international monetary system. Since the 1960s, both institutions have redirected investments and loans toward development and managing debt crises in low- and middle-income countries in the Global South. Their current position as dominant leaders, brokers, and gatekeepers in international development and finance was secured in the 1980s as a result of structural adjustment policies that they institutionalized, as they argue, in necessary response to the Third World debt crisis of the 1970s. Yet, as communities, activists, and scholars critical of the wb and the imf argue, structural adjustment merely initiated another set of strategies to secure the international circulation and dominance of U.S. and g8 finance capital, especially through Third World countries.[8]

Structural adjustment policies mandated the restructuring of Third World societies to reflect the divided private/public sectors, "free" markets, and state forms of neoliberal capitalist nation-states. Structural adjustment loans that supposedly helped Third World countries to avoid defaulting on prior loans not only deepened debt but also reproduced the loop of default crises and the need for additional loans and debt. The loans also exacted profit through interest rates and the incorporation of deregulated Third World economies into transnational chains of export production and finance. Third World countries were required to reroute resources away from meeting social needs toward building export-driven privatized economies and systems of labor, governance, technology, and finance geared toward the demands of the First World–dominated global market. In South Africa during apartheid, wb project-based loans, such as Eskom power and the Lesotho Highlands Water Project, violated sanctions against supporting the apartheid regime and primarily benefited white communities. With the end of apartheid, the wb's and the imf's relationships with the African National Congress–led

South African government has shifted from lending to structural advising on land reform, housing, health care, public works, child-welfare finance, infrastructure, industrial development, and macroeconomic policy. Overall, structural adjustment in the forms of loans, analysis, and advising has produced the very structures of debt, crisis, poverty, and social inequality it has claimed to remedy.

The turn from structural development to human rights and poverty reduction starting in the first decade of the twenty-first century signals a new level of coordination between the UN, the WB, and the IMF. This shift has given new attention to populations deemed "vulnerable" to the effects of social inequality. The WB has paired its primary goal of ending extreme poverty by 2030 with the second goal of promoting shared prosperity by increasing economic growth and monitoring the welfare of the poorest and most vulnerable segments in developing and developed countries, including women and youth. The UN has become more concerned with documenting human rights violations on the basis of sexual orientation and gender identity (SOGI) and has included SOGI as "vulnerable grounds" in its human rights systems. Also, the U.S. Department of State under the leadership of Hillary Clinton made LGBT human rights a policy focus. As part of this wave of human rights–based international development, the Williams Institute at the University of California, Los Angeles, is collaborating with the U.S. Agency for International Development (USAID), which partners with the U.S. State Department, and staff members of the WB to produce a research metric and argument linking LGBT human rights to economic development. According to their preliminary research on thirty-nine countries, the exclusionary treatment of LGBT people at the "micro level" results in costs to the economy, including "lost labor time, lost productivity, underinvestment in human capital, and the inefficient allocation of human resources through discrimination in education and hiring practices" (Badgett et al. 2014, 27). At the "macro level," their research suggests a "clear positive correlation between per capita GDP and legal rights for LGB and transgender people across countries" (Badgett et al. 2014, 2).[9] This new research seeks to redirect development-based international funding, including USAID and the WB, toward LGBT populations as "micro" human rights targets with "macro" economic impact. As revealed in this collaborative research project on international LGBT populations, the turn to human rights–based development by the U.S.- and G8-dominated transnational order of finance and governance marks the new penetration of capital and liberal state ideologies into what is perceived as the micro-infrastructure of the developing global human community. In the shift toward micro-infrastructures, people and communities are extracted and isolated from their lived social and historical contexts. They become human "indexes" for macroeconomic development.

With the intensified, coordinated use of human rights frameworks by the transnational order in the early twenty-first century, communities, groups, and social movements that have relied on human rights concepts to make international connections and to broaden the scope of anticolonial nationalisms have had to revise their strategies. Those working at the intersections of anticolonial, racial, economic, gender, and sexual justice, like Iranti-org in South Africa, must not only retool the Western white cis-hetero-fraternity of human rights systems. Now they must also navigate human rights systems that incorporate differentiated social categories of race, gender and gender identity, sexuality, and economic class. Also, white-dominated gay and lesbian U.S. nongovernmental organizations, such as the Human Rights Campaign and the International Gay and Lesbian Human Rights Commission, have used human rights frameworks to advocate for the mainstreaming of gay and lesbian civil rights and have contributed to the nationalizing and transnationalizing of U.S. white and class-privileged gay and lesbian agendas. Centering on the lives of Black LGBTI South Africans, Iranti-org's digital documentation inverts top-down universal narratives about LGBT lives and rights by the transnational U.S.-led human rights complex.[10] While transnational human rights and development systems often instrumentalize the experiences of LGBT people as data and spectacle, Iranti-org records the impact of hate violence on LGBTI Black South Africans in ways that remember the social fabrics of which targeted people are a part. The group also documents the larger social contexts and histories that have made LGBTI people vulnerable to hate violence.

Iranti-org's digital video documentaries provide close-up, careful accounts of the disturbing pattern of rape and murder targeting gender nonconforming Black lesbians in low-income townships and city areas in South Africa. More than seventeen murders of Black lesbians, many of whom were gender nonconforming masculine of center, have been reported in South African townships since 2005. Mass media reports on these hate incidents are nonexistent, trivializing, sensationalizing, or even condoning (of the murders). Police and state response to these hate murders has ranged from complete absence, neglect, and victim blaming to ceremonial attention without follow-up. Iranti-org's media team often provides the only reporting on these incidents. The team has documented the 2013 hate murder of Duduzile Zozo, a twenty-six-year-old gender nonconforming masculine of center Black lesbian from Thokoza township, southeast of Johannesburg. Filmed a few days after the murder and then during the one-year memorial, Iranti-org's videos focus on Duduzile's mother, father, friends, and neighborhood acquaintances. Duduzile's mother and father speak painfully of their loss and of the special place Duduzile held in their family. Duduzile's friends describe how they watched out for each other, resisted being harassed, and enjoyed time together. These accounts provide viewers with intimate, multidimensional views of Duduzile as belonging to a home and community, while nevertheless dealing with harassment and potential danger as a part of everyday life.

Moreover, Iranti-org's videos give us intimate views of the internal architecture of Duduzile's township, Thokoza. Modest homes of plaster, tin, cardboard, and plastic surrounded by fences offer reminders of the townships' histories as confinement areas for Black, "coloured," and Indian South Africans under the racial apartheid system. Under apartheid, nonwhites were dispossessed of their land, property, homes, and livelihoods and forced to migrate to townships on the margins of towns and cities, where they could be segregated from participation in South African economies, politics, and public life. Despite the formal end of systematic apartheid in the 1990s and the emergence of a Black middle-class, Black, mixed-race, and Indian South Africans in townships have not been able to repossess lost land and property and to find sustaining employment. Most townships remain on the geographic and social outskirts, further marginalized by the neoliberal development projects undertaken by the South African state. Yet townships have continued to flourish as spaces of community building, creative reimagining, informal economic development, and political organizing, despite and in response to their ongoing histories of racial and economic oppression. During apartheid, townships enforced racial and class hierarchies *spatially* between whites and nonwhites and also divides between different nonwhite groups. They became hubs for political organizing and uprising across ethnic, racial, and class divides. In Black townships like Thokoza, neoliberal modes of development after the formal end of apartheid have continued to impoverish and dispossess, while producing gender, sexual, ethnic, and class divides between community members who negotiate the persistence of apartheid's legacy. Duduzile Zozo (named in Zulu and Xhosa languages) was the primary breadwinner for the Zozo family. Duduzile embodied a convergence of differences overwritten by histories of subjugation—and also possibilities in the process of becoming. This convergence of strife and possibility was perceived with fear, dread, intimidation, and desire by the neighbor a few streets down who sought violently to "verify" and impose gender/sex/sexuality on Duduzile's body. He raped and killed Duduzile and placed her lifeless body *to be found just outside*—across the street from—her family home.[11]

Iranti-org's video documentaries on the hate murder of Duduzile Zozo provide not only an account of her death but an account of her life in relationship to the family, friends, and community members who cared for her. The videos insist on more than a "document" of this traumatic event.[12] They insist on remembering the stories of Duduzile's life in the vernaculars of her home, community, and township—vernaculars embedded with cues about the broader social histories that frame her life and death in Thokosa. In doing the work of vernacular documentation, Iranti-org's digital videos resist the translation of racially, gender, and sexually marginalized people of the Global South (and Global North) into mere data, spectacle, and categories for knowledge collection that will profit a twenty-first-century transnational cultural economy fueled increasingly by fusing human rights to development and finance. Moreover, Iranti-org's videos are the products of mobilizations that brought together Thokosa community members and organizations, such as Ihawu and Forum for the Empowerment of Women, to commemorate Duduzile's life a year after Duduzile's murder. Mobilizations like these have put pressure on police and government officials to respond to the hate violence targeting Duduzile Zozo and other gender and sexually variant low-income Black South Africans and to be accountable to communities considered disposable through apartheid's ongoing legacy.

Tanwarin Sukkhapisit and Transnational Cultural Finance

Tanwarin Sukkhapisit is a gender nonconforming Thai kathoey English teacher turned filmmaker who has gone from having her first independent feature banned by the Thailand Cultural Ministry to being awarded best picture for her second independent feature by the Thai Film Director Association.[13] Her first digital independent film, *Insects in the Backyard* (Thailand, 2010), offers windows into the estranged lives of widowed kathoey mother Tanya and her two teenage children, Jenny and Johnny. More a stringing together of separate vignettes than narrative, the film moves between Tanya's failed attempts at domesticity and parenting and Jenny's and Johnny's melancholic

FIGURE 4.3. Jabu Pereira and the Iranti-org media team at Duduzile Zozo's memorial one year after her 2013 murder (June 29, 2014). Courtesy of Jabu Pereira.

searches for comfort far from home. Rather than mourning the loss of the gender conforming heterosexual middle-class family or moralizing about it, however, Sukkhapisit's film seizes on scenes of estrangement to comically expose the confinements of binary gender and sexuality as they are enforced by the nuclear family structure.

The family's brokenness is first described as an effect of Tanya's kathoey gender nonconforming embodiment, which displaces conventional positions and roles within the family. Although Tanya is Jenny's and Johnny's birth parent, she refers to herself and is referred to by her children as their sister. This mistaken naming of family position shows the degraded and rejected place assigned to Tanya because she is kathoey. Yet it also shows how gender nonconformity within the family structure disassembles and opens up family roles and positions to ambiguity, subversive chaos, and rescripting. Tanya is dislocated not only from the positions of birth mother and father but from any recognized position within family and home. Sukkhapisit's film shows Tanya's defamiliarized and unhomed state by interrupting everyday scenes of domesticity with dream-states. Scenes of Tanya sitting lonely at the dining room table after her children have refused to eat her home-cooked meals are intercut with segments of raw sensuality. Dazed, ecstatic, and longing, Tanya wanders through lush natural landscapes or has rough sex in parts of the house. Tanya's moments of wandering are echoed by Jenny's and Johnny's movements between Bangkok's confined commercial spaces and rural vil-

FIGURE 4.4. Director Tanwarin Sukkhapisit as Tanya in *Insects in the Backyard* (2010). Courtesy of Tanwarin Sukkhapisit.

lages and towns like Nong Khai on the northeastern border of Thailand and Laos. In their roving, Jenny and Johnny experiment with nonheterosexual coupled sex and intimacy. Together, these moments of wandering call into question the "real" or most significant storylines in the film as they break up and provide transitions between story threads. They express alienation from (and boredom with) the conventional times, spaces, and relationships of domestic family and public city life. They also introduce the possibility of more expansive embodiments of gender, sexuality, and family that do not rely on biology's scripting of family roles (mother, father, and other as mutually exclusive), binary gender (female or male), and binary sexuality (hetero- or homosexuality).

Yet *Insects*'s moments of wandering remain framed by the film as an interdependent economy of exchange between rural and urban settings. These moments may offer temporary escapes from family domesticity and city life, but they remain claimed by other economies. Jenny's and Johnny's searches for intimacy lead them to sex work that in turn introduces them to gay, lesbian, and bi- or pansexual practices and kink. Tanya's dream-states in lush natural environments are also performances of Hollywood fantasies and scripts, including Halle Berry in the James Bond film *Die Another Day*. Sukkhapisit's refusal to let sexuality and gender roam "free" highlights the experiences of kathoeys, outcast youth, and gender and sexual deviants—or "insects in the backyard"—who have no space or existence outside the economies of the conventional home, formal or informal work, and desires shaped by dominant media. Outcast lives remain *determined* by economies that disassemble the possibility of nonconventional forms of family, desire, intimacy, and embodiment. *Insects* provides a visceral feeling of determined lives by keeping the stories of each family member separate from one another and also internally fragmented from any stable sense of self and belonging. Sukkhapisit's tight framing and editing produces the felt affect of lives shaped by external structures. Viewers have to connect and keep separate shots and segments to make sense of the story. Our viewing experience is one of peering at/into/through multiple windows capturing feeds from different live sources. The active practices of disassembly and reassembly demanded of us make explicit the technologies and aesthetics that shape our experience of the film. Sukkhapisit's *Insects* is thus more than a film shot and produced using digital technologies. It uses styles, practices, and habits transferred from online computerized interfaces. Counter to the engrossment, identification, and linear progress expected of analog narrative film, the Internet-like windows of *Insects* encourage an experience of viewing that is *external* to the internal worlds framed by the film. Like the experiences of Tanya, Jenny, and Johnny within the film, our viewing of it feels determined by external forces.

Sukkhapisit's deterministic and interactive style of Internet-influenced filmmaking becomes even more apparent in her second independently produced feature, *It Gets Better* (2012). *Insects* and *It Gets Better*, however, were produced and received under dramatically different conditions. While *Insects* was a gritty do-it-yourself collaboration made on less than 500,000 Thai baht (about US$15,760), *It Gets Better* was produced with larger-scale funding, a professionalized production team with "high" production values, and the commercial backing of distributor M Pictures. *Insects* was the first film to be banned under the Thailand Cultural Ministry's 2009 rating system, which liberalized the previous system of monitoring and censorship in place since 1930. The Cultural Ministry considered *Insects* immoral and pornographic and prohibited the film's domestic screening under threat of fines and arrest.

Although banned domestically, *Insects* received attention through the 2010 Bangkok International Film Festival and the 2010 Vancouver International Film Festival, where the film was nominated for the Dragons and Tigers Award for Young Cinema. Sukkhapisit rallied international, national, and local support in protest of the banning of *Insects* and called attention to the Cultural Ministry's censorship of her representation of kathoey experiences. To extend her cultural activism, Sukkhapisit founded Amfine Productions, an independent film company that uses film art to raise awareness and promote understanding about human diversity. She was also elected president of the Thai Film Director Association in 2012. The Thai Film Director Association's awarding of "best picture" to Sukkhapisit's second indie film, *It Gets Better*, in 2013 marks the successful overturning of the marginalization of her earlier *Insects*. *It Gets Better* continues to give serious attention to the lives of gender nonconforming kathoeys. It departs from 1980s mainstream films that depict kathoeys as victims of tragedy and early twenty-first-century mainstream films that present them as outcasts who must prove themselves worthy of national belonging.[14] These earlier film waves provided semisympathetic views of them. Yet they reproduced dominant cultural codes that trivialized and devalued kathoeys. Plots often inflicted emotional and physical suffering on kathoey bodies before "rehabilitating" them toward potential national inclusion. In contrast, Sukkhapisit's films are driven by the desire to produce identification with the complexity of kathoey lives. Also, her films are produced by and feature kathoey and other gender and sexually nonconforming cultural workers.

Yet Sukkhapisit's kathoey-centered films are not absolutely independent in their production values and aesthetics. *It Gets Better* was produced with commercial support and with more mainstream gender conforming heterosexual viewers partially in mind. The film cast nonkathoey Thai pop icon Penpak Sirikul as the leading kathoey character and kathoey music and television celebrity Nuntita Khampiranon as a secondary kathoey character. These two stars are crossovers who have appeared in the Thai national film, television, modeling, and music industries; transnational Hollywood and independent film circuits; and pan-Asian regional media networks. For example, Sirikul appeared in the Hollywood comedy *The Hangover Part II* (2011, dir. Todd Phillips) and pan-Asian film coproductions *The Victim* (2006, dir. Monthon Arayangkoon) and *The Last Executioner* (2014, dir. Tom Waller). Khampiranon gained national and regional attention when she sang in the 2011 *Thailand's Got Talent* television show, which is part of the transnational British *Got Tal-*

FIGURE 4.5. Thai pop icon and Hollywood crossover Penpak Sirikul as Saitarn in Sukkhapisit's *It Gets Better* (2012). Courtesy of Tanwarin Sukkhapisit.

ent television series. This television appearance boosted her devoted YouTube following to celebrity status. Sirikul and Khampiranon provide different portals of identification for *It Gets Better*'s nonkathoey and kathoey viewers, many of whom already have experience with these actresses through multiple cultural technologies, mediums, and genres. Additionally, a storyline divided into three vignettes about a middle-age kathoey femme fatale alienated from her family, a teenage Thai monk questioning his sexuality and gender, and a twentysomething Thai American nonkathoey heterosexual man dealing with his trans/homophobia and his distance from Thai culture provides diverse yet acceptable mainstream stories for cross-identification.

While Sukkhapisit's first indie film, *Insects*, did not have this kind of commercial and mainstream reach, its domestic censorship did not stifle the film's international circulation. In fact, the film's only legal screening in Thailand occurred at the Bangkok 2010 International Film Festival, a festival created by the Royal Thai Government and the Tourism Authority of Thailand to promote transnational cultural tourism. In the time between *Insects* and *It Gets Better*, Sukkhapisit directed her first commercial main-

FIGURE 4.6. Thai music and television celebrity Nuntita Khampiranon as Tonlew in Sukkhapisit's *It Gets Better* (2012). Courtesy of Tanwarin Sukkhapisit.

stream feature, teenage romantic comedy *Hak na'Sarakham* (2011), with Thailand media corporation Sahamongkol Film International. Other commercial features followed, including Thai romantic horror *Threesome / Thoe khao rao phi* (2014b) and the Japanese-Thai coproduced romantic comedy *Fin Sugoi* (2014a). Sukkhapisit uses her profits and connections from commercial mainstream filmmaking to support her (semi-)independent kathoey-focused filmmaking.[15] Sukkhapisit has also managed to introduce kathoey storylines in her nonkathoey commercial mainstream films, especially *Fin Sugoi*, which includes Thai tomboy heartthrob Suppanad Jittaleela, nonkathoey Thai actress Apinya Sakuljaroensuk, and nonkathoey Japanese rock star Makoto Koshinaka.

Sukkhapisit's filmmaking navigates the transnationalizing of Thai and other South/Northeast Asian national cinemas. Since the 1980s, "soft" cultural industries, such as cinema, financial services, and agriculture, have been used in trade negotiations between the United States and South/Northeast Asian countries to balance trade surpluses with the United States in "hard" economic industries like high-tech manufacturing. In response to the demands of U.S. trade negotiators, including the Motion Picture Association of America, South/Northeast Asian countries deregulated protected film industries to provide open markets to foreign films dominated by Hollywood.[16] As a result, 78 percent of the Thai box office and 96 percent of the Taiwanese box office currently go to Hollywood, with Japan providing 10 to 20 percent of Hollywood's profits. Failing South/Northeast film industries impacted by deregulation began restructuring in the 1990s toward conglomerate and financial modes of production, distribution, and marketing powered by transnational venture capital. Restructuring has enabled the new production of South/Northeast Asian blockbusters that linked domestic national genres to transnational Hollywood genres. For example, the South Korean blockbuster *Shiri* (1999, dir. Kang Je-gyu) builds on the familiarity of South Korean spy thrillers, which dramatize the conflict between North and South Korea, while matching the spectacular high-budget action scenes of Hollywood. This transnational translation and hybridizing of genres is not only a strategy used by South/Northeast Asian national cinemas to compete with the dominance of Hollywood imports. It is the aesthetic effect of Hollywood's new direct financial investment in coproducing and codistributing South/Northeast Asian films, including Columbia Pictures' and Warner Bros.' distribution and marketing of Ang Lee's Chinese diaspora film *Crouching Tiger, Hidden Dragon* (2000). In addition to Hollywood's penetration of South/Northeast Asian films, Bliss Cua Lim (2009, 190–244) argues that a formula-exhausted Hollywood has "cannibalized" the content and aesthetics of new Asian cinemas through remakes, such as DreamWorks' remake of Hideo Nakata's *Ringu* (1998) and Paramount's remake of Danny and Oxide Chun Pang's *The Eye / Gin Gwai* (2002). These Hollywood remakes reenergize the interest of American viewers through familiar yet "foreign" intergenres, while also capturing transnational audiences, including those who watched the Asian original of the Hollywood remake.[17] Thus, deregulation has produced *transnationally* nationalized film economies and intergeneric films in South/Northeast Asian cinemas and in Hollywood.

Deregulation also has initiated pan-Asian regional film coproductions and intertexts in an effort to share the costs, risks, and labor of conglomerate finance filmmaking that seeks to match the standards of Hollywood and to cultivate networked regional film and media markets. More so perhaps than other South/Northeast Asian cinemas, the Thai film industry has relied on pan-Asian regional coproduction as a response to transnational Hollywood's competition and investment. The first genuinely collaborative pan-Asian coproduction was Kim Jee-woon, Nonzee Nimibutr, and Peter Ho-Sun Chan's *Three* (2002), a horror film made up of three shorts directed in three locations and styles in Thailand, South Korea, and Hong Kong. However, the first pan-Asian film with broad commercial success was the Pang brothers' *The Eye / Gin Gwai* (2002), which featured stars from Hong Kong, Thailand,

Singapore, and Taiwan and was set in Thailand and Hong Kong. *The Eye / Gin Gwai* was remade by Hollywood in David Moreau and Xavier Palud's Paramount film *The Eye* (2008), which starred Jessica Alba.

The American and transnational traffic of pan-Asian regional films starting in the early twenty-first century has introduced a new collection of self-reflexively pan-Asian images into American and Western racial imaginings of Asianness. The converging of different Asian ethnicities, nationalities, and geographies within the single text of a pan-Asian regional film may perpetuate Orientalist perceptions of West, South, and East Asians as racially ethnic differentiated foreigners to the modern United States and West. Yet American and Western viewers must also confront the markedly *familiar* modern and "post"-modern mise-en-scènes and storylines of pan-Asian films. The countercultural imaginings of pan-ethnic Asian American racial identity and politics must also negotiate a new relationship to the regional (rather than racial) and market/industry/finance-driven creation of pan-ethnic Asianness. The American East Asian cinemas craze that began in the 1990s is far from over. The Hollywood conglomerate system has continued to reconfigure to better incorporate and capitalize on this ongoing fascination, including outsourced studio branches in different regions of Asia and "crossing-over" Asian national and regional filmmakers into Hollywood filmmaking.[18] The remake remains Hollywood's primary strategy for containing—and profiting from—the economic and cultural impacts of pan-Asian regional films. In Hollywood remakes of pan-Asian films, the mise-en-scènes, storylines, and characters are translated to erase all traces of the remakes' Asian origins (Lim 2009, 190–244). This erasure positions the Hollywood remake as the original (versus a copy) and affirms its Americanness. Remakes usually translate the Asian casts of pan-Asian films into all-white casts, with the exception of a few films using African American and Latinx American actresses and actors in mostly minor roles. This racial translation of casting continues to disappear Asians, Asian Americans, and other nonwhite racial groups from the scripts and visual landscapes through which Americanness is imagined.

Despite the Thai film industry's involvement in pan-Asian regional coproduction and Hollywood's transnational economies, the Thai national cinema boom that began in 1997 has yet to find a large-scale American and transnational following outside Thailand and the South/Northeast Asian region. To date, Hollywood has not been heavily involved in the coproduction, distribution, and marketing of Thai films and has not remade them or "crossed-over"

Thai filmmakers. Nevertheless, Thai commercial films, such as *The Iron La-dies* (2000, dir. Youngyooth Thongkonthun) and *Beautiful Boxer* (2004, dir. Ekachai Uekrongtham), have found subcultural and "niche" followings in the United States through independent film circuits. Although Thai film and media conglomerates supported by Hollywood finance produced these two films, they have been exhibited, distributed, and marketed in the United States through independent film festivals and film distributors, like Strand and Regent Releasing, interested in gender and sexually nonconforming themed content. Both *The Iron Ladies* and *Beautiful Boxer* are part of the second wave of Thai commercial mainstream kathoey-themed films, which represent kathoeys more sympathetically. In the United States, these mainstream kathoey films have gained subcultural or niche followings at gay and lesbian independent film festivals, such as the San Francisco International Lesbian and Gay Film Festival and Los Angeles Outfest, which have a growing interest in programming transgender and Asian transnational films.

Sukkhapisit's *It Gets Better* self-reflexively navigates the increasingly complex entanglements between transnational, regional, and national film cultural economies. The film harnesses commercial support in aspects of its casting, production, and distribution in order to target more mainstream Thai and transnational viewers, especially American viewers. In addition to casting nonkathoey heterosexual Thai pop icon and Hollywood-crossover Penpak Sirikul in the lead kathoey role (Saitarn), *It Gets Better*'s vignettes include the perspectives of a twentysomething nonkathoey heterosexual Thai American man (Tonmai) struggling with his trans/homophobia and a teenage Thai monk (Din) questioning his sexuality and gender. These nonkathoey and questioning story threads provide potential points of cross-identification for viewers who may have little or no familiarity with gender and sexually nonconforming people and issues. Yet the film ultimately threads these diverse storylines back to kathoey experiences. The film's climax reveals that the leading middle-aged kathoey character (Saitarn/Sirikul) *is* the questioning teenager (Din) and also the deceased parent of the trans/homophobic nonkathoey heterosexual man (Tonmai). Similar to *Insects in the Backyard*, *It Gets Better* uses digital aesthetics to provide diverse story-windows that are fundamentally determined by external forces. While *Insects*' determinist digital style disassembles any unified view of the film's kathoey family, *It Gets Better*'s determinist digital style works through the smooth reassembly of different story-windows into a single transmission—a biological one. Not only is the kathoey main character (Saitarn/Sirikul) the same person as the questioning teenage monk (Din); she is also part of an intergenerational lineage that links her biologically to a nonkathoey heterosexual son (Tonmai) and a nonkathoey elderly father with whom she is reunited. This biological line, however, is neither linear nor contained in a single body. In multiple scenes, Saitarn appears in the same time and place as her younger self, Din, and her son, Tonmai, who has never met the mother whom he thought was his father. Thus, *It Gets Better* works through a biological determinism that always loops back to kathoey experiences and that radically alters the function and concept of biology to include multiple embodiments, temporalities, and modes of relating to biological kin. In contrast to Dan Savage's *It Gets Better* transnational YouTube video project, Sukkhapisit's film by the same name seems to argue for the potential multiplicity of embodied experience, living time, and family in the present tense and for the importance of understanding and addressing how gender and sexual variant youth negotiate their lives as they are, even as we attempt to imagine and activate better futures.

micha cárdenas and Transnational Auto-Technological Networks

U.S.-based Latinx queer trans femme media theorist, artist, and activist micha cárdenas works across the borders of cultural economies, media technologies, cultural forms, and communities. cárdenas is assistant professor of art and design: games and playable media at the University of California, Santa Cruz. Her trans media theories situate the emergence of trans-embodied identities and cultural expression within late twentieth- and early twenty-first-century social and political contexts. In the collaboratively written and edited collection *The Transreal: Political Aesthetics of Crossing Realities* (2012), cárdenas describes what she calls a "transreal" aesthetics in the work of contemporary media artists Blast Theory, Mez Breeze, and Reza Negarestani and in her own work with Elle Mehrmand. Transreality is a counteraesthetics that remixes and reconstructs dominant social reality. It calls attention to the virtual manipulation and fragmentation of reality by contemporary conditions that include "war, economic collapse, the contemporary slavery of the Prison Industrial Complex and daily violence against people around the world" (29). By cocreating transreality in connection with multiple artists, participants, and social conditions, cárdenas mobilizes a transreal aesthetics shaped by differentiated yet interconnected experiences of social embodiment as a new basis for collective political action. cárdenas's version of transreality responds to the daily erasure of her identity and body by dominant cisgender binary reality.

> The transreal emerged as a response to the daily experience, with varying degrees of violence or banality, of being told that as a queer femme transgender woman my gender was not real, my sexuality was not real and even my body was not real. At times this critique came viciously from so-called feminists who didn't share my vision of what feminism could mean, and it continues to happen on a daily basis in my interactions with people who want to tell me that I am a man. The transreal is the embracing of an identity that is a combination of my "real" body that I was born with and my personal history with another identity that I have written in flesh, in words, in pixels, in 3-dimensional models and across multiple strata of communications technologies. To say that I am transreal is a strategy for embracing a gender that exceeds daily reality on Planet Earth and that says back to all the people who have tried to make me choose between man or woman that I choose to be a shape-shifter, a dragon and a light wave. (29–30)

Transreality affirms cárdenas's layered sense and history of embodiment as *real* and overrides cisgender binary claims to know what is reality.[19]

cárdenas's agility in crossing and mixing realities builds on the border consciousness created by queer Chicanx feminist poet theorist Gloria Anzaldúa. In *Borderlands / La Frontera: The New Mestiza* (1987), Anzaldúa contrasts white American conceptions of Aryan racial purity with Mexican philosopher José Vasconcelos's "*una raza mestiza*," or mestiza race. Vasconcelos envisioned a modern Mexican national identity based on a mixture of races, or a "fifth race embracing the four major races of the world" (Anzaldúa 1987, 100; Vasconcelos 1997, 7–42).[20] Although Anzaldúa cites Vasconcelos's nationalist concept of mestiza, she ultimately appropriates the concept for a "new *mestiza* consciousness, *una conciencia de mujer* . . . a consciousness of the Borderlands" (Anzaldúa 1987, 100). Anzaldúa's new mestiza does not seek to produce a new racial hierarchy based on a hybridity. Instead, it recognizes and accepts the struggles and contradictions that come with the converging of races within mixed-race people: "*El choque de un alma atrapado entre el mundo del espíritu y el mundo de la técnica a veces la deja entullada.* Cradled in one culture, sandwiched between two cultures, straddling all three cultures and their value systems, *la mestiza* undergoes a struggle of flesh, a struggle of borders, an inner war" (100).

The new mestiza refuses to transcend the contending cultural systems that structure mixed-race consciousness: "The new *mestiza* copes by developing a tolerance for contradictions, a tolerance for ambiguity. She learns to be an Indian in Mexican culture, to be Mexican from an Anglo point of view. She learns to juggle cultures. She has a plural personality, she operates in a pluralistic mode—nothing is thrust out, the good the bad and the ugly, nothing rejected, nothing abandoned. Not only does she sustain contradictions, she turns the ambivalence into something else" (101). She synthesizes the multiple racial orders within her while preserving the Indian rejected by dominant Mexican national identity and the Indian and the Mexican rejected by dominant U.S. Anglo national identity.

Anzaldúa's new mestiza is a third consciousness that assembles through —rather than beyond—differences. It is a borderland identity created by queer women of color who have been outcast by all dominant national, racial, and hetero-patriarchal communities.

> As a *mestiza* I have no country, my homeland cast me out; yet all countries are mine because I am every woman's sister or potential lover. (As a lesbian I have no race, my own people disclaim me; but I am all races because there is the queer of me in all races.) I am culture-less because, as a feminist, I challenge the collective cultural/religious male-derived beliefs of Indo-Hispanics and Anglos; yet I am cultured because I am participating in the creation of yet another culture, a new story to explain the world and our participation in it, a new value system with images and symbols that connect us to each other and to the planet. (102–3)

The new mestiza is a counteruniversal produced by and for those outside the borders of dominant cultures in disidentification from those securely inside the borders. She embodies and remembers the other nations that underlie the current borders enforced by the U.S. nation-state in the Southwest, Aztlán.

> This land was Mexican once,
> was Indian always
> And is.
> And will be again. (3)

Anzaldúa's new mestiza reclaims the American Southwest not so much for Mexico as for the indigenous Indians who are the original peoples of the continuous lands of the North, Central, and South Americas and their mestizo descendants. She returns the Americas to its Native peoples and to women of color who have been subjugated by the dominant hetero-masculinities of nation-states.

As a first-generation Colombian American who grew up in the U.S. Southeast and the Caribbean city of Miami, Florida, cárdenas embodies the contending geopolitical borders, cultures, and histories of Anzaldúa's new mestiza consciousness. She also extends Anzaldúa's nonbinary borderlands to include mixed-gender trans women of color and to counter the new boundless territories of twenty-first-century U.S. empire. As a member of the cyber activist and artist collective Electronic Disturbance Theater (EDT), cárdenas coproduced the digital video *Transborder Immigrant Tool: Transition* (2009) with Brett Stalbaum, Amy Sara Carroll, Elle Mehrmand, and Ricardo Dominguez. The video begins with a voice that evokes Anzaldúa's words, "We have a tradition of migration, a tradition of long walks. Today we are witnessing *la migración de los pueblos mexicanos*, the return odyssey to the historical/mythological Aztlán." The voicing of Anzaldúa's poetics overlays live imagery of someone walking through a desert landscape with a cell phone in hand and an animated image of a navigational compass in the corner of the screen. The video, therefore, enlivens Anzaldúa's remembering of the Indian roots of Mexican migration in the Southwest through live footage of embodied movement through the borderlands between the United States and Mexico. It does so through the mixing of mediums (sound, movement, video, animation) rather than through the representational coherence and depth perception of dominant film imagery. This mixed media is made apparent through the appearance of an animated screen within the video, the modulating speaking voice, and the flashes and changes in color in the live imagery.

In addition, the video links the mixing of mediums to the network of digital media technologies that enforce and police the territorial boundaries of the United States. The cell phone in the video uses an application still under development by the EDT to lead migrants crossing the U.S.-Mexico border to much-needed water sources, while sustaining their spirits with poetry. The migrant users' interface with the "transborder immigrant tool" is the animated navigational compass viewers see onscreen in the opening segment of the video. The EDT's transborder immigrant application uses U.S. Global Positioning System (GPS) technologies against their intended purposes. A space-based navigation system, GPS was developed by the U.S. military, Department of Defense, university researchers, and corporations in the mid-1970s as a "surgical strike" weapon that would minimize collateral damage during the Cold War (Parks 2001, 209–10). It is made up of twenty-four NAVSTAR satellites that orbit the earth and transmit time and position information to GPS receivers throughout the world.[21] The corporate public release of GPS in 1989 for popular consumption coincides with its greater systematic use by the U.S. military beginning with the 1990 Gulf War. The same satellite system used by the U.S. military and government to guide missiles and soldiers and to police civilians is used by corporations to track and *orient* the position of consumers toward corporate venues and products. With the linking of GPS with Internet-based social media, consumer-users can now map their distance from home, food, entertainment, sex, and social intimacy using their cell phones or other computerized devices. The EDT's transborder immigrant tool subverts U.S. military, state, and corporate uses of GPS by reorienting it toward the survival needs of borderland migrants, who are considered expendable and criminal by dominant U.S. institutions.

Moreover, EDT's video about the transborder immigrant tool exposes and counters the ideologies of technological neutrality and utility presumed by U.S. Cold War information technologies. The video transitions between footage of a migrant on the ground and images of the U.S.-Mexico border at the Rio Grande from satellite, microchip cells, and a cell phone tower. A modulating speaking voice suggests links between biochemical and information systems: "mitochondria . . . imagine the chip's transliteralization and you have arrived at the energies of the Global Positioning System." The video situates GPS and the cell phone used to access it within the broader network of information technologies that have restructured the U.S. transnational state and economy since World War II. Satellites, cell phone towers, and the underground and undersea cables discussed in chapter 2 provide what Lisa Parks and Nicole Starosielski describe as the global media infrastructure that facilitates the movement and distribution of "audiovisual signal traffic" around the world (2015, 4). This largely invisible media infrastructure has extended the reach of U.S. liberal state capitalism not only transnationally but *globally* into the core and exterior orbit of the Earth. This infrastructure enables the second-to-second electronic communication and coordination on which U.S. systems of policing, surveillance, war, governance, finance, and commerce rely domestically and transnationally. It has also facilitated the scientific penetration and instrumentalizing of the inner recesses of organisms at the biomolecular level. As Donna Haraway has argued playfully in her iconic cyborg manifesto, late industrialism's technical or "informatic" dominance has ruptured the boundaries between human and animal, animal-human (organism) and machine, and physical and nonphysical worlds (1991: 149–82). As illustrated by current research on the potential storing of digital data in DNA, biomolecular life is part of the growing global information network. The EDT's video about the transborder immigrant tool exposes the vast scales above, below, and within that this network penetrates to expand the reach and power of the U.S. police, military, state, and capitalist economy. It recodes technological transcendentalism through the embodied, erotic poetics of the trans racialized and engendered migrant on the Native ancestral borderlands of the U.S. nation-state: "This Bridge Called my Back, my heart, my head, my cock, my cunt, my tunnel. Vision: You. Are. Crossing. Into. Me" (Electronic Disturbance Theater/b.a.n.g. lab 2010). Through the cosmology of Mayan border-crossing, the *Transborder Immigrant Tool: Transition* imagines a different kind of network as both origin and future of digital technologies—one that responds to and connects the needs and urges for sustenance and redistributive justice in the transborder migrant, the GPS consumer-user, and the media art viewer and producer.

cárdenas's collaboration "Local Autonomy Networks (Autonets)" repurposes digital technologies to build autonomous community-based networks that reduce violence against women, lesbian, gay, bisexual, transgender, queer, and intersex (LGBTQI) people, people of color, and other groups who survive violence on a daily basis. The project creates a fashion line of mesh, networked, electronic clothing that will allow community members wearing them to communicate one's location and to respond if someone needs help. These Autonets rely on a localized communication network separate from the U.S. corporate-state-military digital infrastructure. The Autonets clothing line and other networks, including offline face-to-face social agreements developed by the Local Autonomy Networks project, seek to increase community safety, interdependence, and self-reliance in ways that counter the state, police, public, militia, and intimate violence experienced by women, LGBTQI people, people of color, and other groups impacted by violence. The project is inspired by "community based, anti-racist, prison abolitionist responses to gendered violence."[22] It is being developed collectively through workshops, performances, presentations, and discussions across art, activist, and academic venues in ways that center horizontal knowledge production in queer, transgender, gender violence survivor, and migrant communities. So far, the project has worked with groups who want to create safety for queer youth of color in Detroit, trans and gender nonconforming people of color in

FIGURE 4.7. *Autonets: We Already Know and We Don't Yet Know*, Hemispheric Institute of Performance and Politics VIII Encuentro, São Paulo, Brazil (January 2013), with micha cárdenas, Tomaz Capobanco, Joana Fittipaldi, Frantz Jerome, Aisha Jordan, Benjamin Lundberg, Lily Mengesha, Alessandra Renzi. Photo by Fran Pollitt. Courtesy of micha cárdenas.

Los Angeles, and sex workers in Toronto, Canada, and to prevent disappearances in Bogotá, Colombia. After a year and a half of collaborations in these locations, however, cárdenas and her collaborators have come to realize that digital technologies—even when hacked to make more accessible—remain out of reach for survival- and low-income people. They have decided to focus on building nondigital social networks and agreements that will lay the groundwork for community safety, resilience, and autonomy.

The low- to zero-tech approaches created by the Local Autonomy Networks project and cárdenas's other collaborations reengage technology in ways that allow for embodied social mobilization. Far from taking a purist stance against technology, these collaborations repurpose technology through trans and queer of color, migrant, and non-Western imaginations that value social collectivity and communicability. Within white Western colonial modernity, technology has been imagined and objectified as the binary opposite (or determining limit) of human life and nature (Bradley 2011; Campbell 2011; Clough 2000). For instance, classical Western metaphysics conceived of the body as a material technology in opposition to the immaterial human soul and mind. The body is an unmoving, unconscious, artificial instrument that, at best, houses human existence and rational thought and, at worst, threatens to dumb down the human into a "thing." Sixteenth- and seventeenth-century Western modern science began to blur classical oppositions between technology and the human through mechanistic theories that compared life to machinery. In the nineteenth century, the energetic perspective of Western thermodynamic science wore away divisions between technology and the human even further. Computer and biological sciences in the mid-twentieth century introduced an informational view of human life that went beyond crossing the boundaries between technology and the human. They positioned technology at the genesis of life as code and programming. This informational perspective was the product of the intensification of white Western colonial modernity's anxious externalizing and control over aspects of human life and nature through the specter of technology—only to find technology at the origins of life itself already organized as a prerational system.

Thus, the American cybernetic revolution in the transition between World War II and the Cold War was theorized as technology's organic return to human nature and life, even as cybernetic technologies were used to perpetrate U.S. state violence. According to Norbert Wiener in 1949, the computer is analogous to the human nervous system in its functioning through binary or digital code: "The all-or-none character of the discharge of the neurons is precisely analogous to the single choice made in determining a digit on the binary scale, which more than one of us had already contemplated as the most satisfactory basis of computing-machine design. The synapse is nothing but a mechanism for determining whether a certain combination of outputs from other select elements will or will not act as an adequate stimulus for the discharge of the next element, and must have its precise analogue in the computing machine" (1949, 14).

Wiener makes this analogy between the computer and nervous system at a moment when the neurosciences have found the central nervous system to be an integrated system that operates through "circular processes, emerging from the nervous system into the muscles, and reentering the nervous system through the sense organs" (8). In other words, computers are like embodied nervous systems, which already operate as technical or computer systems. Wiener envisions computers as the central nervous system that will loop through and steer communication between different sectors of science, the political economy, and society.[23] The new connectivity and conductivity created by computers as distributed synapses across the social body will allow for greater flexibility in responding to "stimuli" or "feedback" (14, 6–7). Wiener also suggests that it will lessen what he describes as the territorial wars between specialized fields: "specialized fields [in the sciences] are continually growing and invading new territory. The result is like what occurred when the Oregon country was being invaded simultaneously by the United States settlers, the British, the Mexicans, and the Russians—an inextricable tangle of exploration, nomenclature and laws" (2).

Despite Wiener's more cautious approach to technological advancement, his cybernetic thought is both an extension and a product of a renewed U.S. imperialism that reaches beyond territorial conquest and colonization. The cybernetic principles that birthed the Internet and the digital revolution have helped to build a networked technological infrastructure that expands the circulation of American capital, the infiltration of U.S. military, police, and security, and the administrative systems of the state. The cybernetic infrastructure supports the growth of decentralized dominant networks of power that claim merely to respond automatically and naturally to their environments rather than being held responsible for the power they hold and the decisions they make. Cyber-networks, therefore, embody the auto-technical functioning of U.S. transnational state capitalism and empire after World War II: war waged supposedly for peace and security; economic exploitation and dispossession for human development; and state violence, imprisonment, and policing for multicultural social integration.

The autonomous local networks created by cárdenas and her collaborators attempt to repurpose not only digital networks but ultimately the cybernetic principles that underlie U.S. technology-driven imperialism and state capitalism in the twenty-first century. Cybernetic technologies were conceived to disperse, connect, and make communicable different sectors of the U.S. political economy in order to better concentrate and control power, wealth, and knowledge in the state, corporations, the military, *and universities*. Autonomous local networks break away from technically automated networks to build locally determined networks based on social interdependence. UN-STOPPABLE, cárdenas's collaboration with Black Lives Matter (BLM) Network cofounder Patrisse Cullors, art healer Edxie Betts, artist software developer Chris Head, researcher and media artist Josefina Garcia-Turner, and programmer Kate Sohng,[24] is working to develop bulletproof clothing to protect the lives of Black people targeted for murder by U.S. state terror, especially Black trans women. The project is a response to a question raised by Cul-

FIGURE 4.8. *UNSTOPPABLE*, materials testing (2015). Photo by Brett Stalbaum.
courtesy of micha cárdenas.

lors in her opening keynote speech at the 2015 Allied Media Conference.
Wearing a shirt designed by Foremost and Damon Turner with the words
"BULLETPROOF #BlackLivesMatter" emblazoned across her chest, Cullors
asked, "What would technology for black lives be?" *UNSTOPPABLE* takes its
name from the words of Sylvia Rivera: "a lot of heads were bashed [at Stone-
wall]. But it didn't hurt their true feelings—they all came back for more and
more. Nothing—that's when you could tell that nothing could stop us at that
time or any time in the future."[25]

The project uses art as direct action to stop the bullets fired to kill Black
people and to kill the possibility of Black movement toward liberation.
Against the "stopping power" of firearms used to kill Black lives and movement, cárdenas, Cullors, Betts, Head, Garcia-Turner, and Sohng are working to build and shield "unstoppable" Black communities. *UNSTOPPABLE* is
developing its line of bulletproof clothing at low to no cost as a do-it-yourself
module to be distributed widely in different communities. Its design process
is aimed toward opening up discussions in communities across the United
States about multiple forms of white supremacist state violence and strategiz-
ing on community-based safety. Like other local autonomous networks in
cárdenas's collaborations, *UNSTOPPABLE* appropriates the cybernetic logic
of connectivity, communicability, and localized difference across different
sectors and environments, including art, university, media, and nonprofit
organizational sectors. But rather than building technological networks that

FIGURE 4.9. *UNSTOPPABLE*, kevlar tube dress worn by Edxie Betts (2015).
Photo by micha cárdenas. courtesy of micha cárdenas.

uproot and translate local value and meaning into information to be circulated as capital, *UNSTOPPABLE* and other local autonomy networks strive to create groups that support locally embodied social needs and relationships.

This anti-cybernetic approach dovetails with the locally rooted and intersectional movement building of the BLM Network. From its inception, the hashtag created by queer Black women political and cultural organizers Alicia Garza, Patrisse Cullors, and Opal Tometi highlighted connections between the civilian murder of Trayvon Martin by George Zimmerman in Sanford, Florida; Zimmerman's acquittal under the protection of Florida's Stand Your Ground law by an almost exclusively white civilian jury in 2012; and the multiple court-condoned police murders of unarmed Black women, men, and children in 2014, including the lesser-known case of Gabriella Nevarez (Sacramento, California) and the more publicized cases of Mike Brown (Ferguson, Missouri), Eric Garner (New York City), and Tamir Rice (Cleveland, Ohio). BLM's response to these murders urged communities to understand these murders as the result of the state-sponsored entrenchment of anti-Black violence and racism in police and court systems and civil society at large rather than private acts of violence and discrimination by individual officers and civilians. In addition to addressing forms of violence that are more directly traceable to the U.S. state, BLM also identifies Black poverty and genocide; the assault on Black women and their children and families; the disposal, fetishizing, and profiting off of Black queer and trans folks; the relegating to the shadows of undocumented Black immigrants; the use of Black girls as negotiating chips during times of conflict and war; and Darwinian experiments that attempt to squeeze Black folks living with disabilities and different abilities into boxes of normality defined by white supremacy *all* as forms of state violence.[26] BLM's centering of women and girls; queer, trans, poor, incarcerated, and undocumented people; and people with disabilities in (re)building a movement for Black liberation intervenes in what I have described in the introduction as the post-1965 state's efforts to construct a multicultural society through external and internal technologies of racial gendering and sexuality, criminalization, pathologization, and economic exploitation.

Nonetheless, the workings of state violence and state-sponsored relational exposure to multiple forms of violence as they impact Black women and trans and gender nonconforming Black people remain structurally invisible. #SayHerName, launched by the African American Policy Forum, and the larger coalitional Movement for Black Lives have called attention to the police killings, attacks, and rapes targeting Black cis women and girls such as Korryn Gaines, Jessica Williams, Gynnya McMillen, Sandra Bland, Tanisha Anderson, Aiyana Stanley-Jones, Rekia Boyd, Denise Stewart, and Alesia Thomas and Black trans women and gender nonconforming people including Mya Hall, Kayla Moore, Duanna Johnson, Nizah Morris, and the New Jersey 7. Black trans women organizers and cultural workers such as Miss Major Griffin-Gracy, Janetta Johnson, Chandi Moore, CeCe McDonald, Ashlee Marie Preston, Elle Hearns, Tourmaline, Wriply Bennet, Aaryn Lang, Janet Mock, and Laverne Cox are mobilizing specifically to address the state, public, and intimate violence affecting Black trans women and girls and have worked to center the lives, leadership, and vision of trans women in Black liberation movement building (J. Chen 2017).

Echoing the networked organizing of the Movement for Black Lives, *UN-STOPPABLE* reharnesses the material that is technology toward purposes counter to U.S. and Western technical rationality. *UNSTOPPABLE*'s bulletproof clothing design relies on recycled rubber tires to potentially armor Black communities, especially Black trans women, targeted by police terror and multiple forms of state violence. It reuses the rubber tires discarded by a U.S. automobile industry that has provided the motor for advanced industrial capitalism. From the last decade of the nineteenth century to the mid-twentieth century, the auto industry provided a module for automated assembly-line production using subdivided, serial, specialized labor.

Mass-produced automobiles sparked a technological revolution in mobility or movement.[27] UNSTOPPABLE repurposes the rubber waste from the now transnational conglomerate U.S. auto industry for a different form or even cosmology of movement. Instead of movement invested in achieving a genocidal state of modern progress, circulation, and accumulation as goals in and of themselves, UNSTOPPABLE is working to uphold and ensure the survival, livelihood, and mobility of those targeted as disposable racial, gender, and sexual threats to the U.S. state and society. The project builds movement and *a* movement based on locally activated social commitments to protecting and fighting for the lives of Black trans women and Black people. The UNSTOPPABLE movement is thus based on what cárdenas has described as "creating relations through the stitch, of finding means to connect groups of people who have formerly been separated," rather than "connectivity" through horizontal hierarchies of division as manifested in dominant technological networks (2016, 6).[28] In addition to shared commitments to protect Black lives, the UNSTOPPABLE collaboration has connected U.S. state violence against Black people to state violence as it occurs transnationally as a continued effect of Western imperial state-building, especially in the Global South.[29] The synthetic and natural rubber retooled by UNSTOPPABLE also holds its own potential material relations in the rubber plantations of Southeast Asia and Africa and in the indigenous rubber trees of the Brazilian Amazon. These possibilities for movement through stitching are being activated by those of Black, Latinx, Asian, Arab, and Indigenous lineages whose historical bodies have been made to bear the violent burden of becoming technology to cultivate the transnational U.S. settler nation-state and its economy.

CONCLUSION

Trans Voice in the House

A rhizomatic reading of *latinidad* suggests the process through which contested constructions of identity work to constitute one another, emphasizing "and" over "is" as a
way to think about differences. So *latinidad* is about the "dimensions" or "the directions
in motion" of history and culture and geography and language and self-named identities. Even if individual narratives used to chart these discourses contradict or exclude
one another, the site of rupture will itself serve as a new site of knowledge production. —JUANA MARÍA RODRÍGUEZ, *Queer Latinidad: Identity Practices, Discursive Spaces*
(2003)

Diasporic populations find themselves in circumstances in which the sense-making
capacity of vision, the significance of vision, is monopolized from a hostile perspective
. . . the fundamental predicament of African Americans is a sensory one. —LINDON
BARRETT, *Blackness and Value: Seeing Double* (1998)

On June 24, 2015, undocumented trans Chicanx/Latinx activist Jennicet
Gutiérrez interrupted then president Barack Obama during his speech at the
first LGBT Pride celebration hosted by the White House. As Obama began,
"Over the years we've gathered to celebrate pride month, and I've told you
that I'm so hopeful about what we can accomplish. I've told you that the civil
rights of LGBT Americans . . . ," Gutiérrez spoke out from the crowd of invited
guests: "President Obama, release all LGBTQ immigrants from detention centers . . . Stop the torture and abuse of trans women in detention centers . . . I
am a trans woman . . . I am tired of the abuse. I am tired of the violence . . .
Not one more deportation." She continued to call for an end to detention and

deportation while the other predominantly white LGBT guests tried to silence her with "sh's" and "boo's." For a split second, it seemed as if Obama recognized Gutiérrez's words openly as a form of engagement, when he paused, looked up, and said, perhaps instinctively, a softly intonated "Yeah?" But, upon *seeing* her, this pause moved quickly into a refusal to engage Gutiérrez and a diminishing of her capacity and "right" to address him. Obama shook his head and finger and scolded "no, no, no, no," followed by, "Listen, you're in my house" and "Shame on you," while those attending the event chanted Obama's name. Gutiérrez was "escorted" out of the event by security. But for about two minutes, her presence and voice in the White House called attention to the approximately sixty-five immigrant trans women—mostly Latinx women from Mexico and Central America—in immigrant detention daily, among the approximately thirty thousand migrants and asylum seekers in detention daily across the country (Human Rights Watch 2016). Trans women in detention are routinely subjected to sexual assault and other forms of abuse and harassment by ICE officers, facility guards, and other detainees in the men's detention facilities where they are most often confined. They are also targeted for solitary confinement for indefinite periods of time. In media coverage following the White House celebration, Gutiérrez pointed out: "Immigrant trans women are 12 times more likely to face discrimination because of our gender identity. If we add our immigration status to the equation, the discrimination increases. Transgender immigrants make up one out of every 500 people in detention, but we account for one out of five confirmed sexual abuse cases in ICE custody" (Gutiérrez 2015). Her action drew public attention through social media and television and online news circuits based on mobile phone videos that documented the event.

Despite the subjective immediacy and objectivity attributed to popular uses of mobile video to document events "as they happen," there are discrepancies in what the videos uploaded on YouTube capture about Obama's speech at the White House LGBT Pride celebration. Because of differences in distance from the stage, framing, lighting, and surroundings, some of the videos show no record of Obama's split second informal acknowledgment of Gutiérrez's questioning. In other instances, the videos do relay that moment but it is easy to miss unless the videos are replayed. Additionally, this moment when Obama responds almost automatically through body motions and intonated voice ("yeah?") works on a gestural register that cannot be readily seen or heard within the Western scopic regime that rules over the order of the senses. Gutiérrez's voice activates an embodied openness be-

FIGURE C.1. Jennicet Gutiérrez at the White House (June 24, 2015).
Courtesy of Jennicet Gutiérrez.

yond communicative language that remembers the other racial histories of the senses. Fred Moten has described a Black aesthetic redistribution of the sensible based on the *performative* phonic expressiveness and senses of Black embodiment and interiority shaped historically by chattel slavery's absolute visual objectification (which attempted to render Blackness as pure body) and resistance against it (Moten 2003). This different racially constituted and performed order of material embodiment and sense makes possible a broader relationship to gender and kinship with the feminine than allowed in the "prevailing social fiction of the Father's name, the Father's law" (Moten 2003, 15). This sensible material—and gender ambivalent—excess in the racial embodiment of Black masculinity was visually managed through the excessive public imagining of Obama as a respectable cis-heterosexual father-and-husband-in-chief while it also provided an exploitable communicable affect that conveyed an intimacy in his style of governing. Kehinde Wiley's commissioned portrait of Obama, which is arguably the least regal of Wiley's paintings, stages the tension in these unsynthesized contradictions.

Nevertheless, Obama's practices of governing continued and amplified the state's legacy of targeting, confining, and annihilating those considered outside the bounds of the nation. His eight years in office included the deportation of over three million migrants, focusing especially on those criminalized; wars and military campaigns in Afghanistan, Iraq, Syria, Somalia, Yemen, Pakistan, and Lybia; new technologies with concentrated killing capacity, including over five hundred drone attacks; and the expansion of surveillance powers as part of counterterrorism efforts that include the FBI's monitoring of "black identity extremists."[1] Additionally, they included producing the upper class aspiring cisgender heterosexual reproductive family as the faultline for respectability, while making initial strides toward the state recognition of LGBT people based on this prerequisite normalcy through his efforts to end bans on gay marriage and LGBT service in the military. The yearly number of reported trans people murdered, most of whom were trans women of color, continued to rise during Obama's presidency and still continue to rise under the Trump administration.

The LGBT Pride celebration at the White House in 2015 was an attempt to normalize relations between the state and queer and trans people, building on the normalized relations between the state and Black communities and communities of color performed by Obama's presidency. The gathering was hosted in the executive home of the U.S. president and first family and the symbolic seat of the U.S. government. With the exception of John Adams and his son, John Quincy Adams, each of the early presidents were slaveholders (Holland 2016). The Obamas were the first Black Americans who were not slaves to have lived in the White House. Obama's reprimand, "Listen, you're in my house," performs his claim to the house that was a slave estate as the paternal head of household. As shown in the fixed physical framing of almost all of the videos of the event, the LGBT guests in the house were fixated on the image of Obama and his speech and did not register the sound of Gutiérrez's voice, much less her message, enough to turn their bodies or phones toward the source of the sound. In most of the videos, therefore, Gutiérrez does not appear at all and her barely audible voice remains disembodied and spatially dislocated. Drawing from Mary Ann Doane's discussion of cinematic voice located outside the visible space of the cinema screen and within the acoustic space of the theater as enveloping and unifying the spectator's body

FIGURE C.2. Gutiérrez chanting "not one more deportation" as she is "escorted" out of the White House LGBT Pride event (June 24, 2015). From Not One More. "White House Pride Event Interrupted Over LGBTQ Detention." YouTube Video, 2:40, June 24, 2015. https://www.youtube.com/watch?v=vv9wRNuptC8&t=1s.

in her classic essay "The Voice in the Cinema" (1980), one might argue that, even before Gutiérrez is physically removed from the celebration, Obama and guests have dissociated her voice and body and pushed them outside the frame of the visible and audible in the space of the private and political event. This externalization of Gutiérrez, which risks being repeated by viewers of the event's videos, gives Obama and guests a sense of spatially bound unity and presence. With greater attention to spatial relationships, Doane's argument provides a theory of cinematic embodiment through sound that furthers Jacques Derrida's critique of the self-authorizing voice of Western metaphysics and Roland Barthes's attempt to disentangle the material "grain of the voice" from language (Derrida 1973; Barthes 1977). Yet, these theories tend to universalize a particular racial gender form and history of subjectivity that cannot sense Gutiérrez's trans migrant voice.

Gutiérrez's embodied presence, voice, and demand disrupted the private spatial enclosures of the event's normalized citizenship. If the voice of the Western subject is thought to communicate an unmediated self-presence, or natural inner "soul," that performs the boundary between inner and outer world and between bodies, trans voices, or trans voice practices, are so often the targets of regulation because they are perceived to be at odds with their gender embodiment, presentation, and/or identity. This perception of incongruence attempts to forcibly map binary cisgender onto trans practices that exceed the image and language of the body and voice as natural signs for gender as sex.[2] Gutiérrez's heterogeneously textured voice, which was not hermetically sealed through the racial, class, and (cis)gender privileges of uninterrupted self-referencing, offered the possibility of a more porous relationship between bodies—a relationship sealed off and out by Obama and event guests. Gutiérrez's action at the White House, demanding the release of LGBTQ immigrants in detention and a stop to the torture of trans women in detention, made visible the regulated boundaries of embodiment that enable and support the construction of the geopolitical borders claiming the U.S. nation-state.

The presidential inauguration of Donald Trump in January 2017 brought stark changes to U.S. immigration policy and the immigration system. The Trump administration's overtly racist regionally and nationally targeted agendas on immigration, which hark back to pre-1960s anti-Asian immigration policies, have been implemented through executive orders and memoranda that have added thousands of officers to Border Patrol and ICE; spiked interior arrests and *removals* (this term replaced *deportation* in 1996 and is distinct from a category of informal "voluntary" deportations called *returns*) of noncitizens; banned the entry of migrants from majority-Muslim countries (initially Iran, Iraq, Libya, Somalia, Sudan, Syria, and Yemen, with Iraq and Sudan recently dropped and Venezuela and North Korea newly added); cancelled the Deferred Action for Childhood Arrivals (DACA) program (still being challenged in the court system); ended Temporary Protected Status for noncitizens from Sudan, Nicaragua, Haiti, El Salvador, Nepal, and Honduras so far; and reduced refugee admissions to their lowest numbers since resettlement procedures were established in 1980.[3] The administration's "zero-tolerance" policy beginning in May 2018 separated migrant children from their parents and placed them in separate detention facilities. Although Trump has issued an executive order purportedly ending the policy, there is no plan in place to reunify families, and the order threatens detention with no time limit for families detained together. Trump has also proposed restrictions to family reunification–based green cards, the most common avenue for authorized migration, and to the diversity visa lottery.

Trump's broad attack on migrants and migration as threats to national and economic security further mobilize and entangle racial discourses targeting the alien, criminal, terrorist, and savage. The most visible symbol of Trump's anti-immigrant agenda has been his proposed construction of a wall along the U.S.-Mexico border, a process that has reportedly begun. Whether it is completed or not, the image of the wall continues to produce and naturalize a preexisting territorial and social boundary that only needs to be made visible and enforced through military-police-prison, legal, economic, and physical blockades. It builds on the racialized fortification of the southern border by Border Patrol to enable the selective and expendable recruitment of masculine migrant agricultural labor by the U.S. government through the Bracero Program from 1941 to 1964 and, starting in the 1950s, to also support federal law enforcement's growing focus on narcotics control (Hernandez 2010). The 1965 Immigrant Act, which placed a systematic national quota on immigration within the Western Hemisphere for the first time, continued to solidify the U.S.-Mexico border as what Walter Mignolo has described as "colonial difference" (2012, 3–90). The establishment of the U.S. southern border through the U.S. invasion of Indigenous and Mexican Southwest territories and their annexation into the northern body of the U.S. through the 1848 Treaty of Guadalupe Hidalgo, followed by the U.S. seizure of Puerto Rico, Guam, and the Philippines and military occupation of Cuba through the 1898 Spanish-American War, marked the ascendance of the U.S. as an international imperial power. The rise of the Anglo-U.S. empire overwrote the geography and geopolitical world imaginary of the Spanish empire and further submerged and subalternized the Indigenous, Black, Arab, Asian, and mestizo knowledges and social systems of Latin Americas in the Caribbean, Mexico, and Central and South America, deemed the American and global "south." The U.S. southern border unites the territorial body, political rule, and distinct yet relational (settler) "colonial difference" of the U.S. within the Western Hemisphere and global system as a descendant of the British empire. As María Josefina Saldaña-Portillo has argued, the Treaty of Guadalupe Hidalgo rationalized U.S. conquest, territorial encroachment, and political disenfranchisement through the casting of Mexicans as "half-breeds," who were unfit for self-governing because of their barbarous indigenous essence (2016, 108–53). The Treaty offered the patronized reinstatement of a diminished form of citizenship to Mexicans, contingent on their adoption of an Anglo racial taxonomy that required the rejection of their indigenous and afromestizo heritages and collusion in the expulsion of Comanche, Apache, Seri, and Kiowa tribes from the Southwest geography claimed by the U.S. (Saldaña-Portillo 2016, 108–53). Anglo colonization of Southwest territories followed the forced removal of Southeast Cherokee, Chickasaw, Choctaw, Creek, and Semiole tribes from their lands through the 1830 Indian Removal Act. The Treaty superimposed a neocolonial Anglo racial geography based on expunging Indigenous and Black peoples onto a national Mexican racial geography that reduced the territorial and political dimensions of Indigenous identity to cultural ethnic traits. This Mexican geography was interarticulated with a prior colonial Spanish racial geography that segregated out Indigenous peoples while retaining aspects of their territorial and political autonomy (Saldaña-Portillo 2016, 108–53). The U.S. fortification of the southern border attempts to control the multiple spaces and times of identities and territories that continue to survive and thrive through the overlayered colonial geographies of the southern Americas.

Since the 1980s, immigration policy and law enforcement practices of migrant interdiction, detention, and deportation have extended the spatial and temporal reach of the U.S. state. The Reagan administration's "war on drugs" maintained the white racial order through the mass criminalization and incarceration of Black and Latinx communities. The 1984 Comprehensive Crime Control Act, followed by the Anti-Drug Abuse Acts of 1986 and 1988, imposed mandatory minimum sentencing for drug-related offenses and restricted the possibility of release on parole, thereby swelling the prison population and creating a crisis in prison overcrowding which called for more funding and expansion of the prison system. Accompanying this legislation, the 1986 Immigration Reform and Control Act, which created the current Criminal Alien Program under ICE, made unauthorized migrants convicted of an offense subject to deportation and brought migrants squarely under the mantle of criminalization as "criminal aliens" in addition to illegality. Reagan's antidrug policies also included designating drug trafficking a threat to national security, authorizing military involvement in antidrug activities, and increasing the ranks of Border Patrol to take leadership in drug interdiction.[4] Moreover, the Reagan administration used military "deterrence" to intercept, detain, and deport migrants and asylum seekers before they reached U.S. territories, even as its military campaigns and funding assisted anti-communist insurgencies in locations worldwide, including Afghanistan, Angola, Cambodia, Ethiopia, Mozambique, and Nicaragua. The Clinton administration further criminalized migration by increasing the categories of crimes that warranted deportation, including a particularly gendering and sexualizing category of crimes described as "moral turpitude"; placing restrictions on due process; establishing mandatory detention as a general enforcement practice for noncitizens, including permanent residents with convictions; and building an information system of classification and surveillance for "criminal aliens" for coordinated use by law enforcement at federal, state, and local levels (Macías-Rojas 2018). The 1996 Illegal Immigration Reform and Immigrant Responsibility Act and Antiterrorism and Effective Death Penalty Act grafted "criminal aliens" with "terrorist aliens" by fusing together counterterrorism provisions targeting Muslim Middle Eastern, and Arab immigrants, domestic crime bills aimed at Black and Latinx communities in the criminal justice system, and criminal alien deportation measures affecting Latin American and Caribbean immigrants caught in the drug war. Following the 9/11 attacks, immigration policy and federal immigration bureaucracy were reorganized to address national security and immigration and border enforcement as national priorities. Immediately after 9/11, the government arrested without warrant and detained without charge more than one thousand two hundred people (total number still unknown) from majority-Muslim countries on suspicion of terrorism and also deported over one thousand Muslims mostly based on minor immigration and criminal charges (Shiekh 2011). The creation of the Department of Homeland Security by the second Bush administration in 2002, the largest reorganization of the federal government since the establishment of the Defense Department after World War II; greater information gathering and sharing between federal, state, and local law enforcement and intelligence agencies and between law enforcement in different countries; more resources for the militarization of the U.S.-Mexico border and greater attention to the U.S.-Canada border, transportation systems, and deterrence beyond the U.S. land base; and more systematic enforcement focused on identifying and removing "criminal" and "terrorist" noncitizens from the U.S. interior have made immigration and border enforcement synonymous with U.S. national security, military expansion, and international diplomacy.[5]

Under Clinton, the term *removal* replaced *deportation* to indicate deportations initiated through official order. Deportation, however, occurs through official and informal practices, such as expedited deportations that circumvent due process all together that are deemed part of apprehending migrants or *returning* them, a term used to describe "voluntary" departure. The temporal and spatial discreteness of the terms (*apprehension, removal, return*) used to describe migrant policing, imprisonment, and expulsion abstracts the elongated and repetitious times and spaces of state surveillance and force, temporally incrementalized detention, and stripping from social and spatial relationships. A 2016 report by the American Immigration Council, for instance, found that Border Patrol routinely holds migrants undergoing initial processing in holding cells, often referred to as *hieleras* in Spanish for "freezers" or "iceboxes, for days and sometimes even months without adequate food, water, and medical care, although these small concrete rooms (with concrete benches and no beds) are not adequate for overnight custody.[6] Holding practices like these and strategies like noncitizen "voluntary" returns, which can result in criminal charges that then legally warrant arrest and detention when noncitizens come back to the border a second time (since "return" often means likely death), reveal the rationalized uses of military-police-"civil" carceral violence by the neoliberal, neocolonial state to continually produce, fortify, and expand the border.

As of May 2017, there are 2.5 million noncitizens in the U.S. under supervision by the Department of Homeland Security, with 1.4 million of this population waiting for the outcome of their cases, which may bring their deportation.[7] According to a 2016 report published by Human Rights Watch (HRW) based on interviews with trans migrant women, predominantly from Mexico and Central America, held in detention between 2011 and 2015, there are approximately sixty-five trans women in detention on any given day among a nationally detained population of approximately thirty thousand migrants, based on ICE estimates. The report suggests that trans migrant women have been greatly impacted by mandatory custody policies that require the use of detention as a primary means of enforcement for large categories of noncitizens, including asylum seekers and permanent residents detained as a result of mostly low-level criminal convictions, based on 1996 laws mentioned earlier. Trans migrant women are held in prison-like "civil" immigration detention facilities and in jails and prisons within the criminal justice system as their asylum cases undergo court proceedings, often for convictions such as drug possession and sex work (considered a crime under the category of "moral turpitude"), or for expedited or reinstated deportation without court proceedings. According to the HRW report, high levels of poverty, violence, societal discrimination, and police profiling faced by trans women contribute to their disproportionate involvement with the criminal justice system and make them particularly vulnerable to detention under mandatory custody immigration policies. Trans women are routinely placed under custody and detention in men's detention facilities, jails, and prisons, where they experience disproportionately high rates of sexual assault and verbal, physical, and sexual abuse by men who are guards, facility staff, detainees, and prisoners. A 2014 investigation by Fusion Media Group found that about seventy-five trans migrants (90 percent trans women and 10 percent trans men) were held in detention by ICE each night across the country, making up less than 1 percent of the estimated forty thousand people held in detention each night across the country. Yet, trans detainees make up one out of five confirmed instances of reported sexual assault in immigration detention facilities.[8] Under detention, trans women often endure solitary confinement and other forms of physical isolation by guards as forms of targeted punishment, sometimes under the guise of protecting them from other detainees and prisoners. In many instances, the Fusion report found that trans women were sexually assaulted and abused by guards while under solitary confinement. Additionally, access to medical care, including life-sustaining HIV medication and treatment, gender-affirming hormone replacement therapy, and mental health services, has been denied or delayed for trans women in detention. In July 2007, Victoria Arellano, a twenty-three-year-old Mexican trans woman, died in ICE custody after medical staff refused to provide her access to her HIV medication. In May 2018, Roxana Hernández, a thirty-three-year-old Honduran trans woman who traveled to San Diego, California, through Mexico as part of a caravan of Central American migrants seeking asylum, died in ICE custody from HIV-related complications following a five-day detention in an "icebox" holding cell at extremely low temperatures, with inadequate food and medical care, and with lights on 24 hours a day.[9] Hernández, who continues to be misgendered in ICE and news reports after her death, was fleeing the gender-based violence she faced as a trans woman in Honduras, where she had been targeted and raped by members of the MS-13 gang. She had been transferred to a trans-segregated unit of the Cibola County Correctional Center in Milan, New Mexico, after her initial detention at San Ysidro Port of Entry in San Diego, California.

Migrant and trans and queer justice organizers and groups, including Jennicet Gutiérrez and FAMILIA: TQLM (Trans Queer Liberation Movement); Isa Noyola and the Transgender Law Center; Pueblo Sin Fronteras, which organized the caravan of Central American asylum seekers to the U.S.; Al Otro Lado; and Diversidad Sin Fronteras are calling for ICE to be held accountable for Hernández's death and for an end to ICE's violent detention of trans women and an end to all detention. The targeted sexual assault, abuse, and neglect of trans migrant women in detention shows the faultiness of the idea of "civil" detention and imprisonment. Gender-based violence, including sexual violence and what Deborah Miranda has called "gendercide" in describing the systematic extermination of third-gender California Indian joyas by Spanish colonizers from the sixteenth to the early nineteenth century, has been a normalized facet of European territorial conquest, occupation, and colonization (Miranda 2010; Smith 2015). While trans-segregated detention units may keep trans women from the routine punitive practice of being housed with detained men, they do not protect trans women from sexual assault, abuse, solitary confinement, and the withholding of medical care by guards. Under the Obama administration, ICE established its first trans- and gay-specific detention "pod" at the Santa Ana City Jail in California in 2011 in response to legal pressure exerted on behalf of LGBT migrants who reported widespread sexual violence and long-term isolation in detention. In 2014, the pod was split in two to confine trans women and gay or bisexual cismen separately. ICE had intended to use the unit, which by 2015 held about half of the trans population in detention, as a flagship model for other LGBT-specific detention facilities throughout the country and to project a more "civil" image of its treatment of LGBT migrants. By 2014, the #EndTransDetention campaign, which was created by a coalition that included FAMILIA: TQLM, the Transgender Law Center, Orange County Immigrant Youth United, and DeColores Queer OC, had begun protesting outside the Santa Ana unit based on reports of trans women having experienced abusive strip searches, withholding or restricting access to medical services, including hormone replacement therapy, and unreasonable use of solitary confinement by guards and facility staff (Human Rights Watch 2016). The coalition called for the release of trans women held in the Santa Ana facility and in all detention facilities, an end to all immigrant detention, and the cancellation of the City of Santa Ana's contract with ICE to detain trans and queer migrants. It revealed that the City of Santa Ana was making $7 million each year through the detention of trans and queer migrants and that the City was planning to expand its detention facilities by one hundred beds to add an additional $2.2 million a year to its profits to repay the Santa Ana City Jail's mounting debt, which will reach $27 million by 2024. The campaign also called attention to the tighter financial and bureaucratic collaboration between "civic" immigration detention facilities and state and federal jails and prisons. Within a two-year span, the local and national organizing efforts of the #EndTransDetention campaign seized a series of wins. By February 2016, the coalition had persuaded the Santa Ana City Council to forgo expanding its facilities to accommodate more ICE detentions. In May 2016, following a hunger strike undertaken by organizers Jennicet Gutiérrez, Deyaneira García, and Jorge Gutierrez, joined by Orange County Immigrant Youth United, FAMILIA: TQLM, and DeColores Queer OC, the city council voted to stop renting space to ICE when its

FIGURE C.3. Supporter Angela Pereira and hunger strikers Deyaneira Garcia, Jorge Gutierrez, and Jennicet Gutiérrez (*left to right*) call for an end to the detention of transgender undocumented immigrants and to Santa Ana's collaboration with ICE (May 16, 2016). Nick Gerda/Voice of OC.

contract expires in 2020, and in December 2016, the city council voted to reduce the maximum number of beds rented to ICE to 128. By the end of May 2017, ICE had terminated its detention contract with the City of Santa Ana because it found the reduction of bed rentals inefficient. Despite organizers' calls to release all trans women held in the Santa Ana unit, the trans detainees were transferred to other detention facilities, including the trans-segregated Cibola County Correctional Center in Milan, New Mexico, where Roxana Hernández died under detention in May 2018.[10] Although the detention center in New Mexico is located in a more remote location, organizers and communities in New Mexico and nationwide, including those involved in the #EndTransDetention campaign, continue to activate the possibility of imagining futures without ICE, detention centers, and prisons.

Notes

INTRODUCTION

1. See Malcolm Gladwell's *The Tipping Point* (2006).

2. I am referring, for instance, to Miss Major's more recent live talks at the book launch for *Trap Door: Trans Cultural Production and the Politics of Visibility* (2017), edited by Tourmaline (Reina Gossett), Eric Stanley, and Johanna Burton, on February 2, 2018, at the New Museum in New York City and at her keynote screening of *MAJOR!* (2015) at the Queer Places, Practices, and Lives Symposium III at the Ohio State University in Columbus, on May 13, 2017.

3. This quote is drawn from *La Vida* (1966). A similar passage can be found in *Five Families* (1959): "In two of the families, the Gómez and the Gutiérrez, the wives have a great deal of influence and use it, although even here they show some subservience to their husbands. It is interesting that in one of these families the husband is impotent and in the other the husband has mild homosexual tendencies. This suggests that in the strongly male-oriented Mexican culture only men who are aging, impotent, homosexual, or "bewitched" are unable to carry out the authoritarian role of the husband" (Lewis 1959, 17).

4. My description draws from Susan Stryker's definition in *Transgender History* (2008) and Julia Serano's provisional and updated discussion in http://juliaserano .blogspot.com/2014/12/julia-seranos-compendium-on-cisgender.html, accessed April 24, 2018.

5. See BQIC Facebook page, accessed April 24, 2018, https://www.facebook.com/pg /blackqueercolumbus/about/?ref=page_internal; Black Pride 4 homepage, accessed April 24, 2018, https://blackpride4.wordpress.com/. See also Erica Thompson, "Community Feature: Black Pride 4 Inspire Community to Examine Pride, Protest and Police Response," *Columbus Alive*, June 28, 2017, http://www.columbusalive.com /entertainment/20170628/community-feature-black-pride-4-inspire-community-to -examine-pride-protest-and-police-response; Encarnacion Pyle, "Protesters Express Anger at Stonewall over Treatment, Pride Parade Arrest," *Columbus Dispatch*, July 18, 2017, http://www.dispatch.com/news/20170718/protesters-express-anger-at-stonewall -over-treatment-pride-parade-arrest.

6. See the U.S. Department of Defense's website for information on the different regions of unified combatant command, accessed April 28, 2018, https://www.defense.gov/.

7. The post-9/11 moment has brought a renewed focus on social theorist Michel Foucault's notion of biopolitics in American academic and intellectual communities, especially with the publication of English translations of Foucault's lectures at the Collège de France from 1975 to 1979 in *"Society Must Be Defended"* (2003); *Security, Territory, Population* (2007); and *The Birth of Biopolitics* (2008). My discussion of Foucault's biopolitics focuses on his analysis of the security state, preceding his more systematic discussion of *governance* and *governmentality*. His public lectures on biopolitics coincide with his three print publications entitled *The History of Sexuality* (1978).

8. See Janetta Johnson and the TGI Justice family, "Expanding Black Trans Safety: An Open Letter to Our Beloved Community," TGI Justice, blog, March 13, 2017, http://www.tgijp.org/blog/blacktranssafety.

ONE. CULTURES

1. See Mel Baggs's blog for updates on hir activism and advocacy and hir self-description, accessed June 28, 2018, https://ballastexistenz.wordpress.com/. Baggs identifies as genderless and uses sie/hir, xe/xyr/xem, ze/zer/zem, ze/hir pronouns; accessed June 28, 2018, https://genderneutralpronoun.wordpress.com/tag/sie-and-hir/.

2. Also refer to the Autism Society's information and advocacy on DSM-5, accessed July 2, 2018, http://www.autism-society.org/what-is/diagnosis/diagnostic-classifications/ and http://www.autism-society.org/releases/autism-society-responds-to-approved-dsm-5-autism-definition/.

3. See Lucas Crawford's discussion of this recoding of "gender identity disorder" to "gender dysphoria" in the DSM, which he has described as the lodging of gender affect in the "hermetically sealed interiors of the self, psyche, soul, or mind" (2015, 166).

4. See Eve Sedgwick's analysis of the depathologizing of homosexuality in the DSM and in psych-medical institutions as a redistribution of pathology toward gender variance in "How to Bring Your Kids Up Gay" (1991).

5. Refer to Leti Volpp's vital work on the gendered cultural and political ramifications of anti-Asian policies and laws in "Divesting Citizenship" (2005) and other work.

6. For more in-depth discussions of the politics and aesthetics of mimesis within Western histories of modernity and enlightenment, see Walter Benjamin's "Doctrine of the Similar" (1933), Max Horkheimer and Theodor Adorno's *Dialectic of Enlightenment: Philosophical Fragments* (2002), Michael Taussig's *Mimesis and Alterity: A Particular History of the Senses* (1993), Homi Bhabba's "Of Mimicry and Man: The Ambivalence of Colonial Discourse" (1994), and Rey Chow's "Sacrifice, Mimesis, and the Theorizing of Victimhood (A Speculative Essay)" (2006).

7. Zavé's website info: http://zavemartohardjono.com/ for description of work and portfolio, as well as links to articles discussing their artwork and activism.

8. In *Stunning Males and Powerful Females: Gender and Tradition in East Javanese*

Dance (2015), Sunardi provides an important intervention in the cis-masculine emphasis of Benedict Anderson's analysis of spiritual charisma and political power in Javanese
society in *Language and Power: Exploring Political Cultures in Indonesia* (1990). She uses
"female" and "male" pointedly to refer to female- and male-bodied and biologically
sexed people in contrast to feminine and masculine gender roles and presentations.
Although this distinction helps to deconstruct gender roles and values assigned based
on (the interpretation of) biological sex, it tends to contribute to naturalizing sex as
binary biological essence, untouched by the social and cultural constructions that
shape gender.

9. Against the fetishizing of ballroom culture in dominant heterosexual culture
and white gay subcultures, Marlon M. Bailey has produced an ethnography of Black
ballroom communities in Detroit that recognizes their collective labor of reworking
conventional gender and sexual identities and meanings—and their relationships to
one another. If Black bodies are subjected to visual regimes that police and normalize
their gender outside and inside Black communities, the ballroom offers the possibility
of refashioning gender and sexual subjectivities in ways that unlock binary femininity and masculinity and heterosexuality from their overriding claims on Black bodies
(Bailey 2013, 29–76).

TWO. NETWORKS

1. For greater discussion of Cheang Shu Lea's work, see Eve Oishi's essay "Collective
Orgasm" (2007) and Ella Shohat's (2001) collection on multicultural feminism.

2. In addition to viewers' own suspicion about the authentic human status of Deckard, certain interviews with Ridley Scott have "confirmed" that Deckard himself is a
Replicant. See *Blade Runner* ([1982] 2007, dir. Scott).

3. On Hollywood's archives of anti-Arab and anti-Asian Orientalist imagery, see the
work of Celine Parreñas Shimizu (2007, 2012) and Jack Shaheen (2001).

4. In *The War of Desire and Technology at the Close of the Mechanical Age* (1996),
Allucquère Rosanne Stone interrupts scientifically driven narratives that represent
communications technology in the virtual age as purely "prosthetic" tools that extend
or replace human agency. Instead, she argues that computerized technologies are based
in and help to create experiences of social interaction that transform the identities,
boundaries, and relationships between technology and nature, human and machine,
human and human, and human and self. For Stone, the gendered body itself is also a
virtual "prosthesis" that provides zones of dynamic interaction, boundary shifting, and
communicated meaning. This argument goes even further than displacing the social
ordering of the body through the hierarchy of primary to secondary biological signs for
sex. It displaces the body itself as the originary "home" and image for what is conceived
of as the human spirit/soul/mind.

5. On the racially gendered figuring of Asian American women through legal, public,
and cinematic discourses, see the work of Laura Hyun Yi Kang (2002).

6. This period of liberalization included the loosening and then lifting of Hollywood
Production Codes by 1968. The codes censored not only the onscreen representation

of homosexuality and other sexual or erotic practices deemed perverse but also erotic relationships between white and nonwhite subjects.

7. For Lev Manovich, new media is the "shift of all culture to computer-mediated forms of production, distribution, and communication" (2001, 19). The convergence of computing and media technologies, including film, has realized the potential for nonlinearity already present in cinema.

8. I would include the "unskilled" assembly work done by Third World women and girls in export processing zones along the international chain of corporate production in this categorization of "secondary" intimate labor. Like work in service, leisure, entertainment, and sex industries, assembly work is not valued culturally or commercially within formal chains of productivity within the imaginary of global capital.

9. My claim builds on the work of Lisa Duggan (2003) and Dean Spade (2011) in appropriating the predominantly white Euro-American leftist critique of neoliberalism (and the material conditions the term describes) toward a focus on dispossessed racial, sexual, and gender social identities, cultures, and communities that remain illegible within paradigms of class and political economics, including trans women of color doing survival work.

10. On theories of autonomy under conditions of deindustrialization, see the work of Grace Lee Boggs (2012). On the technological infrastructure that has facilitated deindustrialization while enabling unintended autonomous exploits, see the work of Alexander Galloway and Eugene Thacker (2007).

11. In using the term *public sphere*, I am referring to Jürgen Habermas's (1991) intervention in conventional political theories of civil society by emphasizing the mediating role of print culture in facilitating popular participation in a bourgeois public sphere constituted as a rational sphere of action and decision-making, independent from the authority of the state and family.

12. The original performance of UKI, part 1, was located at the Hangar Studio, Barcelona, where the junkyard set was built.

13. For more elaboration on the structural impact of high-tech digital economy on countries and local communities in southern Africa, refer to Sokari Ekine's work (2010).

14. For further elaboration on my use of the term *trans media*, see my essay on "transmedia" co-written with Lissette Olivares in *Transgender Studies Quarterly* (2014).

THREE. MEMORY

1. See Kierna Mayo's piece published May 18, 2011, in *Marie Claire*'s Love & Sex section: https://www.marieclaire.com/sex-love/advice/a6075/born-male/.

2. See Pheng Cheah's (2003) work on the appropriation of the Western imperial bildungsroman by postcolonial novelists.

3. Although then U.S. president Grover Cleveland and commissioner James Blount condemned the overthrow, the government actively sponsored the white settler oligarchy's gradual dispossession of Native Hawaiians through military support and occupation (Trask 1999).

FOUR. MOVEMENT

1. See the United Nations website for details on Human Rights Day: http://www .un.org/en/events/humanrightsday/.

2. The *Daily Beast* is an operating business of media and Internet conglomerate IAC (InterActiveCorp), which owns 150 brands and products in 100 countries. IAC's chairman and chief executive since 1995 has been Barry Diller, former chairman and chief executive of Fox and Paramount Pictures Corporation. For documentation of the *Daily Beast*'s "Quorum: Global LGBT Voices" event on Human Rights Day 2014, see http://quorum.thedailybeast.com/.

3. For more information on TED talks, see www.ted.com/about/our-organization#.

4. See also the UN Universal Declaration of Human Rights (1948, 2015) and information on the UN Development Programme's Human Development Index (HDI) and Inequality-adjusted Human Development Index (IHDI) at http://hdr.undp.org/en /content/human-development-index-hdi.

5. For the WB's and IMF's implementation of UN Millennium Goals and their tracking of progress toward goals, see http://datatopics.worldbank.org/mdgs/ and http:// www.imf.org/external/np/exr/facts/mdg.htm.

6. The seventeen UN Sustainable Development Goals are: no poverty; zero hunger; good health and well-being; quality education; gender equality; clean water and sanitation; affordable and clean energy; decent work and economic growth; industry, innovation, and infrastructure; reduced inequalities; sustainable cities and communities; responsible consumption and production; climate action; life below water; life on land; peace, justice and strong institutions; partnerships for the goals. See http://www.un.org/sustainabledevelopment/blog/2015/12/sustainable-development -goals-kick-off-with-start-of-new-year/.

7. The International Monetary Fund (IMF) and the International Bank for Reconstruction and Development (IBRD) were the two original Bretton Woods institutions established in 1944. The IBRD is now one of five institutions that make up the World Bank Group.

8. G8 (Group of 8) stands for the seven countries and one region considered the leading advanced economies in the world. France, West Germany, Italy, Japan, the United Kingdom, the United States, Russia, and the European Union make up the G8, although Russia's membership has been suspended since 2014. The reference originates from the 1975 governmental summit held in France.

9. I attended a symposium on November 11, 2014, in Washington, DC, where researchers from the UCLA Williams Institute presented their preliminary findings on LGBT rights and international human and economic development.

10. Intersex people have not been included in transnational research rubrics like the Williams Institute's or the International Gay and Lesbian Human Rights Commission's. In the United States, intersex social identities and activisms have emerged separately from (and often in tension with) LGBT, queer, and transgender social identities and activisms.

11. Because of mobilizing efforts by Iranti-org and other community groups, Duduzille's murderer was the first to be charged with a hate crime in the South African court system.

12. See the work of Fatimah Tobing Rony (1996) and Michael Renov (1993, 2004) on the overdetermined origins and uses of documentary cinema.

13. The Thai term *kathoey* refers to a gender variant expression that would be categorized along the transfeminine spectrum in the United States. Kathoey describes not only gender expression and embodiment but also a marginalized social caste. I have chosen to use the Thai term rather than imposing the American term *transgender*. At the same time, my argument is that kathoey social identities and cultures have been shaped by transnational and regional cultural technologies. See Peter Jackson's (2011) extensive work on Thai queer and transgender media cultures.

14. See Serhat Unaldi's and Brett Farmer's essays on Thai cinema and television in *Queer Bangkok: Twenty-First-Century Markets, Media, and Rights* (Jackson 2011). Prior to filmmaking, Sukkhapisit had experience playing kathoey buffoon characters on Thai television shows.

15. According to Peter Jackson (2011), there is no government funding for independent filmmaking in Thailand. Commercial film conglomerates dominate the industry.

16. See the work of Darrell Davis and Emilie Yueh-yu Yeh (2008), Toby Miller (2005), and Chris Berry, Jonathan Mackintosh, and Nicola Liscutin (2009) on the transnational film trade.

17. The Pang brothers' pan-Asian regional coproduction *The Eye/Gin Gwai* (2002) grossed $13,733,856 at the Hong Kong box office, while David Moreau and Xavier Palud's Paramount remake of *The Eye* (2008) grossed $56,964,642 (with $25,545,945 of this amount grossed outside the United States).

18. Examples of Asian filmmakers who have crossed over into Hollywood include Hideo Nakata and Chan-wook Park.

19. See also micha cárdenas and Barbara Fornssler's *Trans Desire/Affective Cyborgs* (2010).

20. For more on Vasconcelos's concept of mestizaje and its use in identifying Latin American racial specificity, see Licia Fiol-Matta's (2002) work on Chilean writer, educator, and diplomat Gabriela Mistral.

21. See the work of Hiawatha Bray (2014) for a longer discussion of the history of GPS.

22. See cárdenas's description of her Local Autonomy Networks (Autonets) project at https://faculty.washington.edu/michamc/autonets/.

23. The term *cybernetics* is derived from the Greek term *kybernetike*, which means "governance" or the "art of steering."

24. See "About UNSTOPPABLE," November 29, 2015, https://faculty.washington .edu/michamc/wordpress-unstoppable/2015/11/29/about/.

25. See "About UNSTOPPABLE," November 29, 2015, https://faculty.washington. edu/michamc/wordpress-unstoppable/2015/11/29/about/ and also, for original source of quote of Sylvia Rivera, see Dave Isay's radio documentary *Remembering Stonewall* (1989) and Tourmaline's online distribution of an excerpt from the documentary's transcript at http://thespiritwas.tumblr.com/post/18108920192 /sylvia-rivera-nypd-reflect-on-stonewall.

26. See the #BLM website, http://blacklivesmatter.com/, and Alicia Garza's "A Herstory of the #BlackLivesMatter Movement" (2014).

27. See Paul Virilio's ([1977] 1986) body of work on the accelerated speeds of transmission and communication enabled by modern technologies.

28. cárdenas's theorizing of the "stitch" works alongside and in distinction from the "cut," as theorized by Sarah Kember and Joanna Zylinska (2012), and the "fold" by Gilles Deleuze (1993) in thinking about the relationship between social bodies and their surroundings. For cárdenas, the stitch offers a less violent conceptualizing of the social relationship—one that joins for healing and creation. It is a conceptual creation that draws from the material practice of object making through sewing, which is primarily practiced by women, especially women in the Global South. The stitch also resonates for transgender people who undergo body modification (cárdenas 2016, 4–8).

29. See Eden Medina's (2011) research on the cybernetic systems envisioned by the Chilean government under Salvador Allende to manage the country's economy in the 1970s. Although the cybernetic systems were never implemented in Chile, their vision and principles were exported for potential adoption by the Uruguayan government in the 1980s and Colombian government agencies in the 1990s.

CONCLUSION

1. For more information, see the Migration Policy Institute's "The Obama Record on Deportations: Deporter in Chief or Not?" (2017), accessed June 26, 2018, https://www.migrationpolicy.org/article/obama-record-deportations-deporter-chief-or-not; The New York Times's "The F.B.I.'s Dangerous Crackdown on 'Black Identity Extremists,'" accessed June 26, 2018, https://www.nytimes.com/2017/11/15/opinion/black-identity -extremism-fbi-trump.html.

2. Lal Zimman's sociophonetic ethnography (2014) with transmasculine communities in the San Francisco Bay Area suggests a "multi-layered approach to gender" that takes into account the ways in which sex, gender identity, gender assignment, gender presentation, and sexuality shape phonetic expression and that conveys the complexity of transmasculine appropriations of semiotic resources to align or disalign themselves with a range of masculinities. Annette Schlicter has argued, "Voice . . . cannot be clearly positioned as either sensible or intelligible; it is not necessarily contained by culture or nature" (2011, 43). Providing a critique of the role of voice in Judith Butler's theory of gender performativity, she emphasizes that the voice is not an indicator of gender and is itself performative.

3. The information from this section relies on the Migration Policy Institute's reports "Revving Up the Deportation Machinery: Enforcement under Trump and the Push-back" (May 2018) and "Immigration under Trump: A Review of Policy Shifts in the Year Since the Election" (December 2017) and the Pew Research Center's "Key Facts about U.S. Immigration Policies and Proposed Changes" (February 26, 2018): https://www.migrationpolicy.org/research/revving-deportation-machinery-under-trump -and-pushback, accessed June 26, 2018; https://www.migrationpolicy.org/research /immigration-under-trump-review-policy-shifts, accessed June 26, 2018; and http://www.pewresearch.org/fact-tank/2018/02/26/key-facts-about-u-s-immigration-policies -and-proposed-changes/, accessed June 26, 2018.

4. Information in this section draws from the Migration Policy Institute's report "US Border Enforcement: From Horseback to High-Tech" (2005), accessed June 26, 2018, https://www.migrationpolicy.org/research/us-border-enforcement-horseback-high -tech, and Patrisia Macías-Rojas's book *From Deportation to Prison* (2016) and article "Immigration and the War on Crime: Law and Order Politics and the Illegal Immigra- tion Reform and Immigrant Responsibility Act of 1996" in the *Journal on Migration and Human Security* 6, no. 1 (2018): 1–25.

5. See the Migration Policy Institute's reports "Post-9/11 Policies Dramatically Alter the U.S. Immigration Landscape" (2011), accessed June 28, 2018, https://www .migrationpolicy.org/article/post-911-policies-dramatically-alter-us-immigration -landscape, and "The People Perceived as a Threat to Security: Arab Americans Since September 11" (2006), accessed June 28, 2018, https://www.migrationpolicy.org/article /people-perceived-threat-security-arab-americans-september-11; and also Irum Shiekh's *Detained without Cause: Muslims' Stories of Detention and Deportation in America after 9/11* (2011).

6. See the American Immigration Council's report "Detained beyond the Limit: Prolonged Confinement by U.S. Customs and Border Protection along the Southwest Border" (August 2016), accessed June 26, 2018, https://www.americanimmigration council.org/research/prolonged-detention-us-customs-border-protection.

7. See https://www.pri.org/stories/2017-05-23/immigration-detention-soars-23 -million-people-are-also-regularly-checking, accessed June 28, 2018.

8. See Fusion Media Group's report "'Do You See How Much I'm Suffering Here?' Abuse against Transgender Women in U.S. Immigration Detention" (2016), accessed June 26, 2018, http://interactive.fusion.net/trans/.

9. See statement by Pueblo Sin Fronteras on Roxana Hernández's death, accessed June 28, 2018, https://www.facebook.com/diversidadsinfronteraz/posts /378858885957426, and Colorlines article on Hernández's death, accessed June 28, 2018, https://www.colorlines.com/articles/transgender-woman-dies-ice-custody.

10. See multiple news articles on the trans-specific unit in Santa Ana, California, accessed June 28, 2018, https://www.ocregister.com/2017/05/09/remaining-ice -detainees-at-santa-ana-jail-transferred-out-monday/; https://rewire.news/article/2016 /05/17/hunger-strikers-ice-transgender-immigrant/; https://www.vice.com/en_us /article/43g5jd/why-is-ice-closing-its-only-detention-center-for-transgender-detainees -v24n5; and https://splinternews.com/how-trans-ice-detainees-ended-up-in-a-men-s -detention-c-1795818417.

References

Alexander, Michelle. 2012. *The New Jim Crow: Mass Incarceration in the Age of Color-blindness*. New York: The New Press.

American Immigration Council. 2016. "Detained beyond the Limit: Prolonged Confinement by U.S. Customs and Border Protection along the Southwest Border." Accessed on June 26, 2018. https://www.americanimmigrationcouncil.org/research/prolonged-detention-us-customs-border-protection.

Anderson, Benedict R., OG. 2006. *Language and Power: Exploring Political Cultures in Indonesia*. Jakarta: Equinox.

Angelou, Maya. 1970. *I Know Why the Caged Bird Sings*. New York: Random House.

Anzaldúa, Gloria. 1987. *Borderlands/La Frontera: The New Mestiza*. San Francisco: Aunt Lute Books.

Anzaldúa, Gloria, and AnaLouise Keating. 2015. *Light in the Dark = Luz En Lo Oscuro: Rewriting Identity, Spirituality, Reality*. Durham, NC: Duke University Press.

Aoki, Ryka. 2012. *Seasonal Velocities: Poems, Stories, and Essays*. Los Angeles: Trans-Genre.

Assistant Secretary of Labor (Daniel Patrick Moynihan), Office of Policy Planning and Research. 1965. "The Negro Family: The Case for National Action." United States Department of Labor. Accessed on May 20, 2017. https://www.dol.gov/oasam/programs/history/webid-meynihan.htm.

Badgett, M. V. Lee, Sheila Nezhad, Kees Waaldijk, and Yana van der Meulen Rodgers. 2014. *The Relationship between LGBT Inclusion and Economic Development: An Analysis of Emerging Economies*. Los Angeles: The Williams Institute, UCLA School of Law. Accessed on June 3, 2017. williamsinstitute.law.ucla.edu/wp-content/uploads/lgbt-inclusion-and-development-november-2014.pdf.

Bailey, Marlon M. 2013. *Butch Queens up in Pumps: Gender, Performance, and Ballroom Culture in Detroit*. Ann Arbor: University of Michigan Press.

Baird, Bruce, and Rosemary Candelario. 2019. "Introduction: Dance Experience, Dance of Darkness, Global Butoh: The Evolution of a New Dance Form." In *The Routledge Companion to Butoh Performance*, edited by Bruce Baird and Rosemary Candelario, 1–22. New York: Routledge.

Barbin, Herculine. 1980. *Herculine Barbin: Being the Recently Discovered Memoirs of a Nineteenth-Century French Hermaphrodite*. Translated by Richard McDougall. Introduction by Michel Foucault. New York: Pantheon Books.

Barrett, Lindon. 1998. *Blackness and Value: Seeing Double*. Cambridge: Cambridge University Press.

Barthes, Roland. 1977. "The Grain of the Voice." In *Image, Music, Text*, translated by Stephen Heath, 179–89. London: Fontana Press.

Bassichis, Morgan, Alexander Lee, and Dean Spade. 2015. "Building an Abolitionist Trans and Queer Movement with Everything We've Got." In *Captive Genders: Trans Embodiment and the Prison Industrial Complex*, 2nd ed., edited by Eric A. Stanley and Nat Smith, 21–46. Oakland: AK Press.

Benjamin, Walter, and Knut Tarnowski. 1933. "Doctrine of the Similar." *German Critique*, no. 17 (spring 1979): 65–69.

Berry, Chris, Jonathan D. Mackintosh, and Nicola Liscutin. 2009. *Cultural Industries and Cultural Studies in Northeast Asia: What a Difference a Region Makes*. Hong Kong: Hong Kong University Press.

Beydoun, Khaled A., and Justin Hansford. 2017. "The F.B.I.'s Dangerous Crackdown on 'Black Identity Extremists.'" *New York Times*, November 15. Accessed June 26, 2018. https://www.nytimes.com/2017/11/15/opinion/black-identity-extremism-fbi-trump.html.

Bhabba, Homi K. 1994. "Of Mimicry and Man: The Ambivalence of Colonial Discourse." In *The Location of Culture*, 121–31. New York: Routledge.

Blake, Debra. 2008. *Chicana Sexuality and Gender: Cultural Refiguring in Literature, Oral History, and Art*. Durham, NC: Duke University Press.

Boggs, Grace Lee. 2012. *The Next American Revolution: Sustainable Activism for the Twenty-First Century*. Berkeley: University of California Press.

Bond, Patrick. 2003. *Against Global Apartheid: South Africa Meets the World Bank, IMF, and International Finance*. 2nd ed. Lansdowne, South Africa: University of Cape Town Press.

BQIC and Blackpride4. "Black Pride 4." Accessed April 24, 2018. https://blackpride4.wordpress.com/.

Bradley, Arthur. 2011. *Originary Technicity: The Theory of Technology from Marx to Derrida*. Houndmills, Basingstoke, UK: Palgrave Macmillan.

Bray, Hiawatha. 2014. *You Are Here: From the Compass to GPS, the History and Future of How We Find Ourselves*. New York: Basic Books.

Bruyneel, Kevin. 2007. *The Third Space of Sovereignty: The Postcolonial Politics of U.S.-Indigenous Relations*. Minneapolis: University of Minnesota Press.

Butler, Judith. 1990. *Gender Trouble: Feminism and the Subversion of Identity*. New York: Routledge.

Butler, Judith. 1993. *Bodies That Matter: On the Discursive Limits of "Sex."* New York: Routledge.

Butler, Judith. 2006. *Precarious Life: The Powers of Mourning and Violence*. London: Verso.

Butler, Judith. 2018. *Notes toward a Performative Theory of Assembly*. Cambridge, MA: Harvard University Press.

Byrd, Jodi A. 2011. *The Transit of Empire: Indigenous Critiques of Colonialism*. Minneapolis: University of Minnesota Press.

Campbell, Timothy C. 2011. *Improper Life Technology and Biopolitics from Heidegger to Agamben*. Minneapolis: University of Minnesota Press.

cárdenas, micha. 2011. *The Transreal: Political Aesthetics of Crossing Realities*. Edited by Zach Blas and Wolfgang Schirmacher. New York: Atropos.

cárdenas, micha. 2016. "Trans of Color Poetics: Stitching Bodies, Concepts and Algorithms." *Scholar and Feminist Online* 13.3–14.1. Web.

cárdenas, micha, and Barbara Fornssler. 2010. *Trans Desire/Affective Cyborgs*. New York: Atropos.

Castells, Manuel. 1996. *The Rise of the Network Society*. Malden, MA: Blackwell.

Castells, Manuel. 2013. *Communication Power*. Oxford: Oxford University Press.

Chen, Jian. 2017. "#BlackLivesMatter and the State of Asian/America." *Journal of Asian American Studies* 20, no. 2: 265–71.

Chen, Jian, and Lissette Olivares. 2014. "Transmedia." *Transgender Studies Quarterly* 1, no. 1: 245–48.

Chow, Rey. 2006. *The Age of the World Target: Self-Referentiality in War, Theory, and Comparative Work*. Durham, NC: Duke University Press.

Chow, Rey. 2012. "Sacrifice, Mimesis, and the Theorizing of Victimhood." In *Entanglements, or Transmedial Thinking about Capture*, 81–106. Durham, NC: Duke University Press.

Chun, Wendy Hui Kyong. 2013. *Programmed Visions: Software and Memory*. Cambridge, MA: MIT Press.

Clare, Eli. 2017. *Brilliant Imperfection: Grappling with Cure*. Durham, NC: Duke University Press.

Clough, Patricia Ticineto. 2000. *Autoaffection: Unconscious Thought in the Age of Teletechnology*. Minneapolis: University of Minnesota Press.

Corazón, Lovemme. 2013. *Trauma Queen: A Memoir*. Toronto: Biyuti.

Costantini, Christina, Jorge Rivas, and Kistofer Ríos. 2014. "'Do You See How Much I'm Suffering Here?' Abuse against Transgender Women in U.S. Immigration Detention." *Fusion*, November 17. Accessed June 26, 2018. http://interactive.fusion.net /trans.

Couser, G. Thomas. 2012. *Memoir: An Introduction*. New York: Oxford University Press.

Crawford, Lucas. 2015. "Woolf's 'Einfühlung': An Alternative Theory of Transgender Affect." *Mosaic: An Interdisciplinary Critical Journal* 48, no. 1 (Queer/Affect, March 2015): 165–81.

Crenshaw, Kimberlé. 1989. "Demarginalizing the Intersection of Race and Sex: A Black Feminist Critique of Antidiscrimination Doctrine, Feminist Theory and Antiracist Politics." *University of Chicago Legal Forum*, no. 1: 139–67.

Davis, Angela Y. 2003. *Are Prisons Obsolete?* New York: Seven Stories.

Davis, Darrell William, and Emilie Yueh-yu Yeh. 2008. *East Asian Screen Industries*. London: British Film Institute.

Day, Iyko. 2016. *Alien Capital: Asian Racialization and the Logic of Settler Colonial Capitalism*. Durham, NC: Duke University Press.

Deleuze, Gilles. 1993. *The Fold: Leibniz and the Baroque*. Minneapolis: University of Minnesota Press.

Denetdale, Jennifer Nez. 2017. "Return to 'The Uprising at Beautiful Mountain in 1913' Marriage and Sexuality in the Making of the Modern Navajo Nation." In *Critically Sovereign: Indigenous Gender, Sexuality, and Feminist Studies*, edited by Joanne Barker, 69–98. Durham, NC: Duke University Press.

Derrida, Jacques. 1973. "The Voice That Keeps Silence." In *Speech and Phenomena, and Other Essays on Husserl's Theory of Signs*, translated by David Allison and Newton Garver, 70–87. Evanston, IL: Northwestern University Press.

Derrida, Jacques. 1982. "White Mythology." In *Margins of Philosophy*, translated by Alan Bass, 207–72. Chicago: University of Chicago Press.

Dibia, I Wayan, and Rucina Ballinger. 2012. *Balinese Dance, Drama and Music: A Guide to the Performing Arts of Bali*. North Clarendon, VT: Tuttle.

Doane, Mary Ann. 1980. "The Voice in the Cinema: The Articulation of Body and Space." *Yale French Studies*, no. 60, Cinema/Sound: 33–50.

Doroshow, Ceyenne, with Audacia Ray. 2012. *Cooking in Heels: A Memoir Cookbook*. New York: Red Umbrella Project.

Drescher, Jack. 2013. "Gender Identity Diagnoses: History and Controversies." In *Gender Dysphoria and Disorders of Sex Development Progress in Care and Knowledge*, edited by Baudewijntje P. C. Kreukels, Thomas D. Steensma, and Annelou L. C. de Vries, 137–50. New York: Springer.

Driskill, Qwo-Li. 2016. *Asegi Stories: Cherokee Queer and Two-Spirit Memory*. Tucson: University of Arizona Press.

DSM-3: *Diagnostic and Statistical Manual of Mental Disorders*, 3rd ed. 1980. Arliington, VA: American Psychiatric Association.

DSM-4: *Diagnostic and Statistical Manual of Mental Disorders*, 4th ed. 1994. Arliington, VA: American Psychiatric Association.

DSM-5: *Diagnostic and Statistical Manual of Mental Disorders*, 5th ed. 2013. Arliington, VA: American Psychiatric Association.

Duggan, Lisa. 2003. *The Twilight of Equality? Neoliberalism, Cultural Politics, and the Attack on Democracy*. Boston: Beacon.

Edwards, Paul N. 1997. *The Closed World: Computers and the Politics of Discourse in Cold War America*. Cambridge, MA: MIT Press.

Ekine, Sokari. 2010. SMS *Uprising: Mobile Activism in Africa*. Oxford: Pambazuka.

Electronic Disturbance Theater/b.a.n.g. lab. 2010. *Sustenance: A Play for All Trans [ ] Borders*. Printed Matter, Inc. thing.net/~rdom/Sustenance.pdf.

Ellison, Treva. 2016. "The Strangeness of Progress and the Uncertainty of Blackness." In *No Tea, No Shade: New Writings in Black Queer Studies*, edited by E. Patrick Johnson, 323–45. Durham, NC: Duke University Press.

Eng, David L. 2007. *Racial Castration: Managing Masculinity in Asian America*. Durham, NC: Duke University Press.

Espiritu, Yen Le. 1992. *Asian American Panethnicity: Bridging Institutions and Identities*. Philadelphia: Temple University Press.

Espiritu, Yen Le. 2008. *Asian American Women and Men: Labor, Laws, and Love*. Lanham, MD: Rowman and Littlefield.

Fajardo, Kale Bantigue. 2014. *Filipino Crosscurrents: Oceanographies of Seafaring, Masculinities, and Globalization*. Minneapolis: University of Minnesota Press.

Farmer, Brett. 2011. "Loves of Siam: Contemporary Thai Cinema and Vernacular Queerness." In *Queer Bangkok: Twenty-First-Century Markets, Media, and Rights*, edited by Peter Jackson, 81–98. Hong Kong: Hong Kong University Press.

Feinberg, Leslie. 1992. *Transgender Liberation: A Movement Whose Time Has Come*. New York: World View Forum.

Ferguson, Roderick A. 2003. *Aberrations in Black: Toward a Queer of Color Critique*. Minneapolis: University of Minnesota Press.

Fiol-Matta, Licia. 2002. *Queer Mother for the Nation: The State and Gabriela Mistral*. Minneapolis: University of Minnesota Press.

Flores, Andrew R., Jody L. Herman, Gary J. Gates, and Taylor N. T. Brown. 2016. *How Many Adults Identify as Transgender in the United States*. The Williams Institute, UCLA School of Law. Accessed on June 3, 2017. williamsinstitute.law.ucla.edu/wp-content/uploads/How-Many-Adults-Identify-as-Transgender-in-the-United-States.pdf.

Foucault, Michel. 1978. *The History of Sexuality*, Volume 1: *An Introduction*. Translated by Robert Hurley. New York: Pantheon.

Foucault, Michel. 2003. *"Society Must Be Defended": Lectures at the Collège de France, 1975–1976*. Edited by Mauro Bertani and Alessandro Fontana. Translated by David Macey. New York: Picador.

Foucault, Michel. 2007. *Security, Territory, Population: Lectures at the Collège de France, 1977–1978*. Edited by Michel Senellart. Translated by Graham Burchell. Basingstoke, UK: Palgrave Macmillan.

Foucault, Michel. 2008. *The Birth of Biopolitics: Lectures at the Collège de France, 1978–1979*. New York: Palgrave Macmillan.

Friedberg, Anne. 2006. *The Virtual Window: From Alberti to Microsoft*. Cambridge, MA: MIT Press.

Fujikane, Candace, and Jonathan Y. Okamura. 2008. *Asian Settler Colonialism: From Local Governance to the Habits of Everyday Life in Hawai'i*. Honolulu: University of Hawai'i Press.

Fung, Richard. 1991. "Looking for My Penis: The Eroticized Asian in Gay Video Porn." In *How Do I Look? Queer Film & Video*, edited by Bad Object-Choices, 145–68. Seattle: Bay Press.

Garza, Alicia. 2014. "A Herstory of the #BlackLivesMatter Movement." *The Feminist Wire*, October 7. Accessed on June 3, 2017. thefeministwire.com/2014/10/black livesmatter-2.

Galloway, Alexander, and Eugene Thacker. 2007. *The Exploit: A Theory of Networks*. Minneapolis: University of Minnesota Press.

Geary, Daniel. 2017. *Beyond Civil Rights: The Moynihan Report and Its Legacy*. Philadelphia: University of Pennsylvania Press.

Gilmore, Ruth Wilson. 2007. *Golden Gulag: Prisons, Surplus, Crisis, and Opposition in Globalizing California*. Berkeley: University of California Press.

Gittlen, Ariela. 2016. "In Her New Film, Wu Tsang Unveils the Queer History of One of China's Most Famous Poets." *Art Sy*, March 21. Accessed on March 7, 2017. https://www.artsy.net/article/artsy-editorial-wu-tsang-unveils-the-queer-history-of-one-of-china-s-most-famous-poets.

Gladwell, Malcolm 2006. *The Tipping Point: How Little Things Can Make a Big Difference*. New York: Little, Brown.

Go, Julian. 2005. "Modes of Rule in America's Overseas Empire: The Philippines, Puerto Rico Guam, and Samoa." In *The Louisiana Purchase and American Expansion, 1803–1898*, edited by Sanford Levinson and Bartholomew H. Sparrow, 209–30. Lanham, MD: Rowman and Littlefield.

Go, Julian. 2011. *Patterns of Empire: The British and American Empires, 1688 to the Present*. Cambridge: Cambridge University Press.

Gopinath, Gayatri. 2007. *Impossible Desires: Queer Diasporas and South Asian Public Cultures*. Calcutta: Seagull Books.

Gossett, Che. 2013. "Silhouettes of Defiance: Memorializing Historical Sites of Queer and Transgender Resistance in an Age of Neoliberal Inclusivity." In *The Transgender Studies Reader*, Volume 2, edited by Susan Stryker and Aren Aizura, 580–90. New York: Routledge.

Gossett, Che. 2015. "Abolitionist Imaginings: A Conversation with Bo Brown, Reina Gossett [Tourmaline], and Dylan Rodríguez." In *Captive Genders: Trans Embodiment and the Prison Industrial Complex*, 2nd ed., edited by Eric A. Stanley and Nat Smith, 357–78. Oakland: AK Press.

Gossett, Reina [Tourmaline], Eric A. Stanley, and Johanna Burton. 2017. *Trap Door: Trans Cultural Production and the Politics of Visibilty*. Cambridge, MA: MIT Press.

Gutiérrez, Jennicet. 2015. "I Interrupted Obama Because We Need to Be Heard." *Washington Blade*, June 25. https://www.washingtonblade.com/.

Habermas, Jürgen. 1991. *The Structural Transformation of the Public Sphere: An Inquiry into a Category of Bourgeois Society*. Cambridge, MA: MIT Press.

Haritaworn, Jin. 2015. *Queer Lovers and Hateful Others: Regenerating Violent Times and Places*. London: Pluto Press.

Haritaworn, Jin, Adi Kuntsman, and Silvia Posocco. 2014. "Introduction." In *Queer Necropolitics*, edited by Jin Haritaworn, Adi Kuntsman, and Silvia Posocco, 1–28. New York: Routledge.

Harris, Keith. 2006. *Boys, Boyz, Bois: The Ethics of Black Masculinity in Film and Popular Media*. New York: Routledge.

Harris, Marvin. 1964. *Patterns of Race in the Americas*. Westport, CT: Greenwood.

Hartman, Saidiya V. 1997. *Scenes of Subjection: Terror, Slavery, and Self-Making in Nineteenth-Century America*. New York: Oxford University Press.

Hartman, Saidiya V. 2007. *Lose Your Mother: A Journey Along the Atlantic Slave Route*. New York: Farrar, Straus and Giroux.

Hartman, Saidiya V. 2002. "The Time of Slavery." *South Atlantic Quarterly* 101, no. 4 (fall): 757–77.

Hartman, Saidiya V. 2016. "The Belly of the World: A Note on Black Women's Labors." *Souls* 18, no. 1: 166–73.

Harvey, David. 1990. *The Condition of Postmodernity: An Enquiry into the Origins of Cultural Change*. Malden, MA: Blackwell.

Hauʻofa, Epeli. 2008. *We Are the Ocean: Selected Works*. Honolulu: University of Hawaiʻi Press.

Hernandez, Kelly Lytle. 2010. *Migra!: A History of the U.S. Border Patrol*. Berkeley: University of California Press.

Holland, Jesse J. 2016. *The Invisibles: The Untold Story of African American Slaves in the White House*. Guilford, CT: Lyons Press.

Hong, Grace Kyungwon, and Roderick A. Ferguson. 2011. *Strange Affinities: The Gender and Sexual Politics of Comparative Racialization*. Durham, NC: Duke University Press.

Human Rights Watch. 2016. "'Do You See How Much I'm Suffering Here?' Abuse against Transgender Women in US Immigration Detention." Accessed on April 24, 2018. https://www.hrw.org/sites/default/files/report_pdf/us0316_web.pdf.

Hunter, Nan D. 2006. "Contextualizing the Sexuality Debates: A Chronology 1966–2005." In *Sex Wars: Sexual Dissent and Political Culture*, edited by Lisa Duggan and Nan D. Hunter, 15–28. New York: Routledge.

Hurston, Zora Neale. [1937] 1990. *Their Eyes Were Watching God: A Novel*. New York: Perennial Library.

Jackson, Peter A. 2011. *Queer Bangkok: Twenty-First-Century Markets, Media, and Rights*. Hong Kong: Hong Kong University Press.

Jacobs, Harriet A. 1973. *Incidents in the Life of a Slave Girl*. Edited by Lydia Maria Child. New York: Harcourt Brace Jovanovich.

Johnson, Janetta, and TGI Justice. "Expanding Black Trans Safety: An Open Letter to Our Beloved Community." Accessed March 13, 2017. http://www.tgijp.org/blog/blacktranssafety.

Kang, Laura Hyun Yi. 2002. *Compositional Subjects: Enfiguring Asian/American Women*. Durham, NC: Duke University Press.

Kauanui, J. Kēhaulani. 2008. *Hawaiian Blood: Colonialism and the Politics of Sovereignty and Indigeneity*. Durham, NC: Duke University Press.

Keeling, Kara. 2007. *The Witch's Flight: The Cinematic, the Black Femme, and the Image of Common Sense*. Durham, NC: Duke University Press.

Kelley, Robin D. G. 1997. *Yo' Mama's Disfunktional!: Fighting the Culture Wars in Urban America*. Boston: Beacon.

Kember, Sarah, and Joanna Zylinska. 2012. *Life after New Media: Mediation as a Vital Process*. Cambridge, MA: MIT Press.

Kim, Jodi. 2010. *Ends of Empire: Asian American Critique and the Cold War*. Minneapolis: University of Minnesota Press.

Kina, Laura. 2016. "Liminal Possibilities: Queering Mixed-Race Asian American Strategies in the Art of Maya Mackrandilal and Zavé Gayatri Martohardjono." In *Queering Contemporary Asian American Art*, edited by Laura Kina and Jan Christian Bernabe, 138–51. Seattle: University of Washington Press.

Kusno, Abidin. 2013. *After the New Order: Space, Politics, and Jakarta*. Honolulu: University of Hawai'i Press.

Kwong, Jessica. 2017. "Remaining ICE Detainees at Santa Ana Jail Transferred Out Monday." *The Orange County Register*, May 9. Accessed June 28, 2018. https://www.ocregister.com/2017/05/09/remaining-ice-detainees-at-santa-ana-jail-transferred-out-monday.

Lady Chablis, with Theodore Bouloukos. 1996. *Hiding My Candy: The Autobiography of the Grand Empress of Savannah*. New York: Pocket Books.

Lewis, Oscar. 1959. *Five Families; Mexican Case Studies in the Culture of Poverty*. New York: Basic Books.

Lewis, Oscar. 1966. "The Culture of Poverty." *Scientific American* 215, no. 4 (October): 19–25.

Lewis, Oscar. 1966. *La Vida: A Puerto Rican Family in the Culture of Poverty*. San Juan: Random.

Liberation Newspaper of the Party for Socialism and Liberation. 2015. "Interview with Jennicet Gutiérrez." YouTube Video, 25:47, September 28. https://www.liberationnews.org/interview-jennicet-gutierrez.

Lim, Bliss Cua. 2009. *Translating Time: Cinema, the Fantastic, and Temporal Critique*. Durham, NC: Duke University Press.

Lim, Eng-Beng. 2013. *Brown Boys and Rice Queens: Spellbinding Performance in the Asias*. New York: New York University Press.

Lippit, Akira Mizuta. 2005. *Atomic Light (Shadow Optics)*. Minneapolis: University of Minnesota Press.

LiPuma, Edward, and Benjamin Lee. 2004. *Financial Derivatives and the Globalization of Risk*. Durham, NC: Duke University Press.

Lorde, Audre. 1982. *Zami: A New Spelling of My Name*. Trumansburg, NY: Crossing.

Lowe, Lisa. 2007. *Immigrant Acts: On Asian American Cultural Politics*. Durham, NC: Duke University Press.

Loyd, Jenna M., and Alison Mountz. 2018. *Boats, Borders, and Bases: Race, the Cold War, and the Rise of Migration Detention in the United States*. Berkeley: University of California Press.

Luibhéid, Eithne. 2002. *Entry Denied: Controlling Sexuality at the Border*. Minneapolis: University of Minnesota Press.

Lüthje, Boy, Stefanie Hürtgen, Peter Pawlicki, and Martina Sproll. 2013. *From Silicon Valley to Shenzhen: Global Production and Work in the IT Industry*. Lanham, MD: Rowman and Littlefield.

Macías-Rojas, Patrisia. 2016. *From Deportation to Prison: The Politics of Immigration Enforcement in Post-Civil Rights America*. New York: New York University Press.

Macías-Rojas, Patrisia. 2018. "Immigration and the War on Crime: Law and Order Politics and the Illegal Immigration Reform and Immigrant Responsibility Act of 1996." *Journal on Migration and Human Security* 6, no. 1: 1–25.

Manovich, Lev. 2001. *The Language of New Media*. Cambridge, MA: MIT Press.

Marx, Karl. 1999. *The Eighteenth Brumaire of Louis Bonaparte*. Marx/Engels Internet

Archive. Accessed on June 3, 2017. marxists.org/archive/marx/works/download
/pdf/18th-Brumaire.pdf.

Mbembe, Achille. 2003. *On the Postcolony.* Berkeley: University of California Press.

McLuhan, Marshall. 1994. *Understanding Media: The Extensions of Man.* Cambridge,
MA: MIT Press.

Medina, Eden. 2011. *Cybernetic Revolutionaries: Technology and Politics in Allende's
Chile.* Cambridge, MA: MIT Press.

Melamed, Jodi. 2011. *Represent and Destroy: Rationalizing Violence in the New Racial
Capitalism.* Minneapolis: University of Minnesota Press.

Mercer, Kobena. 1994. *Welcome to the Jungle: New Positions in Black Cultural Studies.*
New York: Routledge.

Meyerowitz, Joanne. 2004. *How Sex Changed: A History of Transsexuality in the United
States.* Cambridge, MA: Harvard University Press.

Mignolo, Walter D. 2012. *Local Histories/Global Designs: Coloniality, Subaltern Knowledges, and Border Thinking.* Princeton, NJ: Princeton University Press.

Migration Policy Institute. 2005. "US Border Enforcement: From Horseback to High-
Tech." Accessed on June 26, 2018. https://www.migrationpolicy.org/research
/us-border-enforcement-horseback-high-tech.

Migration Policy Institute. 2006. "The People Perceived as a Threat to Security:
Arab Americans Since September 11." Accessed on June 28, 2018. https://www
.migrationpolicy.org/article/people-perceived-threat-security-arab-americans
-september-11.

Migration Policy Institute. 2011. "Post-9/11 Policies Dramatically Alter the U.S. Immigration Landscape." Accessed on June 28, 2018. https://www.migrationpolicy.org
/article/post-911-policies-dramatically-alter-us-immigration-landscape.

Migration Policy Institute. 2017. "Immigration under Trump: A Review of Policy
Shifts in the Year Since the Election." Accessed on June 26, 2018. https://www
.migrationpolicy.org/research/revving-deportation-machinery-under-trump-and
-pushback.

Migration Policy Institute. 2017. "The Obama Record on Deportations: Deporter in
Chief or Not?" Accessed on June 26, 2018. https://www.migrationpolicy.org/article
/obama-record-deportations-deporter-chief-or-not.

Migration Policy Institute. 2018. "Revving Up the Deportation Machinery: Enforcement under Trump and the Pushback." Accessed on June 26, 2018. https://www
.migrationpolicy.org/research/immigration-under-trump-review-policy-shifts.

Miller, Toby. 2005. *Global Hollywood.* 2nd ed. London: BFI.

Mitchell, W. J. T. 2005. *What Do Pictures Want?: The Lives and Loves of Images.* Chicago: University of Chicago Press.

Miranda, Deborah. 2010. "Extermination of the *Joyas*: Gendercide in Spanish California." *GLQ: A Journal of Lesbian and Gay Studies* 16, no. 1–2: 253–84.

Miranda, Deborah. 2013. *Bad Indians: A Tribal Memoir.* Berkeley, CA: Heyday.

Mock, Janet. 2014. *Redefining Realness: My Path to Womanhood, Identity, Love and So
Much More.* New York: Atria Books.

Mock, Janet, and Kierna Mayo. 2011. "I Was Born a Boy." *Marie Claire*, May 18. Accessed on June 3, 2017. marieclaire.com/sex-love/advice/a6075/born-male.

Moten, Fred. 2003. *In the Break: The Aesthetics of the Black Radical Tradition*. Minneapolis: University of Minnesota Press.

Motley, Dena. 1967. "The Culture of Poverty in Puerto Rico and New York." *Social Security Bulletin*. Accessed on May 20, 2017. https://www.ssa.gov/policy/docs/ssb /v30n9/v30n9p18.pdf.

Muñoz, José Esteban. 1999. *Disidentifications: Queers of Color and the Performance of Politics*. Minneapolis: University of Minnesota Press.

Nakamura, Lisa. 2008. *Digitizing Race: Visual Cultures of the Internet*. Minneapolis: University of Minnesota Press.

Nama, Adilifu. 2008. *Black Space: Imagining Race in Science Fiction Film*. Austin: University of Texas Press.

Newman, Toni. 2014. *I Rise: The Transformation of Toni Newman*. Edited by Kevin Hogan. Hollywood, CA: SPI Productions.

Ngai, Mae M. 2014. *Impossible Subjects: Illegal Aliens and the Making of Modern America*. Princeton, NJ: Princeton University Press.

Nguyen, Hoang Tan. 2014. *A View from the Bottom: Asian American Masculinity and Sexual Representation*. Durham, NC: Duke University Press.

Nguyen, Mimi Thi. 2012. *The Gift of Freedom: War, Debt, and Other Refugee Passages*. Durham, NC: Duke University Press.

Nichols, Bill. 2010. *Introduction to Documentary*. Bloomington: Indiana University Press.

Nothing, Ehn, ed. 2006. *Street Transvestite Action Revolutionaries: Survival, Revolt, and Queer Antagonist Struggle*. New York: Untorelli Press.

Obama, Barack. 2006. *The Audacity of Hope: Thoughts on Reclaiming the American Dream*. New York: Crown.

Ochoa, Marcia. 2014. *Queen for a Day: Transformistas, Beauty Queens, and the Performance of Femininity in Venezuela*. Durham, NC: Duke University Press.

Oishi, Eve. 2007. "'Collective Orgasm': The Eco-Cyber-Pornography of Shu Lea Cheang." *WSQ: Women's Studies Quarterly* 35, no. 1–2 (spring/summer).

Omi, Michael, and Howard Winant. 2015. *Racial Formation in the United States*. New York: Routledge.

Parks, Lisa. 2001. "Plotting the Personal: Global Positioning Satellites and Interactive Media." *Ecumene* 8, no. 2 (April): 209–22.

Parks, Lisa D., and Nicole Starosielski. 2015. *Signal Traffic: Critical Studies of Media Infrastructures*. Urbana: University of Illinois Press.

Petersen, William. 1966. "Success Story, Japanese-American Style." *New York Times*, January 9. Accessed on May 20, 2017. http://inside.sfuhs.org/dept/history/US _History_reader/Chapter14/modelminority.pdf.

Pew Research Center. 2018. "Key Facts about U.S. Immigration Policies and Proposed Changes." Accessed on June 26, 2018. http://www.pewresearch.org/fact-tank /2018/02/26/key-facts-about-u-s-immigration-policies-and-proposed-changes.

Piepzna-Samarasinha, Leah Lakshmi. 2016. *Dirty River: A Queer Femme of Color Dreaming Her Way Home*. Vancouver: Arsenal Pulp Press.

Ponce, Martin Joseph. 2012. *Beyond the Nation: Diasporic Filipino Literature and Queer Reading.* New York: New York University Press.

Poster, Mark. 1990. *The Mode of Information: Poststructuralism and Social Context.* Chicago: University of Chicago Press.

Preciado, Paul B. 2013. *Testo Junkie: Sex, Drugs, and Biopolitics in the Pharmacopornographic Era.* New York: The Feminist Press at CUNY.

Puar, Jasbir K. 2017. *Terrorist Assemblages: Homonationalism in Queer Times.* Durham, NC: Duke University Press.

Pueblo Sin Fronteras, 2018. "Statement by Pueblo Sin Fronteras, Al Otro Lado, and Diversidad Sin Fronteras," Facebook, May 29. https://www.facebook.com/diversidadsinfronteraz/posts/378858885957426.

Pyle, Encarnacion. 2017. "Protesters Express Anger at Stonewall over Treatment, Pride Parade Arrest," *Columbus Dispatch*, July 18. Accessed on April 24, 2018. http://www.dispatch.com/news/20170718/protesters-express-anger-at-stonewall-over-treatment-pride-parade-arrest.

Rak, Julie. 2004. "Are Memoirs Autobiography? A Consideration of Genre and Public Identity." *Genre* 37 (fall/winter): 483–504.

Richardson, Matt. 2013. *Queer Limit of Black Memory: Black Lesbian Literature and Irresolution.* Columbus: Ohio State University Press.

Rinaldi, Tiziana. 2017. "As Immigration Detention Soars, 2.3 Million People Are Also Regularly Checking in with Immigration Agents." *PRI*, May 23. Accessed on June 28, 2018. https://www.pri.org/stories/2017-05-23/immigration-detention-soars-23-million-people-are-also-regularly-checking.

Robinson, Cedric J. 1983. *Black Marxism: The Making of the Black Radical Tradition.* Chapel Hill: University of North Carolina Press.

Rodríguez, Dylan. 2005. "Asian-American Studies in the Age of the Prison Industrial Complex: Departures and Re-narrations." *Review of Education, Pedagogy, and Cultural Studies* 27, no. 3: 241–63.

Rodríguez, Juana María. 2003. *Queer Latinidad: Identity Practices, Discursive Spaces.* New York: New York University Press.

Rodríguez, Juana María. 2014. *Sexual Futures, Queer Gestures, and Other Latina Longings.* New York: New York University Press.

Rifkin, Mark. 2012. *The Erotics of Sovereignty: Queer Native Writing in the Era of Self-determination.* Minneapolis: University of Minnesota Press.

Rifkin, Mark. 2015. "Finding Voice in Changing Times: The Politics of Native Self-Representation during the Periods of Removal and Allotment." *The Routledge Companion to Native American Literature*, edited by Deborah L. Madsen, 146–56. London: Routledge.

Rivas, Jorge. 2017. "How Trans ICE Detainees Ended Up in a Men's Detention Center in the Middle of New Mexico." *Splinter*, June 5. Accessed June 28, 2018. https://splinternews.com/how-trans-ice-detainees-ended-up-in-a-men-s-detention-c-1795818417.

Rony, Fatimah Tobing. 1996. *The Third Eye: Race, Cinema, and Ethnographic Spectacle.* Durham, NC: Duke University Press.

Rubin, Gayle. 2011. *Deviations: A Gayle Rubin Reader*. Durham, NC: Duke University Press.

Said, Edward. 1994. *Culture and Imperialism*. New York: Vintage.

Salamon, Gayle. 2010. *Assuming a Body Transgender and Rhetorics of Materiality*. New York: Columbia University Press.

Saldaña-Portillo, María Josefina. 2016. *Indian Given: Racial Geographies across Mexico and the United States*. Durham, NC: Duke University Press.

Sassen, Saskia. 2012. "Expanding the Terrain for Global Capital: When Local Housing Becomes an Electronic Instrument." In *Subprime Cities: The Political Economy of Mortgage Markets*, edited by Manuel B. Aalbers, 74–96. Malden, MA: Blackwell.

Schlichter, Annette. 2011. "Do Voices Matter? Vocality, Materiality, Gender Performativity." *Body and Society* 17, no. 1: 31–52.

Sedgwick, Eve. 1991. "How to Bring Your Kids up Gay." *Social Text*, no. 29: 18–27.

Serano, Julia. 2014. "Julia Serano's Compendium on Cisgender, Cissexual, Cissexism, Cisgenderism, Cis Privilege, and the Cis/trans Distinction." Accessed April 24, 2018. http://juliaserano.blogspot.com/2014/12/julia-seranos-compendium-on -cisgender.html.

Serrano, Alfonso. 2018. "Transgender Woman Dies in ICE Custody." *Colorlines*, May 31. Accessed June 28, 2018. https://www.colorlines.com/articles/transgender -woman-dies-ice-custody.

Shah, Nayan. 2011. *Stranger Intimacy: Contesting Race, Sexuality, and the Law in the North American West*. Berkeley: University of California Press.

Shaheen, Jack. 2001. *Reel Bad Arabs: How Hollywood Vilifies a People*. Northampton, MA: Olive Branch.

Sharpe, Christine. 2010. *Monstrous Intimacies: Making Post-Slavery Subjects*. Durham, NC: Duke University Press.

Sharpe, Christine. 2016. *In the Wake: On Blackness and Being*. Durham, NC: Duke University Press.

Shiekh, Irum. 2011. *Detained without Cause: Muslims' Stories of Detention and Deportation in America after 9/11*. New York: Palgrave Macmillan.

Shigematsu, Setsu, and Keith L. Camacho. 2010. "Introduction: Militarized Currents, Decolonizing Futures." In *Militarized Currents: Toward a Decolonized Future in Asia and the Pacific*, edited by Setsu Shigematsu and Keith L. Camacho, 15–41. Minneapolis: University of Minnesota Press.

Shimakawa, Karen. 2002. *National Abjection: The Asian American Body Onstage*. Durham, NC: Duke University Press.

Shimizu, Celine Parreñas. 2007. *The Hypersexuality of Race: Performing Asian/ American Women on Screen and Scene*. Durham, NC: Duke University Press.

Shimizu, Celine Parreñas. 2012. *Straitjacket Sexualities: Unbinding Asian American Manhoods in the Movies*. Stanford, CA: Stanford University Press.

Shohat, Ella. 1990. "Gender in Hollywood's Orient." *Middle East Report*, No. 162, Lebanon's War (January–February): 40–42.

Silva, Noenoe K. 2004. *Aloha Betrayed: Native Hawaiian Resistance to American Colonialism*. Durham, NC: Duke University Press.

Skwiot, Christine. 2010. *The Purposes of Paradise: U.S. Tourism and Empire in Cuba and Hawai'i*. Philadelphia: University of Pennsylvania Press.

Smith, Andrea. 2005. *Conquest: Sexual Violence and American Indian Genocide*. Cambridge, MA: South End Press.

Smith, Sidonie, and Julia Watson. 2010. *Reading Autobiography: A Guide for Interpreting Life Narratives*. Minneapolis: University of Minnesota Press.

Smith-Hefner, Nancy J. 2007. "Javanese Women and the Veil in Post-Suharto Indonesia." *Journal of Asian Studies* 66, no. 2 (May): 389–420.

Snorton, C. Riley. 2014. *Nobody Is Supposed to Know: Black Sexuality on the Down Low*. Minneapolis: University of Minnesota Press.

Sobchack, Vivian. 2001. *Screening Space: The American Science Fiction Film*. New Brunswick, NJ: Rutgers University Press.

Spade, Dean. 2011. *Normal Life: Administrative Violence, Critical Trans Politics and the Limits of Law*. Cambridge, MA: South End Press.

Spillers, Hortense J. 2003. *Black, White, and in Color: Essays on American Literature and Culture*. Chicago: University of Chicago Press.

Stahl, Aviva. 2017. "Transgender Prisoners Suffer Abuse at Record Numbers." *Vice*, June 12. Accessed June 28, 2018. https://www.vice.com/en_us/article/43g5jd/why -is-ice-closing-its-only-detention-center-for-transgender-detainees-v24n5.

Stanley, Eric A., and Nat Smith, eds. 2015. *Captive Genders: Trans Embodiment and the Prison Industrial Complex*, 2nd ed. Oakland: AK Press.

Steinmetz, Katy. 2014. "America's Transition." *Time*, June 9, 38–46.

Stiegler, Bernard. 2010. *For a New Critique of Political Economy*, translated by Daniel Ross. Malden, MA: Polity Press.

Stone, Allucquère Rosanne (Sandy). 1996. *The War of Desire and Technology at the Close of the Mechanical Age*. Cambridge, MA: MIT Press.

Stone, Sandy. 1987. "The *Empire* Strikes Back: A Posttranssexual Manifesto." Accessed on June 3, 2017. sandystone.com/empire-strikes-back.pdf.

Stryker, Susan. 2006. "Introduction." In *The Transgender Studies Reader*, Volume 1, edited by Susan Stryker and Stephen Whittle, 1–17. New York: Routledge.

Stryker, Susan. 2008. *Transgender History*. Berkeley, CA: Seal Press.

Stryker, Susan, Paisley Currah, and Lisa Jean Moore. 2008. "Introduction: Trans-, Trans, or Transgender?" *Women's Studies Quarterly* 36, no. 3/4, Trans- (fall-winter): 11–22.

Sunardi, Christina. 2015. *Stunning Males and Powerful Females: Gender and Tradition in East Javanese Dance*. Urbana: University of Illinois Press.

Sunder Rajan, Kaushik. 2006. *Biocapital: The Constitution of Postgenomic Life*. Durham, NC: Duke University Press.

Taussig, Michael T. 1993. *Mimesis and Alterity: A Particular History of the Senses*. New York: Routledge.

Taylor, Diana. 2016. *Performance*. Durham, NC: Duke University Press.

Teaiwa, Teresia K. 1994. "bikinis and other s/pacific n/oceans." *The Contemporary Pacific* 6, no. 1 (January): 87–109. Honolulu: University of Hawai'i.

Thom, Kai Cheng. 2017. *Fierce Femmes and Notorious Liars: A Dangerous Trans Girls Confabulous Memoir*. Montreal: Metonymy Press.

Thomas, Heather, and Tom Boellstorff. 2017. "Beyond the Spectrum: Rethinking Autism." *Disability Studies Quarterly* 37, no. 1. Accessed on April 24, 2018. http://dsq-sds.org/article/view/5375/4551.

Thompson, Erica. 2017. "Community Feature: Black Pride 4 Inspire Community to Examine Pride, Protest and Police Response." *Columbus Alive*, June 28. Accessed on April 24, 2018. http://www.columbusalive.com/entertainment/20170628 /community-feature-black-pride-4-inspire-community-to-examine-pride-protest -and-police-response.

Thoreau, Henry David. [1854] 1995. *Walden, and On the Duty of Civil Disobedience.* The Project Gutenberg. Ebook.

Trask, Haunani-Kay. 1999. *From a Native Daughter: Colonialism and Sovereignty in Hawai'i.* Honolulu: University of Hawai'i Press.

Trinh T. Minh-Ha. 2011. *Elsewhere, within Here: Immigration, Refugeeism and the Boundary Event.* London: Routledge.

Umberger, Emily. 1996. "Art and Imperial Strategy in Tenochtitlan." In *Aztec Imperial Strategies*, edited by Frances F. Berdan et al., 85–108. Washington, DC: Dumbarton Oaks Research Library and Collection.

Unaldi, Serhat. 2011. "Back in the Spotlight: The Cinematic Regime of Representation of *Kathoeys* and Gay Men in Thailand." In *Queer Bangkok: Twenty-First-Century Markets, Media, and Rights,* edited by Peter Jackson, 59–80. Hong Kong: Hong Kong University Press.

United Nations. 1948. "The Universal Declaration of Human Rights." Accessed on June 3, 2017. ohchr.org/EN/UDHR/Documents/UDHR_Translations/eng.pdf.

United Nations. 2015. "The Millennium Development Goals Report 2015." Accessed on June 3, 2017. un.org/millenniumgoals/2015_MDG_Report/pdf/MDG%202015 %20rev%20(July%201).pdf.

United Nations General Assembly. 1948. "International Bill of Human Rights." Accessed on June 3, 2017. ohchr.org/Documents/Publications/Compilation1.1en.pdf.

United Nations General Assembly. 2000. "Resolution Adopted by the General Assembly: United Nations Millennium Declaration." Accessed on June 3, 2017. un.org /millennium/declaration/ares552e.pdf.

United Nations General Assembly. 2015. "Resolution Adopted by the General Assembly on 25 September 2015: Transforming Our World: The 2030 Agenda for Sustainable Development." Accessed on June 3, 2017. unfpa.org/sites/default/files /resource-pdf/Resolution_A_RES_70_1_EN.pdf.

U.S. Congress (43rd). 1875. "Chap. 141—An act supplementary to the acts in relation to immigration" (Page Act). Accessed April 28, 2018. https://www.loc.gov/law/help /statutes-at-large/43rd-congress/session-2/c43s2ch141.pdf.

U.S. Congress (79th). 1946. "Chapter 945: An act to place Chinese wives of American citizens on a nonquota basis" (War Brides Act). Accessed April 28, 2018. https:// www.loc.gov/law/help/statutes-at-large/79th-congress/session-2/c79s2ch945.pdf.

U.S. Department of Defense. Accessed April 28, 2018. https://www.defense.gov/.

U.S. News and World Report. 1966. "Success Story of One Minority Group in U.S."

December 26, 1966. Accessed on May 20, 2017. https://www.dartmouth.edu
/~hist32/Hist33/US%20News%20&%20World%20Report.pdf.

Vasconcelos, José. 1997. *The Cosmic Race/La Raza Cosmica*. Translated by Didier T. Jaén. Baltimore: Johns Hopkins University Press.

Vasquez, Tina. 2016. "Hunger Strikers to ICE: End Transgender Immigrant Detention." *Rewire.News*, May 17. Accessed on June 28, 2018. https://rewire.news /article/2016/05/17/hunger-strikers-ice-transgender-immigrant.

Virilio, Paul. 2006. *Speed and Politics*. Translated by Mark Polizzotti. Los Angeles: Semiotext(e).

Volpp, Leti. 2005. "Divesting Citizenship: On Asian American History and the Loss of Citizenship through Marriage." 53 *UCLA Law Review* 405.

Weaver, Matthew. 2015. "Transgender Woman Heckles Barack Obama at White House Gay Pride Event." *The Guardian*, June 25. Accessed on June 26, 2018. https:// www.theguardian.com/us-news/2015/jun/25/barack-obama-heckled-transgender -woman-gay-pride-white-house.

Wiener, Norbert. 1949. *Extrapolation, Interpolation, and Smoothing of Stationary Time Series with Engineering Applications*. Cambridge, MA: MIT Press.

Wilkinson, Willy. 2015. *Born on the Edge of Race and Gender: A Voice for Cultural Competency*. Oakland, CA: Hapa Papa Press.

Wright, Richard. 1995. *The Color Curtain: A Report on the Bandung Conference*. Jackson: University Press of Mississippi.

Wyma, Chloe. 2012. "'I Dislike the Word Visibility': Wu Tsang on Sexuality, Creativity, and Conquering New York's Museums." *Blouin Artinfo*, February 3. Accessed on September 3, 2014. https://www.blouinartinfo.com/news/story/761447/i-dislike -the-word-visibility-wu-tsang-on-sexuality-creativity-and-conquering-new-yorks -museums.

Yagoda, Ben. 2009. *Memoir: A History*. New York: Riverhead Books.

Zimman, Lal. 2014. "Transmasculinity and the Voice: Gender Assignment, Identity, and Presentation." In *Language and Masculinities: Performances, Intersections, Dislocations*, edited by Tommaso M. Milani, 217–39. New York: Routledge.

FILMOGRAPHY

Arayangkoon, Monthon, dir. 2006. *The Victim/Phii Khon Pen*. New York: Palisades Tartan. DVD.

Baggs, Mel, dir. 2007. "In My Language." *YouTube*. Accessed on June 3, 2017. https:// www.youtube.com/watch?v=JnylM1hI2jc.

cárdenas, micha, dir. 2012. "Find Each Other: Local Autonomy Networks/Autonets." *Vimeo*. Accessed on June 3, 2017. vimeo.com/48938574.

Cheang Shu Lea, dir. 2000. *I.K.U.* Tokyo: Uplink Co. DVD.

Cheang Shu Lea, dir. 2009–present. UKI. Accessed on June 3, 2017. u-k-i.co/index.html.

Electronic Disturbance Theater, dir. 2009. "Transborder Immigrant Tool: Transition." *Vimeo*. Accessed on June 3, 2017. vimeo.com/6109723.

Everett, Karen, dir. 1996. "I Shall Not Be Removed: The Life of Marlon Riggs." Youtube, San Francisco: California Newsreel. Accessed on June 3, 2018. youtube.com /watch?v=kuojQyysroI.

Jee-woon, Kim, Nonzee Nimibutr, and Peter Ho-Sun Chan, dirs. 2002. Three/三更. Santa Monica, CA: Lionsgate. DVD.

Je-gyu, Kang, dir. 1999. Shiri. New York: Samuel Goldwyn Films. DVD.

Lee, Ang, dir. 2000. Crouching Tiger, Hidden Dragon. New York: Sony Pictures Classics. DVD.

Livingston, Jennie, dir. 1990. Paris Is Burning. Santa Monica, CA: Lionsgate. DVD.

Moreau, David, and Xavier Palud, dirs. 2008. The Eye. Santa Monica, CA: Lionsgate. DVD.

Nakata, Hideo, dir. 1998. Ringu. Tokyo: Toho. DVD.

Ophelian, Annalise, and StormMiguel Florez, dirs. 2015. MAJOR! Amazon. Accessed on June 3, 2017. amazon.com/dp/B079HCVBQ2/ref=cm_sw_r_tw_dp _x_TBEDAbAC7VTQS.

Pang, Danny, and Oxide Chun Pang, dirs. 2002. The Eye/Gin Gwai. Hong Kong: Panorama Entertainment. DVD.

Phillips, Todd, dir. 2011. The Hangover Part II. Burbank, CA: Warner Bros. DVD.

Sukkhapisit, Tanwarin, dir. 2010. Insects in the Backyard. Thailand. DVD.

Sukkhapisit, Tanwarin, dir. 2011. Hak na'Sarakham. Thailand.

Sukkhapisit, Tanwarin, dir. 2012. It Gets Better. Thailand.

Sukkhapisit, Tanwarin, dir. 2014a. Fin Sugoi. Thailand.

Sukkhapisit, Tanwarin, dir. 2014b. Threesome/Thoe khao rao phi. Thailand.

Scott, Ridley, dir. [1982] 2007. Blade Runner. 4-disc collector's ed. Burbank, CA: Warner Home Studio. DVD.

Sharma, Parvez, dir. 2007. A Jihad for Love. New York: First Run Features. DVD.

Thongkonthun, Youngyooth, dir. 2000. The Iron Ladies. New York: Digital Media Rights. DVD.

Tsang, Wu, dir. 2008. Shape of a Right Statement.

Tsang, Wu, dir. 2012. Wildness.

Uekrongtham, Ekachai, dir. 2004. Beautiful Boxer. Los Angeles: Regent Releasing. DVD.

Waller, Tom, dir. 2014. The Last Executioner. Toronto: Arrow Entertainment. DVD.

Yozmit. 2011. Transcending Stonewall.

Index

Page numbers followed by *f* indicate illustrations.

Page Law (1875), 15, 45
Pakistan, 138
Palud, Xavier: *The Eye*, 120, 154n17
Panama, 45
Pang Oxide Chun: *The Eye/Gin Gwai*, 119
panopticon, 8
pansori, 32
Paramount Pictures, 119–20, 153n2, 154n17
Paris Is Burning (film), 35–36, 83
Park, Pauline, 7
Park Chan-wook, 154n18
Parks, Lisa, 126
Parreñas Shimizu, Celine, 52
patriarchy, 12, 95; cis-hetero-patriarchy, 7,
    9–10, 15–17, 22, 25, 28–29, 44, 47, 49, 71,
    103, 110; hetero-patriarchy, 13, 22, 93, 96,
    124
Pearl River Lagoon, 91
Pereira, Angela, 147f
Pereira, Jabu, 101–6, 113f
performance studies, 24
performativity, 38, 155
Petersen, William: "Success Story, Japanese-
    American Style," 13–14
phenomenology, 35
Philippines, 8–9, 13, 23–25, 44–45, 99–100,
    141
Phillips, Todd: *The Hangover Part II*, 116
philosophy, 24, 35, 123
Piepzna-Samarasinha, Leah Lakshmi, 78
Placide, Kenita, 101
populism, 3, 45, 80–81, 86
pornography, 115; postporn, 28, 59; stag films,
    52
Portugal: Portuguese colonialism, 88
postcolonialism, 78, 107
post-Marxism, 24, 61
postmodernism, 61, 70
postporn, 28, 59
poststructuralism, 35
Preciado, Paul B., 4
Preston, Ashlee Marie, 133
prison industrial complex (PIC), 17–19, 122
prisons, 7, 17–19, 25–27, 41, 88–89, 94, 122,
    127, 130, 141–47
privatization, 10, 17, 24, 44, 51, 78, 91, 108. *See
    also* neoliberalism
Production Codes (Hays Code), 151n6

promiscuous sociality, 99
Protestant ethic, 13
psychiatry, 4, 6, 19, 40–42, 77, 84, 104, 150n4
psychoanalysis, 24, 35
Puerto Rico, 12–13, 23, 36, 78, 100, 141; San
    Juan, 11

queer of color critique, 4
Queer Places, Practices, and Lives Sympo-
    sium, 149n2
Quorum: Global LGBT Voices, 101

race, 30, 58, 61–63, 67, 75, 82, 84, 91, 103–7,
    110–12, 120, 123–24, 152n9; colonialism
    and, 22–24, 44–45, 59, 66, 93–94, 142;
    gendered, 3–5, 7, 8, 10–16, 19, 25–28,
    31–32, 35–36, 39–40, 43, 45, 47–54,
    59–60, 64, 66, 68–71, 77, 85, 87–89,
    92–99, 102, 127, 133–34, 137, 139–41,
    151n9; racial capitalism, 8, 17. *See also*
    racism
racial justice, 9, 17, 26–27, 70, 106, 110
racism, 3–5, 7, 9, 11, 14, 28, 47, 62, 68, 103,
    132; anti-racism, 17, 127; Trump's, 140. *See
    also* slavery; white supremacy; yellowface
Rak, Julie, 79–81
Ramayana, 54
Reagan, Ronald, 23, 106, 142
Refugee Act, 15
refugees, 9, 15–16, 23–24, 30, 140. *See also*
    asylum
Renzi, Alessandra, 128f
Republic of Hawaii, 91
restorative justice, 15
Rice, Tamir, 132
Richardson, Matt, 96
Rifkin, Mark, 19, 22
Rivera, Ignacio, 7
Rivera, Sylvia, 7, 30, 131
Rodríguez, Juana María, 13, 135
Rousseau, Jean Jacques, 79
Royal Thai Government, 117
Russia, 101, 130, 153n8. *See also* Soviet Union

Sahamongkol Film International, 118
Saint Laurent, Octavia, 36